BUDDHISM

THE ILLUSTRATED GUIDE

BUDDHISM

THE ILLUSTRATED GUIDE

KEVIN TRAINOR, GENERAL EDITOR

OXFORD
UNIVERSITY PRESS

Oxford University Press

Oxford   New York
Auckland   Bangkok   Buenos Aires
Cape Town   Chennai   Dar es Salaam   Delhi
Hong Kong   Istanbul   Karachi   Kolkata   Kuala Lumpur
Madrid   Melbourne   Mexico City   Mumbai   Nairobi
São Paolo   Shanghai   Singapore   Taibei   Tokyo   Toronto

and associated companies in Berlin

This edition published in 2004 in the United States of America by
Oxford University Press, Inc.
198 Madison Avenue, New York, N.Y. 10016
Oxford is a registered trademark of Oxford University Press

The text uses Sanskrit as the standard language for Buddhist terms, with the
Pali equivalent given in parentheses if appropriate. The principal exception to
this rule is to be found in Part 3: Chapter 2, where the subject matter is the Pali
canon and hence Pali takes precedence. The book also uses terms from other
languages, which are identified either explicitly, or implicitly by context.

Conceived, created, and designed by
Duncan Baird Publishers, London, England

Library of Congress Cataloging-in-Publication Data is available

ISBN: 0-19-517398-8

Project Editor: Peter Bently
Editors: Christopher Westhorp and Joanne Clay
Designers: Paul Reid and Lloyd Tilbury at Cobalt id
Picture Researcher: Cee Weston-Baker
Commissioned Maps: Sallie Alane Reason
Decorative Borders: Sally Taylor

Managing Editor: Diana Loxley

Typeset in Sabon
Color reproduction by Colourscan, Singapore
Printed in Thailand by Imago

NOTES
The abbreviations CE and BCE are used throughout this book:
CE Common Era (the equivalent of AD)
BCE Before the Common Era (the equivalent of BC)

CAPTIONS TO ILLUSTRATIONS ON PAGES 1 AND 2:
Page 1: Tree roots surround a stone head of the Buddha, Ayutthaya, Thailand.
Page 2: A monk in a doorway, Tonle Bati, Cambodia.

10 9 8 7 6 5 4 3 2 1

CONTENTS

INTRODUCTION

The act of "seeing" has a prominent place in the history of Buddhism. Buddhist texts frequently use visual imagery to communicate the nature of the Dharma, a key Buddhist term that denotes both the ultimate truth which the Buddha realized and the actual words through which he communicated that truth to his followers. The Dharma is commonly described as something that one should "come and see" for oneself, and the experience of perceiving the true nature of reality is often described as "knowing and seeing." Just as the Buddha opened his eyes to the ultimate truth (the title "Buddha" means "one who has awoken"), so too his words and glorious physical appearance are said to enlighten those blinded by ignorance, hatred, and desire, guiding them to their own awakening, or enlightenment.

Given this positive emphasis on seeing, it is perhaps surprising to find evidence of some ambivalence in early Buddhist tradition about viewing the Buddha's physical form (see pp.42–5). While Buddhist teaching stresses that the Buddha's physical body, like all compounded things, is subject to decay and death, this does not mean that it has little value. Indeed, Buddhist communities have long celebrated the importance of standing in the Buddha's physical presence, as mediated through bodily relics or images which inspire those trapped in the endless cycle of rebirth (see pp.58–9) with the timeless truth of the Dharma. One commonly cited story suggests the complexity of the issue. In one version, the Buddha visits a monk called Vakkali, who has been seriously ill. Vakkali expresses his frustration that he has not been able to see the Buddha for some time, to which the Buddha replies: "Enough, Vakkali; what good is the sight of this putrid body to you? Vakkali, the one who sees the Dharma sees me; the one who sees me sees the Dharma."

The past quarter century has been marked by a significant reorientation within Buddhist studies in Europe and North America. Nineteenth-century Western scholars tended to portray Buddhism, at least in its original form, as a primarily philosophical and rational quest for personal insight that had little to do with worship of the Buddha or with ritual in general. This earlier scholarship also tended to sift through authoritative Buddhist scriptures for evidence of the historical origins of the tradition, with a particular focus on uncovering the "Buddha's original teachings." However, more recent studies have emphasized the cultural diversity of Buddhist traditions and the central role that ritual has played in the history of Buddhist practice and Buddhist institutions. One may thus speak of a general move to "rematerialize" the history of Buddhism. Implied in this term is both a concern for the material forms around which Buddhist practice has been organized, including relics, images, and the architectural structures in which they are located, and attention to the ways in which Buddhist rituals "embody" Buddhist ideals and values.

This movement away from representing Buddhism as a set of idealized doctrines and picturing it instead through the complexities of human practice has been supported by the results of anthropological research on contemporary Buddhist communities in a wide range of cultural settings. Increasing attention to the history of women's participation in Buddhist tradition and to gender differences is also changing the way Buddhism is understood.

These interpretive shifts within contemporary Western scholarship on Buddhism are well reflected in both the general approach and specific content of *Buddhism: The Illustrated Guide*. The broad outlines of Buddhist teaching are set out in considerable detail so that one can gain an understanding of the religious worldview shared by many Buddhist communities. There is also considerable attention to the wealth of regional forms of Buddhist doctrine and practice, including the emergence of Buddhist communities outside the religion's Asian heartlands. The illustrations highlight the regional and historical diversity of what is, today, truly a world religion. *Buddhism: The Illustrated Guide* is organized in four principal sections:

ORIGINS

This section provides an introduction to the historical and cultural context in which Buddhism arose, including the early Vedic and Brahmanic forms of Indic religion, as well as the rise of urban centers and kingdoms in north India.

The Malla princes dividing the cremated remains of the Buddha. Buddhist tradition records that these princes, who ruled the region in which the Buddha died, sought at first to keep all his relics for themselves, but were persuaded to distribute them for the benefit of the wider Buddhist community (see p.41). This wall painting adorns the Phutthaisawan (Buddhaisawan) Chapel, constructed in 1787 and now part of the Thai National Museum, Bangkok.

Pilgrims in the entrance hallway of the Dalada Maligava ("Temple of the Tooth") in Kandy, Sri Lanka. The temple enshrines one of the most sacred physical relics of the Buddhist world, a tooth of the Buddha, believed to have been brought to Sri Lanka in the 4th century CE. (See also p.110.)

The development of Buddhist biographical tradition is examined next, including the major episodes in the life of the Buddha. This section concludes by sketching the early expansion of Buddhism, with attention to the reign of the great Indian emperor Ashoka (third century BCE), and the rise of Mahayana Buddhism (the "Great Vehicle"). This historical overview incorporates the results of recent scholarship, including archaeological research, that is currently reshaping our understanding of the history of ancient Indian religion.

PRINCIPLES AND PRACTICE

This section begins by outlining the basic Buddhist worldview, including notions of rebirth, *karma*, and the organization of the cosmos ranging from Buddhist hells up to the highest celestial realms. There follows a detailed explication of the fundamental teachings as set out by the Buddha in "the Four Noble Truths." The next chapter examines Buddhist meditation, including the use of *mandala*s and other objects and practices, such as chanting, to focus and transform human consciousness. This is followed by a discussion of the

Buddhist community, from *buddha*s, *bodhisattva*s, and *arhat*s, to the monastic Sangha and the laity. The ensuing chapter highlights common forms of Buddhist ritual practice, such as monastic initiation, devotion, and pilgrimage to important sites such as Bodh Gaya, where the Buddha gained enlightenment. The section concludes with an historical overview of the principal schools of Buddhism and their regional forms, with detailed coverage of the Theravada and Mahayana traditions, including Zen and Vajrayana (Tantra), which are among the best known schools in the West.

HOLY WRITINGS
This section provides a wide ranging and detailed examination of the diversity of Buddhist textual traditions, including both canonical and non-canonical literature. The authors discuss the key issues of the compilation, dissemination, translation, and physical reproduction of the Buddha's teaching after the early centuries in which it was passed on only in oral form. This review considers the various media in which the Dharma has been transmitted, from palm-leaf manuscripts to CD-ROM and the Internet. Much of the section is devoted to a survey of the texts of the core Buddhist canon, the Tripitaka ("Three Baskets"), together with some of the most influential Mahayana and tantric texts.

BUDDHISM TODAY
The final section examines the trends affecting the development of Buddhism in the modern world. The first chapter explores the expanding Buddhist community, including new Buddhist movements in Asia, the rise of burgeoning communities outside Asia comprised of Asian immigrants and Western converts, the changing roles of Buddhist women, and the relationship between Buddhist practice and critical scholarship. The second chapter, and the concluding chapter of the book, explores a number of key social and political issues currently facing Buddhists throughout the world, such as the relationship between Buddhism and politics, the growing influence of Buddhist meditation centers, the impact of Western science and new technology, and the rise of "Engaged Buddhism," a phrase coined by the noted Vietnamese Zen monk Thich Nhat Hanh to describe the commitment of Buddhists to work for social change in accordance with Buddhist teachings.

Also dispersed throughout the book are special "Art and Architecture" feature spreads devoted to particular aspects of the sumptuous iconographic and architectural traditions which Buddhism has inspired over the centuries.

The contributors to *Buddhism: The Illustrated Guide* have sought to provide an accessible and visually engaging introduction to the immense richness of Buddhist ideals and cultural forms. This book invites the reader to explore, through text and pictures, an ancient religious tradition which, in keeping with Buddhist insights, tells a story of constant and inevitable transformation.

Kevin Trainor
Associate Professor of Religion
University of Vermont
Burlington, VT.

PART 1

ORIGINS

A sandstone stela from eastern India, ca. 6th–7th centuries CE, of Siddhartha touching the ground with one hand, his traditional gesture of calling the earth to witness his past meritorious deeds just before his enlightenment. His face has an expression of serenity, capturing the moment of victory over the deva Mara, whose daughter stands next to Siddhartha while a monster hovers nearby (see also pp.34–5).

PART 1 • CHAPTER 1 *Todd T. Lewis*

ANCIENT INDIA: BELIEF AND SOCIETY

CITIES AND KINGDOMS

Bounded to the north by the Himalayas, the world's highest mountain range, and to the south by the Indian Ocean, the Indian subcontinent has constituted a distinct cultural area for several millennia. Since antiquity, the peoples of this region have flourished on fertile alluvial plains watered by great rivers swollen by mountain glaciers and summer monsoon rains.

The region's first urban civilization arose ca. 2500BCE on the Indus River, in modern-day Pakistan. This civilization declined—apparently between 2000BCE and 1750BCE—as its cities were abandoned, due perhaps to one or more factors, including climatic changes, disruption in the courses of rivers, epidemics, invasion or migration, and changing trade patterns. At about the same time, another group appeared, although whether they were migrants from outside India or are best understood as a development of the Indus Valley civilization is a matter of scholarly debate. These peoples called themselves Aryan ("Nobles") and spoke the Indo-European language that later became Sanskrit. The dominant view has been that the Aryans were pastoral migrants who entered the subcontinent from the north or northwest, excelled in mounted warfare, and quickly dominated the local indigenous peoples. Over the succeeding centuries, according to this view, many Aryan clans followed them. Some moved from the Indus to the Ganges plain, subjugating the non-Aryan tribes that they encountered.

This sequence of events has increasingly been challenged by some scholars who believe that the language of the Indus Valley civilization was a member of the Indo-European family rather than Dravidian, which was formerly assumed to be the indigenous linguistic family of the subcontinent, and to which many present-day southern Indian languages belong. These scholars postulate that Aryan culture actually developed among the peoples who remained in the region after the decline of the Indus Valley cities. The old idea that the Aryans were a light-skinned race of immigrants who subjugated a darker-skinned indigenous population has largely been abandoned. Other more recent theories explore the idea that, even if the Aryans were not indigenous, they migrated over a long period, beginning as early as ca. 2200BCE, and became assimilated within a multi-ethnic and partly bilingual culture. Until the Indus Valley script is deciphered, scholarly consensus is likely to remain elusive. However, it is undisputed that Indo-Aryan culture, whatever its ethnic and geographical origins, came to define the region.

Textual and archaeological evidence also suggests the gradual emergence of stable political units and increasing urban settlement in the region. Using iron tools, the migrants cleared the dense jungle and plowed the soil, assisting intensive crop cultivation. The resulting food surpluses supported the growth of specialist groups, towns, and trade.

The formation of city-states from ca. 550BCE onward exerted pressure on the small-scale tribal traditions, centered on a sacrificial religious system, that had characterized generations of Indo-Aryan life in the subcontinent. It was in this era of increasing social complexity that Siddhartha Gautama—the Buddha—was born.

A map of ancient India showing the main Indus Valley sites and the major Buddhist centers. The latter include those places which existed at the time of the Buddha, those which were associated with him during his lifetime, and those which have become associated with Buddhism over the centuries.

CLASS AND HIERARCHY

As Indo-Aryan society developed, it evolved a highly stratified social system in which may be seen the roots of the much later Hindu caste system. As described in the latest sections of the sacred texts called the Vedas (see p.16)—whence the name Vedic that is commonly applied to this era—there were originally four ranked social "classes," or *varna*s (see box, below). To be a member of a *varna*, a person had to be born into it; each group member was assumed to have the same level of innate purity and to possess a very distinct nature and capacity from members of other *varna*s. Ancient texts also identify socially inferior groups such as *chandala*s, who performed tasks that members of higher classes considered to be defiling and whose very touch or shadow was considered polluting. From these developed the "Untouchables," traditional India's most underprivileged social group—Mahatma Gandhi, in protest at their status, referred to them as "Harijans" ("Children of the God [Vishnu]").

According to legal and social codes of later centuries, those born into the same class were obliged to marry only within their group and to perform the traditional "expected duty," or *dharma* (not to be confused with the same word in the sense of the Buddha's teachings) of that group. While it is uncertain to what extent these prescriptions may have applied in earlier Vedic society, the doctrine of class *dharma* came to play a central role in developed Hinduism. As a famous passage in the Bhagavad Gita ("Laws of Manu," ca. second century BCE) states: "Better to do one's own *dharma* badly than another class's *dharma* well."

In developed Hinduism, the *varna* system came to be underpinned by the doctrine of reincarnation, which asserts that those born in the highest

THE FOUR *VARNAS*

The four main *varna*s were headed by the Brahmans, the priestly class. Society depended upon the Brahmans because they ensured that the gods would be worshipped properly, which in turn guaranteed the divine grace needed to sustain the bounty of the land, the regularity of the monsoons, and social harmony. The main *dharma* of the Brahmans was to master the Vedas—which they alone were permitted both to learn and to teach—and their related ritual practices (see pp.16–17).

Ranked below the Brahmans were the Kshatriyas, the aristocratic warrior class, who were expected to rule justly and protect all members of society, especially the Brahmans. Next came the Vaishyas, the mercantile class, specialists in crafts and agriculture who multiplied the wealth of society. Both Kshatriyas and Vaishyas were permitted to learn, but not teach, the Vedas. Later Hindu law codes identify the three highest classes as *dvija* ("twice born"), because their members were considered to be "born again" through religious initiation, which in Hinduism came to be restricted to males. The fourth *varna*, the Shudras, or servants, were workers who performed tasks for their superiors.

Not every person could be easily classified within each of the *varna*s, and over time many subclasses (*jati*s) developed, which to this day vary regionally in their names and functions. Nor were the limitations of *varna* status necessarily strictly observed, as the recorded wealth and prominence of some Shudra *jati*s testify.

varna deserve their status owing to their superior *karma*, the accumulated merit derived from their deeds and behavior in past lives (see p.20). Although the doctrine of reincarnation is not explicit in the Vedic hymns, it was articulated clearly in the later Upanishads (ca. 800–300BCE) and subsequent texts. Hindu theorists argued that caste rules insured social harmony as well as the spiritual progress of dutiful individuals who would move up in birth status in their next lifetimes.

It is most likely that Indo-Aryan society across north India was highly patriarchal, although it is not clear whether gender roles were as precisely defined as they were to be in the later Hindu codes. A few of the Vedic hymns are apparently attributed to female seers, and one woman, named Gargi, plays a role in the Upanishads. However, while their status in early Indian society is the subject of considerable scholarly controversy, by the time of the Manava Dharmashastra ("Laws of Manu"), women were denied initiation into "twice-born" status (see box, opposite) and were prohibited from hearing the Vedas. They were also considered ritually impure while menstruating and after childbirth. As a much cited passage from the Laws of Manu puts it: "In childhood subject to her father, in youth to her husband, and when her husband is dead to her sons, she should never enjoy independence." While the extent to which such strictures were followed is open to debate, there seems little doubt that the lives of women were highly circumscribed by male authority.

A present-day Hindu priest at a temple in Rajasthan, India. His "twice born" caste status (see box, opposite) is denoted by the sacred thread which he wears around his left shoulder.

A WORLD OF SACRIFICE

First referred to in the Upanishads, where it is described as the "seed sound" of all other sounds, the Sanskrit syllable om *had a range of sacred meanings.* Om, *which is understood to consist of three sounds (a-u-m), is repeated by Hindus, Buddhists (particularly in Tibet), and Jains as part of offerings and as a meditation* mantra. *These rocks in Tibet are adorned with the popular* mantra, "Om mani padme hum" ("Om, the Jewel of the Lotus, hum"), *the prayer of* Avalokiteshvara (see pp.137–9).

What is known of early Indic society and religion derives largely from the four Vedas, collections of ancient texts of which the oldest, the Rig Veda, was perhaps first assembled ca. 1200BCE; the others (the Yajur Veda, Sama Veda, and Atharva Veda) were likely collected between three and four centuries later. The Vedas comprise more than one thousand hymns of praise and supplication addressed to the gods; liturgical formulas; and chants, spells, and charms. Composed in an early form of Sanskrit (see sidebar, opposite), the Vedic hymns show no systematic development, ordering, or single mythological framework. It is also likely that the hymns were collected and appreciated by only the most culturally refined social groups of the time. Under the four-class system, it was the Brahmans who controlled

access to these texts and they alone were able to teach them (see box, p.14). The Vedas existed for over two millennia in oral form and were only committed to memory by successive generations of male Brahmans.

Early Vedic religion was centered on sacrifice (*yajna*), the most prestigious of which was the fire ritual called *homa*. The sacrifice was performed by Brahman priests, who memorized the Vedic hymns and particularly the chants that were integral to the performance of this rite. Highly intricate *homa* rituals were performed with the aim of gratifying the numerous deities of the Vedic pantheon with offerings of grain, animal flesh, and clarified butter. Accompanied by the chants of the officiating priests, these offerings were believed to be transformed into fragrant smoke by the god of fire (Agni), who carried them upward to nourish the gods. According to one Vedic perspective on creation, the world arose originally through a primordial act of sacrifice: the gods' offering of a great man (*purusha*) gave rise to all the elements of the cosmos, including the social order—the four *varna*s (see p.14) sprang respectively from the *purusha*'s mouth (the Brahmans), arms (Kshatriyas), thighs (Vaishyas), and feet (Shudras). Vedic texts state that the entire universe is maintained by sacrifice—propitiated and strengthened through these offerings, the deities will sustain creation and insure the prosperity of those who perform sacrifices.

The major Vedic deities, who were all male, were those connected to the sacrifice, martial conquest, exalted mental states, and the maintenance of moral order. As described above, the fire god Agni was essential for the successful performance of the sacrificial ritual. The Vedic warrior deity *par excellence* was Indra and it is to him that the greatest number of Vedic hymns are dedicated. Indra subdued alien deities and was called upon to lead warriors into battle. Soma was conceived to be a divine presence dwelling within a psychoactive substance of the same name, which was consumed by humans and deities before battle and at the end of ritual celebrations. Perhaps it was Soma who inspired the early Hindu seers to probe deeper into the nature of reality. The sky god Varuna was thought to enforce *rita*, the moral order of the Vedic universe, meting out punishments or rewards. The hymns indicate that Varuna was the deity whom humans could approach with personal petitions for forgiveness.

One's destiny after death was partly in the hands of one's descendants. It was believed that one could become an ancestor (*pitri*) and reach a heavenly afterlife (*pitriloka*) as a star, provided that one had lived a moral life and that one's family performed special rituals called *shraddha* in the year following death. However, those who had lived immorally or whose families failed to perform the proper *shraddha* rituals suffered the disintegration of their afterlife spirits and merely dissolved back into the earth.

Vedic religion was therefore marked by faith in the power of the gods, ritual acts aimed at influencing them, and the spiritual resonance of the sacred texts (see sidebar, right). In post-Vedic religion, however, the principal deities of the earliest pantheon became less prominent, and the idea of *rita*, the cosmic order, may lie behind the central Hindu notion of *dharma* ("expected duty," "eternal universal order"), which became closely tied into the ideas of reincarnation and *karma* (see pp.14–15).

A gold coin issued during the reign of Samudragupta (reigned ca. 330–380CE), the images of a horse and a fire bears reference to an ancient Vedic horse sacrifice.

THE SACRED LANGUAGE

The Sanskrit (meaning "cultured," "refined," or "perfected") language is a member of the Indo-European linguistic family, which also includes Latin and English. The language of the Vedic hymns and also a canonical language of Buddhism (see pp.178–9), Sanskrit is one of the world's oldest recorded tongues and was believed to be divine in origin. Sanskrit words, phrases, and prayers are still at the heart of Hindu rituals because they are believed to delight the gods.

In Vedic society a mastery of Sanskrit was the most important knowledge that one could acquire—it was essential for the male Brahmans who memorized the Vedas and it remains the mark of Brahman scholars to this day. As a scholarly language, Sanskrit has remained remarkably unchanged since its grammar was systematized by the Indian scholar Panini around 600BCE. Until recently, the earliest manuscript of the Vedas was from the eighteenth century CE, but a manuscript dating to the eleventh century CE has recently come to light in Nepal—evidence that the Vedas have been written down for some time.

ART AND ARCHITECTURE *Michael Willis*

ANCIENT INDIAN CITIES

The earliest cities in India date to the third millennium BCE and belong to what is known as the Indus Valley civilization. The main centers, Mohenjo Daro and Harappa in modern-day Pakistan, were unique in the ancient world for their urban planning: streets laid out according to a defined grid, substantial homes made of fired brick and built, it seems, to a set number of designs, and, finally, a comprehensive drainage system for waste-water and sewage. The picture that emerges is one of a prosperous, well organized, and somewhat bureaucratic society with a substantial middle class. There were also impressive citadels for the rulers and massive buildings for the collective storage of grains. Only the brick plinths of these structures survive. Industrial activities seem to have been laid out in zones, with specific quarters for the production of dyed textiles and other goods. A notable feature of Indus life seems to have been the lack of a central religious cult: there were no temples or other structures which can be identified as being devoted to religious concerns.

The surviving ruins of the planned urban settlement of Mohenjo Daro reveal its carefully laid out grid pattern, prefiguring the later establishment of large, ordered communities in north India and the development of a social class of traders and an urban élite, both of which provided important patrons of the later Buddhist monastic community.

The Indus Valley civilization went into decline from the mid-second millennium BCE. This seems to have been due to deforestation, climate change, shifting rivers, and an increasing number of migrants from central Asia and beyond. For the next six hundred years, there were no large urban centers but rather a host of evenly distributed villages across the plains of north India. South Asian society at this time was probably very mixed in ethnic and cultural terms but it came to be dominated by the clan and tribal traditions of a group that called themselves Aryan ("Nobles"). Based on their main scriptures, the Vedas (see pp.16–17), Indo-Aryan society is often called "Vedic," although the people to whom the Vedas belonged cannot be located in the archaeological record. One reason why the Vedic hymns are unrelated to the meager archaeological data between ca. 1500BCE and ca. 600BCE is that the hymns were the property of bards and ritual specialists who had little interest in describing everyday life.

The Vedic texts provide a picture of a society that was decentralized, semi-nomadic, and much concerned with warfare and sacrifice. The demands of this predatory tribal culture clashed with those of the states and cities that were beginning to develop along the Ganga, Yamuna, and other great rivers of north India. An increase in agrarian production led to a larger sedentary population and the emergence of walled settlements where there was a degree of social differentiation and craft specialization. By the time of the Buddha, the towns of Hastinapura, Shravasti, Kaushambi, Varanasi, and Pataliputra were bustling centers of political, military, and economic power. Urban life was prosperous and trade flourished. Beside the rulers and intelligentsia, a new class of influential merchants had now appeared. Cities were surrounded by huge moats and ramparts, their gates fortified and their main avenues laid out to accommodate royal processions. While the foundations of some of these ancient fortifications have been traced, no architecture is preserved because it was made of wood, stucco, and other perishable materials. The bas-reliefs at Bharhut and Sanchi (see illustration, right, and p.48) give some idea of the opulent nature of the early cities and the craft skills of the people.

The new urban centers and the patterns of life on which they depended meant that the old Vedic system had to be overthrown or reformed. The Buddha's repeated use of agricultural metaphors in his teaching, his acceptance of traders as key patrons of the monastic community, his insistence on non-violence and his denial of the efficacy of sacrifice can all be read as part of his attempt to provide a new philosophical and religious system for the urban élite of north India. Vedic tradition survived by being reformulated: the sacrificial fire moved to the domestic hearth and rites of passage, rules of conduct, and minor sacrifices were governed by a new body of orthodox writing known as the Grihya *sutra*s ("Domestic aphorisms").

A bas-relief depicting the fire offering, from the site at Sanchi. Vedic traditions survived principally in the household setting, with the sacrificial fire relocated to the domestic hearth. Spectacular rituals of old, such as the horse sacrifice (see illustration, p.17), were preserved as showpieces for the dedication and promotion of the rulers of India's new cities and kingdoms.

AN AGE OF INQUIRY

An early Buddhist text in Pali, the
Samannaphala Sutta, gives an
indication of the breadth and vitality
of religious and philosophical inquiry
in the age when the Buddha taught.
There were materialists who rejected
outright any spiritual explanation of
reality. For example, Ajita Kesakembali
denied the efficacy of sacrifice or
offering, the doctrine of *karma* ("there
is neither the fruit nor result of good
and evil deeds"), and the existence of
"this world or the next." Humans
were purely material beings made up
of the four elements: "It is the doctrine
of fools, this talk of religious gifts.
Fools and wise alike, after death, are
cut off, annihilated, and after death
they do not exist."

The law of *karma* was also denied
by fatalists such as Makkhali Gosala,
for whom all beings were powerless,
"bent this way and that solely by their
fate," and by antinomians such as
Purna Kassapa, who refuted the
existence of any absolute moral laws:
"To him who acts or causes another to
mutilate, punish, cause torment, or
who kills a living creature, who steals,
robs, or commits adultery, to him
acting thus, there is no guilt. . .
Likewise, if he went along the Ganges
River and made sacrifices and alms,
there would be no merit whatsoever. In
generosity, in self-mastery, in speaking
the truth, there is neither good *karma*
nor bad *karma*."

By the mid-second millennium BCE, with the rise of urban settlements on the
Ganges plain (see pp.12–13), new religious and philosophical trends characterized by introspection and cosmic speculation had begun to emerge
alongside the Vedic sacrificial system. The roots of these trends are discernible both within brahmanical groups as well as among non-Brahman
teachers. The Upanishads and other post-Vedic texts refer to the existence
among the Brahmans of a certain type of *muni* ("sage"), who sought to
explain the hidden sources that underlay the power of the ritual sacrifices.
For example, one sage proposed that Agni, the god of fire, was the ultimate
reality behind the sun's fiery presence in the sky, and was inherent in all the
natural world, since fire springs to life from dried vegetation while warmth
indicates life in the human body.

More influential were the speculations that posited an unseen spirit
called Brahman, which had created the world and animated all beings, including humans, through its interior presence as the soul (*atman*). The Upanishads
set out the concept of *samsara*, the cycle of birth, death, and rebirth in the
world, whereby the soul transmigrates after death to a new physical body.
The form in which the soul is reincarnated depends upon the individual's
karma ("action"), the cumulative balance of merit or demerit resulting from
one's actions in all previous lives. The doctrine of *karma*, or moral causality,
became central to both Hinduism and Buddhism (see pp.58–61).

In Hinduism, the ultimate goal of religious life is not to achieve an
ever higher form of rebirth but to escape *samsara* entirely by reuniting the
soul with Brahman. The means to this end is called *yoga* (literally "yoke,"
the idea being that one "yokes" oneself to the divine). By applying mental

*A Pahari depiction of a disciple receiving
instruction from his guru (right). Note the
use of a rosary-like aid to meditation.*

SHRAMANA TEACHERS

Alongside the Brahman *guru*s of the mid-second millennium BCE there were spiritual teachers known as Shramanas ("wanderers"), who renounced society and lived as itinerant ascetics. They rejected the Vedas as revealed texts and denied the religious superiority of the Brahman caste, who in turn were critical of the Shramanas as ascetic social renunciants. In the subsequent history of Indic religions, these two groups remained opponents, often engaging fiercely in religious debate "like cobra and mongoose," as one text puts it.

Debating between ascetics and Brahmans of varying schools was an ancient tradition in India, even to the extent of being sponsored by kings, who would attend them and reward the victor with patronage. Rules for the conduct of debate appear in the earliest sectarian texts, including how to respond to "manifestations of anger, hatred, threat, or violence."

Although the views of the Brahman orthodoxy, in particular its teachings on *karma* (see sidebar, opposite), were challenged vigorously by the Shramanas and others there were also some Shramanas who accepted the assumptions of *samsara* and *karma* but offered distinctive paths to final release from the world of perpetual rebirth and suffering. They included the founders of two traditions that survive today: Mahavira, the founder of Jainism, and the most famous Shramana of all, Siddhartha Gautama, better known as the Buddha.

A Pahari painting of an ascetic yogi *in the* matsyendra *posture. The use of yogic meditation practices to alter states of consciousness played a part in the development of various beliefs about the human soul,* karma, *and* samsara.

techniques that lead to altered states of consciousness and by physically training the body, the spiritual seeker attempts to experience the reality of the soul within and eliminate bad *karma*. To do so requires the guidance of a *guru* ("spiritual teacher"), who can monitor the disciple's development and lead him or her toward final release (*moksha*).

Some *guru*s were Brahmans and over the centuries their views regarding the cosmic Brahman, the individual soul, *karma*, and *yoga* were adopted as the central doctrines of Hinduism. These teachings were used to support the logic of the class system, justifying the status of the highest castes on the grounds of their superior *karma* (see p.14). Later generations of Brahman scholars argued that these teachings were consistent with Vedic revelation.

PART 1 ● CHAPTER 2 *Kevin Trainor*

THE CAREER OF SIDDHARTHA

THE BUDDHA'S BIOGRAPHY

Over the past century and a half, the figure of the Buddha has become widely known outside the regions of Asia where Buddhist traditions originated and flourished. Since the nineteenth century, Westerners have come to know of Buddhism through accounts of the Buddha's life such as the epic poem *The Light of Asia* (1879) by the English poet Sir Edwin Arnold or through works such as *Siddhartha* (1922) by the German writer Hermann Hesse. For more than two millennia, narratives of the Buddha's life have, not surprisingly, played a vital role in the lives of Buddhists throughout Asia, and from them the figure of the Buddha emerges today as through a prism, appearing at one point as a superhuman wonder worker, at another as a rationalist philosopher—he has even been seen by some modern writers as a crusading social reformer. It is noteworthy, then, that the Buddha's biography, in the sense of a comprehensive account of his life from birth to final passing away, appears to have developed only gradually among the Buddha's followers during the first centuries after his death, probably in close conjunction with the development of important pilgrimage sites identified with key events in his evolving life story.

The Buddha is, to be sure, vividly present in the earliest surviving canonical texts, since in most cases these teachings are in the form of dialogues between the Buddha and those whom he taught. Moreover, these texts provide detailed accounts of connected episodes in the Buddha's life, in particular the events up to and following his enlightenment, and the period immediately before his final passing away. But a continuous narrative of his life developed only gradually and in fact *jataka* stories—accounts of the Buddha's previous lives—were, judging from their prominence in the canonical collections (see pp.190–91), of more concern to the early Buddhist community than the details of his early life as Siddhartha Gautama. Buddhist tradition also holds that Gautama was but the latest in a long line of *buddhas* extending infinitely into the past and future (see p.93).

Some scholars have attempted to separate clearly the complex intermingling of the mythic and historical strands of the Buddha biography. Yet despite a considerable amount of research and debate, there is presently no consensus among scholars regarding the historical dates of Gautama Buddha's life. There is a widely accepted tradition that he gained enlightenment

Episodes from the Buddha's career were popular subjects for Buddhist artists, who typically transferred the events of his life to more familiar local settings. This hand-colored Chinese woodblock print of 1818 depicts Prince Siddhartha's excursions from the palace and witnessing of the Four Sights (see pp.28–9 and also illustration on p.59).

at the age of thirty-five and lived to be eighty, but the dates for his life proposed by different traditions of Buddhism and by modern scholars have varied considerably. Western scholarship throughout much of the twentieth century has accepted 486 or 483BCE as the likely date of the Buddha's death, with his birth placed eighty years earlier (566 or 563BCE). In the last twenty years, however, a growing consensus has emerged, based in particular on archaeological evidence, that his death date should be moved later, and many scholars favor a date of around 400BCE.

Whatever the extent of Western scholarship's preoccupation with the quest for the historical Buddha, it is clear that the Buddha's traditional biography has simultaneously stressed both his mundane and supramundane dimensions and that both dimensions have been of fundamental significance for his followers. While at one point the Buddha's biography may exemplify his role as a struggling human being, striving for perfection, at another it reveals his status as a superhuman embodiment of perfect enlightenment. The Buddha represents both the transcendent nature of such enlightenment, unfathomable to his unenlightened followers, and also its accessibility, made present in transforming acts of human communication addressed to a diversity of hearers, each at different stages along their individual paths to enlightenment.

THE LEGEND OF BAARLAM AND JOSAPHAT

While it was only in the nineteenth century that detailed information about the Buddha's life became available to a Western audience, elements of the Buddha's biography formed the basis of a widespread and very popular collection of legends that circulated throughout medieval Europe from the eleventh century. The legends, which appear to have made their way into Christian tradition via Arabic sources, concerned an Indian prince named Josaphat who was converted to Christianity by an ascetic sage named Baarlam. The biblical-sounding name Josaphat derives from the Sanskrit *bodhisattva*, a term used to refer to the Buddha prior to his enlightenment, and many of the details of Josaphat's life closely parallel episodes from the Buddha's youth, including his closeted early life within his father's palace before a transformative encounter with old age, sickness, death, and an ascetic renunciant (see pp.28–9). Josaphat and Baarlam were venerated as Christian saints in both the Greek and Roman churches. Nineteenth-century scholars uncovered the true origins of the saints' lives when accurate information about the life of the Buddha began to appear in Europe.

WONDROUS BIRTH

Traditional accounts of the Buddha's life often begin with stories of his previous lives, in which his exceptional virtues are displayed, for example in his penultimate birth as the prince Vishvantara (Pali, Vessantara), the very embodiment of boundless generosity (see pp.116–17). Following his death as Vishvantara, the *bodhisattva* ("enlightenment being," one who is destined to become a *buddha*) is reborn as a *deva* (deity) in the Tushita heaven, where he awaits the proper time for his final rebirth as Siddhartha. Some accounts tell of the *deva*s entreating him to descend into the human realm and of his choice of an appropriately virtuous woman to become his mother. Such stories emphasize the Buddha's extraordinary merit, accumulated through countless past lives, and also reinforce the message of his superiority over the *deva*s who, although divine beings, nevertheless depend upon a human to realize the ultimate truth that leads to liberation from rebirth, a condition afflicting gods as well as mortals.

In Buddhist legend, the *bodhisattva*'s conception takes an unusual form. His mother Mahamaya, the chief wife of Shuddhodana, the ruler of a small state in the Himalayan foothills, dreams that a great white elephant enters her womb through her right side. A white elephant is a symbol of royal majesty and authority, and court sages predict the future greatness of

PURITY AND GENDER

Traditions associated with the Buddha's mother Mahamaya in Buddhist literature suggest some ambivalence toward women and their role as bearers of children. Birth is often represented negatively as a symbol of the cycle of *samsara* (see p.58) from which the Buddha's teachings provide an escape, and in ancient south Asian cultures pregnancy, birth fluids, and menstruation were associated with pollution. Thus the Buddha's physical purity at birth is emphasized, as is Mahamaya's death shortly after he is born. According to Theravada tradition, her premature death preserves her purity from sexual contact and pregnancy, thus preventing her womb from being defiled by anything less pure than the *bodhisattva*. This tradition also demonstrates her great store of merit, which bears immediate fruit in her rebirth as a male *deva* (a general pattern that applies to the mothers of all *buddha*s). It is stated in the Nidanakatha: "Since the womb in which a *bodhisattva* has lain is like the relic-chamber of a shrine, and no other being can lie in it or occupy it, the mother of the *bodhisattva* dies seven days after the *bodhisattva*'s birth and is reborn in the [heaven of] Tusita [Tushita]."

In this stone relief from his birthplace at Lumbini in Nepal, the future Buddha is born from the right side of his mother Mahamaya (right), who is said to have given birth standing, holding onto the branch of a tree which miraculously lowered itself toward her.

the child, who is destined to become either a universal monarch or a *buddha* (see pp.26–7). While traveling to visit her family for the final stage of her pregnancy, Mahamaya gives birth to her son Siddhartha in a forest grove near Lumbini in present-day Nepal, and many traditions highlight the exceptional nature of the *bodhisattva*'s delivery. As numerous sculptures and paintings depict (see box, opposite), Mahamaya stands during the birth, assisted by a miraculously lowered branch from an overhanging tree. In some versions of the story, Siddhartha emerges painlessly from her right side and is caught in a golden net held by attendant *deva*s. Tradition emphasizes the uncharacteristic purity of the infant who, unlike other babies, emerges spotlessly clean from his mother's womb. The infant's purity is so great that Mahamaya dies a week after his birth (see box, opposite).

Siddhartha's singularity as the only being capable of realizing the ultimate truth is prefigured in the first moments following his birth. He alights from the *deva*s' arms and surveys the world in all directions. Perceiving that no other beings are his equal, he takes seven steps toward the east (the direction he will face when he gains enlightenment) and proclaims his mastery over the entire world, declaring, "I am the chief of the world."

The Birth of the Buddha *from an 18th-century Thai manuscript. The virtuous Mahamaya is giving birth to the* bodhisattva *in a special birthing enclosure. The god Brahma (above left) is shown receiving the Bodhisattva.*

THE "WHEEL TURNER"

A 2nd-century CE panel from the stupa (Buddhist "relic monument") at Amaravati, India, depicting a chakravartin king surrounded by attendants and devotees.

Compared to the lavish biographical detail accorded his conception and birth, the Buddha's early life and adolescence pass by relatively unremarked. One episode describes how as a youth he entered into meditative trance and was miraculously covered by the unwavering shadow of a nearby tree despite the sun's movement across the sky. Another story recounts how he defeated the best archers in the land, despite his complete lack of training.

The narratives repeatedly emphasize the great luxury with which the young *bodhisattva*'s father, Shuddhodana, surrounded him. While there is evidence to suggest that the Buddha was probably the son of an oligarch ruling over a relatively modest tribal republic straddling the present-day border of India and Nepal, the biographies describe his upbringing as one appropriate to the son of a great king, surrounded by enormous wealth and every imaginable pleasure. These descriptions serve to sharpen the contrast between Siddhartha's indulgent youth and his later ascetic renunciation, which was so extreme that he nearly died of starvation. They also contribute to a poignant subplot centered on his father's efforts to isolate him from any hint of human suffering which would cause him to abandon society and give up his potential to become a universal monarch—at his birth, the court sages had predicted that the Buddha would be a *chakravartin* ("wheel turner"), either a righteous universal king or a great enlightened renunciant.

While the story of the Buddha's life appears to resolve the tension between his two possible vocations unequivocally—he renounces society and fulfills the higher good of becoming a perfectly enlightened *buddha*—the history of the relationship between Sangha and state in south and southeast Asia suggests a more complicated intermingling of religious and political ideals. For example, the Buddha comes to function in some Buddhist societies as a sort of "king above kings," who rules *in absentia* over a cosmic hierarchy of celestial and earthly beings. There are also examples of Buddhist monarchs, such as the Dalai Lamas of Tibet, who claimed to be *bodhisattvas*, thereby imbuing their rule with a powerful aura of religious authority.

Despite a long history of scholarship on Buddhism emphasizing the apolitical character of the Buddha's teachings and the otherworldliness of his monastic followers, the history of the great Buddhist civilizations in Asia tells a rather different story of Buddhist engagement with secular rulers. Rather than an example of how an originally pure religious vision becomes corrupted by secular concerns with the passage of time, this phenomenon should be seen as arising from the interrelated ideals of the two wheels, one the wheel of the *chakravartin* king, whose righteous rule reflects the ethical ideals of the Buddha's teaching, the other the wheel of the Dharma, the liberating truth set in motion by the Buddha's first teaching (see pp.36–7). The fruitful tension between these twin ideals has exerted a powerful force on the development of Buddhist societies since at least the third century BCE, when the Indian emperor Ashoka embraced the Dharma and provided a paradigm of Buddhist kingship (see pp.50–53).

THE *MAHAPURUSHA*

The tension between the Buddha's two possible life courses hinges upon a tradition that he was a *mahapurusha*, a "great man." Such exalted beings, by virtue of their countless meritorious deeds in innumerable past lives, are born with an extraordinary physical perfection that sets them apart from ordinary humans, hence the distinctive physical characteristics that render images of the Buddha immediately recognizable.

The notion of the *mahapurusha* has roots that pre-date the appearance of Buddhism. For example, the Rig Veda (10.90) includes a creation myth detailing how the universe emerges from the sacrifice of a cosmic *purusha*. While it is unclear if this influenced later Buddhist notions of the *mahapurusha*, in Buddhist sources the idea has a marked ethical orientation; the extraordinary features of the *mahapurusha*, both physical and mental, are the direct outcome of virtuous deeds performed in past lives. Some Buddhist texts emphasize both the extraordinary beauty of the Buddha's appearance, as well as the benefits available to those who have the good fortune to gaze upon him and hear his voice. Canonical sources detail thirty-two major marks that adorn the bodies of *mahapurusha*s, and some of these are usually represented in images of the Buddha, including the tightly curled hair on his head circling to the right, the hair between his eyebrows, and the image of a wheel on his feet. Some traditions added a further eighty minor marks of a *buddha*.

A monumental sculpture in Pegu, Burma (Myanmar), of the Buddha reclining as he awaits his Final Nirvana (see pp.40–41). It shows the 108 auspicious signs which, in some Buddhist traditions, are said to have adorned the soles of his feet.

THE "FOUR SIGHTS"

Forewarned of the circumstances that will cause his son to reject life in society and set off alone to find a remedy for human suffering, Siddhartha's father surrounds him with sensual pleasures. As a result, the sheltered young man is ignorant of old age, disease, and death.

One day Siddhartha sets out in his chariot from the palace into the city. Some versions of the story describe how his father has the route beautified and guarded so that his son's gaze cannot fall upon anything that might turn his thoughts to suffering. But the *devas*, knowing that the future liberation of all beings rests upon the *bodhisattva*'s encounter with suffering, conjure up the sight of an old man. When he sees the gray-haired man, stooped and trembling over his cane, Siddhartha stares wide-eyed and uncomprehending. He asks Chandaka, his charioteer, what manner of person stands before him, and is told that this is an old man. He asks if this man is unique, but Chandaka replies that the infirmities of old age come to all beings alike. Deeply shaken, Siddhartha returns quickly to the palace.

When his father learns what has happened, he immediately showers him with sensual diversions, but his son is too troubled to enjoy them. On the following day—some traditions recount the four events in one day—Siddhartha sets forth in his chariot, and now the *devas* produce an image of a sick man, his diseased body afflicted with oozing sores. Once again Siddhartha turns to Chandaka for an explanation and is told that all beings are subject to the ravages of disease and pain. Siddhartha hurries home, distraught by what he has witnessed.

THE DANCING GIRLS

Many important themes and tensions in Buddhist tradition can be illustrated by the account of Siddhartha and the dancing girls (see main text). A central insight of the Buddha's teaching—that the human body and its attendant sensual pleasures are transient—is graphically illustrated here. The account also exemplifies specifically male attitudes toward women that reflect gender inequalities in ancient Indian society (see pp.14–15). Variations of this episode occur elsewhere in Buddhist literature—for example, in the story of the householder Yashas, whose similar spiritual awakening at the sight of sleeping women was prefigured by an incident in a past life when he had cremated the corpse of a pregnant woman and had been filled with a sense of disgust at the body's impurity.

Stories such as these, which represent women's bodies as impure and threatening to men, reveal a basic ambivalence toward women that is also reflected in their lower social status. This inequality is apparent, for example, in the traditional accounts of the Buddha's initial reluctance to found the women's monastic community (see p.39) and its institutional subordination to the men's community, despite the recognition that women were fully capable of gaining enlightenment.

It seems likely that the ongoing dialogue—and tensions—about appropriate roles for Buddhist men and women will take on additional force and complexity as Buddhist communities become more widely established in the West and as possibilities for global communication increase (see pp.212–37).

On the third day Siddhartha heads out into the city in his chariot and this time the *deva*s produce a corpse. Seeing the funeral procession from a distance, Siddhartha mistakes it for a parade, but wonders why those participating look so miserable. Chandaka explains that the man has died and that death is the inevitable fate of all beings. Still more deeply troubled, Siddhartha returns quickly to the palace.

On his fourth and final excursion from the palace, the *deva*s create an image of a wandering renunciant, whose tranquil and composed face captures the gaze of the deeply agitated *bodhisattva*. Chandaka explains that this is a person who has gained equanimity by renouncing the cares of the world. Immediately Siddhartha resolves to follow his example.

When Siddhartha returns to the palace, he is surrounded by beautiful women who play enchanting music and dance before him. When he falls asleep, they lie down to rest. After a time the *bodhisattva* awakes and gazes upon the sleeping women. Some of them are drooling, others snoring and grinding their teeth. Suddenly the women, whom he had once seen as sexually arousing, appear to him like corpses strewn about a charnel ground. Prefiguring his future moment of enlightenment beneath the Bodhi tree, the *bodhisattva* awakens to the profoundest truths about the nature of human experience. Everything before him speaks of transience, suffering, and death.

A 19th-century Burmese manuscript illustration of Prince Siddhartha leaving the palace and witnessing the Four Sights. Some Buddhist traditions suggest that these events took place on four successive days, while others recount the incidents within a single day.

THE "GOING FORTH"

The *bodhisattva*'s decision to renounce society was tested in a final scene before his triumphant "going forth" into homelessness. While Siddhartha is said to have married at age sixteen, he did not become a father until he was twenty-nine. On the very day that he resolved to leave his family behind, he learned that his wife Yashodhara had given birth to a son. His response signals his sense of estrangement from worldly concerns—he named his son Rahula, which means "impediment."

Siddhartha clearly felt some sense of loss at the prospect of abandoning his newborn child, for his final act before leaving was to enter the darkened room where his wife and son were sleeping. As Siddhartha gazed upon them, he felt the urge to pick up his son, but overcame his desire because he knew that this would awaken his wife, who would try to prevent his departure. He resolved to return to see the boy after he had gained enlightenment.

In a reenactment of the Buddha's departure from his father's palace and renunciation of his princely life, young boys who are about to be ordained leave their homes dressed as the young prince Siddhartha. During the ordination ceremony—such as this one in Rangoon, Burma (Yangon, Myanmar)—they exchange their princely robes for the simple garments of a monk.

THE BUDDHA'S REUNION WITH HIS SON
It is recorded that the Buddha did in fact see his son again after his enlightenment. When Yashodhara learned that her former husband had come to the palace to receive alms, she sent Rahula, now a young boy, to confront him and demand his inheritance. The Buddha finally responded by ordaining him as a novice monk, much to the dismay of his grandfather, who extracted from the Buddha a promise that he would not ordain children without the permission of their parents.

CHANDAKA

The story of Chandaka, Siddhartha's chariot driver, provides an interesting example of the elaborate biographical traditions that developed around those closest to the young *bodhisattva*. It is said that Chandaka, like the Buddha's wife Yashodhara and his horse Kanthaka, was born at the very instant that the Buddha came into the world. Chandaka also appears as a character in stories of the Buddha's past lives. When the *bodhisattva* renounced the world, Chandaka begged permission to accompany him into a life of renunciation, but Siddhartha refused, insisting that he return to the city. Siddhartha's horse died of a broken heart, and Chandaka returned to Kapilavashtu with a double burden of grief. He later encountered the Buddha after his enlightenment and became a monk, but his former intimate association with the *bodhisattva* filled him with such pride that he committed various transgressions, and the Buddha's final act before passing away was a pronouncement of excommunication on his former charioteer. However, the humbled Chandaka later repented of his misdeeds and attained *nirvana* (Pali, *nibbana*).

Once again, the emotional register of the narrative has shifted. The young man who first experienced disquiet and anxiety in the face of life's ills, and then a powerful revulsion toward sensual desires, now recognized the value of what he was leaving behind even as he resolved to let nothing deter him from attaining his goal.

In a scene widely illustrated throughout the Buddhist world, Siddhartha next mounted his horse and fled the palace, with his faithful chariot driver Chandaka (see box, above) clinging to the horse's tail. Superhuman beings intervened, by holding the horse's hooves suspended above the ground to prevent the sleeping city from waking.

Siddhartha's decision to renounce the world was by no means unprecedented in his day. He was one of many who "went forth" from society as Shramanas, wandering mendicants who committed themselves to lives of physical asceticism, philosophical inquiry, and techniques of mental concentration (see pp.20–21). Traditional accounts of the Buddha's life identify two such figures with whom Siddhartha studied—Alara Kalama and Udraka Ramaputra. From them he learned to attain very high levels of mental trance, but not the liberating insight he was seeking. Disenchanted, Siddhartha turned to extreme forms of asceticism in order to conquer his body's primal demands for food, sleep, sex, and sensual enjoyment.

After six years of harsh ascetic practices Siddhartha was on the verge of dying of starvation. He realized that his death at this point, before he had attained enlightenment, would only lead to continued rebirth, and he resolved to fortify his body with food so that he could make a final effort to gain the truth. He encountered a young woman named Sujata who gave him a meal of milk rice. When the five ascetics who had been following him as their teacher learned that he had eaten, they abandoned him in disgust, convinced that he had given up. Now utterly alone, Siddhartha sat down beneath the sheltering leaves of a pipal tree and vowed to sit in meditation until he had attained enlightenment.

OVERLEAF *This 19th-century Thai painting depicts Siddhartha leaving the palace at night. His faithful charioteer, Chandaka, clings onto the horse's tail. The deities, meanwhile, support his horse's hooves so they make no noise.*

Devas (supernatural beings) and other superhuman entities populate the literature of Buddhism, both in its élite canonical forms and its popular folk variations, and they play important supporting roles in the Buddha's biography. Devas live very long lives—some of them recall previous buddhas—and they intervene at key points in the narrative to keep the bodhisattva's march toward enlightenment on track. Moreover, throughout the story of Siddhartha's quest for enlightenment there is a fruitful tension between the dramatic struggles of a human being who must overcome formidable obstacles as he strives to realize the truth, and a more cosmic perspective from which the bodhisattva's past deeds of merit inevitably come to fruition in this final installment of a story that stretches back over countless lifetimes.

THE "AWAKENING"

Once Siddhartha has sat beneath the pipal tree, the biographies do not move immediately to the conclusion of his quest for inner realization—a journey that has led him from his original aspiration to attain enlightenment through countless lives marked by self-sacrifice and virtuous deeds. Instead the accounts interject a dramatic scene—a final contest between Siddhartha, a solitary human being intent on finding a way out of the cycle of birth, death, and rebirth, and the armies of the *deva* Mara, a supernatural being associated with death and rebirth, and the desires that lead to *samsara*.

The story of Mara's attack on the *bodhisattva* has drawn the attention of countless artists throughout the Buddhist world (see box, opposite). Siddhartha's meditative calm proved so powerful that the deadly forces hurled at him were transformed into flowers of offering that showered gently down upon his head. Siddhartha was equally unmoved when, according to some traditions, Mara sent his beautiful daughters in an attempt to seduce the *bodhisattva*. In a final attempt to unseat him, Mara insisted that he, not Siddhartha, had a right to the throne of enlightenment by virtue of his

The Seat of Enlightenment at Bodh Gaya in Bihar province, northeastern India, is generally dated to the 3rd century BCE (the Mauryan period) and is said to mark the very spot where the Buddha attained enlightenment. It remains a major pilgrimage site (see pp.114–15) and the Bodhi tree there is said to be descended from the original tree under which the Buddha sat.

previous meritorious deeds, and all of Mara's hordes thundered forth their support. In response, the solitary *bodhisattva* reached down and touched the ground, calling upon the earth goddess to bear witness to his countless past deeds of merit. In acknowledgment the earth gave a great shudder, at which Mara's fearsome elephant bowed down before the Buddha in submission, and Mara and his armies fled in terror. At this moment hosts of *deva*s arrived to proclaim Siddhartha's victory and to witness his final illumination.

After this cosmic confrontation, the account of the Buddha's actual enlightenment seems almost anticlimactic. He meditated throughout the three watches of the night, first attaining knowledge of his past lives, then the power to see the past lives of other beings (the "divine eye"), and finally insight into the causally conditioned nature of reality (see pp.60–61 and p.140). As the sun dawned in the east, he gained perfect omniscience. In response, a thundering earthquake resounded throughout the ten thousand surrounding world systems and all of nature was momentarily transformed. Knowing that he had finally attained an end to rebirth, the Buddha uttered his "lion's roar," announcing his victory over the forces of *samsara*. It is from this moment that he is properly called the Buddha, the "Awakened One."

The accounts go on to describe the seven weeks following the Buddha's enlightenment, during which he meditated at seven different places, before deciding to share his liberating knowledge with others (see pp.36–7).

THE DEFEAT OF MARA IN BUDDHIST ART

The striking contrast between the equanimity of the seated figure of Siddhartha, rapt in meditation, and the encircling chaos of Mara's armies, attacking the *bodhisattva* with wave upon wave of violent assaults, invited graphic representation in Buddhist art. The victory over Mara became an important subject for southeast Asian Buddhist artists, beginning around the eleventh century CE as the Theravada tradition grew in prominence in the region. An interesting Thai variation on this scene highlights the role of the earth goddess, who rises up beneath the throne of enlightenment and wrings out her hair. The deluge that rushes forth (symbolizing the *bodhisattva*'s accumulated merits from past virtuous deeds) washes away Mara's hordes.

Many representations of the Mahabodhi shrine at Bodh Gaya, the site of the Buddha's victory over Mara and subsequent enlightenment, appear throughout Burma (Myanmar) and Thailand.

A 19th-century Burmese manuscript painting of the meditating bodhisattva *Shakyamuni being attacked by the forces of Mara, witnessed by the earth goddess as she wrings out her hair, which has been drenched by the water poured out during the donation rituals performed by the* bodhisattva *in past lives.*

THE "FIRST TURNING OF THE DHARMA WHEEL"

THE FIRST LAY BUDDHISTS
The seventh week following the Buddha's enlightenment ended with another encounter that proved symbolically important for the institutionalization of his teachings. While the Buddha was seated in meditation, two merchants named Trapusha and Bhallika stopped to make an offering of food, his first meal since Sujata's offering seven weeks earlier (see p.31). These men became the first lay followers of the Buddha, formally "taking refuge" in the Buddha and his teaching, the Dharma. This foreshadowed what would become the Triple Refuge ritual, following the establishment of the third refuge, the Sangha (see p.38). They then begged the Buddha for something of his to venerate after they left, and he gave them some hairs from his head which they later enshrined in a *stupa* ("relic monument"). Here, in microcosm, appeared the basic pattern of lay support for the Buddhist monastic community (the Sangha).

During the first week following his enlightenment, the Buddha remained seated beneath the pipal—henceforth called the "Bodhi tree" ("enlightenment tree")—experiencing the sublime joy of his perfect liberation. In the second week he stood and gazed unblinkingly upon the tree in gratitude. He spent the third week walking back and forth next to the tree—with each step lotus blossoms sprang up to cushion his feet. In the fourth week he sat in a divinely created jeweled house, contemplating the teachings that later become the Abhidharma collection (see pp.192–3). For the final three weeks the Buddha sat in meditation under three different trees. During the sixth week he was seated under the tree of Muchalinda, a *naga* ("serpent deity"), when a great storm threatened. But Muchalinda rose up and spread out his cobra hood to protect the Buddha from the elements—an episode commonly depicted in Buddha images. At the conclusion of the seventh week, the Buddha considered whether or not to teach the profound truth that he had realized, and a delegation of *deva*s, headed by the great god Brahma, entreated him to share his liberating insight with others.

In one sense, the account of the enlightenment represents the climax of the Buddha's biography, in that it marks the fulfillment, after countless lifetimes, of his quest for liberation. However, the Buddha's first act of teaching can be seen as an event of even greater significance, since from this point the liberation he had achieved became a possibility for the whole of humankind. For some forty-five years following his enlightenment the Buddha was occupied in teaching his insights.

It is said that the Buddha's first thought was to teach his own two teachers, but they had already died. He then turned to his former students, the five ascetics who had lost faith in him when he had turned back from the brink of starvation. The Buddha used his "divine eye" to determine that they were in fact able to benefit from his instruction, and headed toward the deer park in Sarnath, a town a few miles from Varanasi (Benares), where they were residing. The five saw him approaching and resolved to remain seated to show their lack of respect, but as the Buddha got closer he radiated such a powerful aura of loving kindness that they could not resist venerating him. When they used his old name and addressed him familiarly as "friend," the Buddha explained that this form of address was no longer appropriate: he was now the Tathagata, a term reserved for *buddha*s, literally one who has "gone thus" along the path to the realization of perfect enlightenment.

The five ascetics gathered around the Buddha and he began to teach them, an event characterized as the First Turning of the Dharma Wheel. In this discourse he set forth the basic outlines of the truth he had realized under the Bodhi tree, a profound understanding of the nature of reality summarized in the formula known as the Four Noble Truths (see pp.64–71). He also explained the Middle Path that the seeker after enlightenment should follow, avoiding the two extremes of sensual indulgence and harsh asceticism. So effective was his teaching that within a week all of them had become *arhat*s, "worthy ones" who have realized *nirvana* (Pali, *nibbana*).

The Buddha's exceptional effectiveness as a teacher is repeatedly emphasized in both canonical sources and in the later biographies. In part this can be attributed to the supernormal mental attainments gained during his enlightenment. Equipped with a detailed knowledge of his own past lives and with the power to see the past lives of others, the Buddha is said to have had the capacity to teach at a level precisely calibrated to the needs and abilities of his hearers, who as a result made remarkably quick progress toward enlightenment. This unique ability to teach in ways appropriate to a diverse audience, some at the beginning of the path and others on the brink of realization, becomes the basis for the Mahayana doctrine called Skill in Means.

The importance of the First Turning of the Dharma Wheel and the site where it took place are apparent from both textual sources and archaeological remains. In the third century BCE the great emperor Ashoka (see pp.50–53), a Buddhist convert, erected a *stupa* there and an inscribed column. Ashoka's inscription, the so-called Schism Edict, commemorated the scene of the Buddha's first teaching with a reminder to the members of the Buddhist community—the Sangha—of the importance of unity, and prescribed expulsion for those who sowed seeds of dissension.

The Ivolginskiy monastery, near Ulan-Ude in eastern Siberia. The golden Dharma Wheel and two deer symbolize the Buddha's first act of teaching in the deer park at Sarnath and are characteristic features of temples of the Tibetan Buddhist tradition, which was influential across central and northeastern Asia. A spoked wheel has become a common symbol of the Buddhist tradition and in ancient India a wheel could represent the sovereignty of kings. The figure of a wheel is also said to have appeared on the soles of the Buddha's feet (see box, p.27). While many early examples of Buddhist wheels show a multitude of spokes, contemporary versions often have eight, to symbolize the Eightfold Path (see pp.72–9).

THE GROWING SANGHA

A Chinese, Song-dynasty era (960–1279), polychrome bronze figurine of Kashyapa, one of the Buddha's first followers and arhats. He is believed to have presided at the council held in Rajagriha in the wake of the Buddha's death.

The five ascetics who received the Buddha's first teaching after his enlightenment, and who requested permission to "go forth" as ordained followers, became the first members of the Sangha. Thus the nucleus of the Buddhist monastic community was initially comprised of men who had already withdrawn from society and had been living for years as wandering mendicants.

Soon after this initial formation of the Sangha, the Buddha encountered a wealthy young householder named Yashas who, much like the Buddha before his own renunciation, had had an experience of disillusionment with sensual pleasures while gazing on the bodies of sleeping women (see pp.28–9). Yashas was so distraught that he fled into the forest in the middle of the night where he unexpectedly met the Buddha. The Buddha taught him and Yashas gained considerable insight into the Dharma, but did not actually request ordination. The next morning Yashas' father searched for his missing son, and the Buddha used his marvelous powers to hide Yashas from his father's sight. While the Buddha instructed the father, Yashas gained enlightenment and became an *arhat* ("worthy one;" see p.96). Yashas' father became a male lay follower (*upasaka*) of the Buddha—one who recited the Triple Refuge because the third refuge, the Sangha, had now been established—and the Buddha allowed him to see his son who had been seated in front of him all along.

Recognizing that his son could not revert to lay life, Yashas' father invited the Buddha to his home to receive alms, attended by Yashas. When they arrived, the Buddha taught Yashas' mother—who was the first woman to recite the Triple Refuge and become a female lay follower (*upasika*). Four of Yashas' wealthy young friends arrived, heard the Buddha's teaching and were ordained, becoming *arhat*s as well. Finally, word spread and fifty more friends came to see the Buddha, received ordination, and quickly gained *nirvana*. The Buddha sent these sixty enlightened men out to spread his teaching, saying: "Travel forth, monks, for the benefit of the many, for the happiness of the many, out of compassion for the world, for the well-being, benefit, and happiness of gods and humans. Two should not go together. Teach, monks, the Dharma which is delightful from beginning to end."

While tradition suggests that the earliest followers of the Buddha were from socially prominent families, the Sangha attracted people from all levels of society. In principle, the early Sangha was open to all males, although the Vinaya (text defining monastic discipline) describes the Buddha gradually excluding various groups, such as debtors, criminals, deserters, and those with physical deformities. This seems to reflect his concern to avoid criticism of the movement, which was dependent upon support from the laity for its material needs and for recruiting future generations of monks. As the community began to accept younger men, a twofold ordination developed, with boys entering the community as novices under the guidance of monastic preceptors, and men older than nineteen eligible for full ordination as *bhikshu*s, subject to the full discipline defined in the Vinaya.

After the Sangha had been in existence for five years, the Buddha's aunt and foster mother, Mahaprajapati, approached him seeking to join the Sangha. Traditional accounts record that the Buddha initially refused, but relented when his close attendant Ananda intervened on her behalf, and the nuns agreed to eight additional rules that subordinated their community to the community of monks. These accounts unequivocally affirm that women are fully capable of attaining *nirvana*; the Buddha's initial resistance appears to reflect a concern to ensure lay support and to avoid complications resulting from groups of male and female renunciants living in close proximity (see also pp.98–9).

The Sangha's original peripatetic lifestyle also gradually shifted to a more settled mode of life as lay donors established permanent monastic residences and local communities of Buddhist monastics developed reciprocal relationships with particular lay communities. The ideals of solitude and complete isolation from social ties lived on in the Sangha, but only a minority of monastics adhered to them as the Buddhist movement became better established.

Monks carrying bowls for receiving their daily alms from lay householders—a tradition dating back to the earliest years of Buddhist monasticism. Wat Suan Mokkhaphalaram, Thailand.

THE FINAL NIRVANA

Events during the forty-five-year period from the Buddha's enlightenment and establishment of the Sangha up to his death are represented in early canonical sources mostly by unconnected individual dialogues between the Buddha and his followers. Canonical sources do, however, preserve a lengthy biographical account of the weeks leading up to his Final Nirvana (*parinirvana*), or Great Final Nirvana (*mahaparinirvana*)—an event that marked both the ultimate completion of his own quest for total liberation from *samsara* and a crucial moment in the life of his community.

Buddhist tradition embodies a fundamental tension concerning the Buddha's role in his followers' ongoing practice. On the one hand, the Buddha's teaching stresses that everyone must realize the truth for him- or herself—the Buddha can only point the way, which he does through his teachings. On the other hand, the tradition also celebrates the extraordinary efficacy of personal encounters with the Buddha.

As the richness of Buddhist art attests, truth in the abstract is of less use to suffering beings than truth embodied and accessible through the

The Buddha's Final Nirvana, an 18th-century painting from Dambulla Rajamahavihara, Sri Lanka. In some artistic representations of the death of the Buddha—who is typically shown, as here, lying between two trees—his followers react with varying degrees of grief or equanimity according to their own relative progress along the path to nirvana.

senses. The accounts of the Buddha's death vividly illustrate this point. Ananda figures prominently in these final scenes and he provides a kind of emotional center to the narrative, for he had been the Buddha's personal servant for twenty-five years but had not himself realized *nirvana*. When the Buddha heard that Ananda was weeping at the prospect of his death, he took him aside and recalled Ananda's countless acts of loving kindness toward him, assuring Ananda that he would soon gain enlightenment.

It is recorded that the Buddha died from food poisoning after a final meal offered by the blacksmith Chunda. Knowing that the food he was about to consume was deadly, the Buddha made sure that no one else ate it. He contracted acute dysentery, but overcame the pain and traveled on. Finally, outside the town of Kushinagara, he lay down on his right side between two shala trees, his head facing north. Withdrawing into himself, he ascended through successive levels of profound meditative trance and finally passed away. At that moment, it is said, the entire universe shook violently.

The Buddha's final words were: "All contingent things pass away; strive onward [toward *nirvana*] with diligence." These words highlight both the inevitability of death—even for perfectly enlightened *buddha*s—and the importance of self-discipline and self-realization. In short, the Buddha told his followers: you are on your own. And yet, things are not so simple. For an earlier passage describes the Buddha giving detailed instructions for cremating his body and preserving his corporeal remains; as befits both enlightened beings and *chakravartin* kings, his relics were to be enshrined in relic monuments (*stupa*s or *chaitya*s) situated in public places. Moreover, the Buddha, in another passage, encourages the practice of visiting the four places associated with his birth, enlightenment, first teaching, and death. While the Buddha himself may no longer be directly available to his followers, his liberating presence continues to be manifested in diverse material forms: through his recollected words of instruction; contact with pilgrimage sites; and material objects that mediate his presence, whether by virtue of a direct physical connection (as with corporeal relics) or a physical resemblance (images).

DIVISION OF THE RELICS

Early accounts of the Buddha's death include the story of how his cremated remains were divided into portions and distributed among local rulers who enshrined them throughout northern India. What is more telling, however, is the description of how the Mallas, in whose territory the Buddha died, initially sought to keep all the relics for themselves (see illustration, p.7). When a terrible war was about to ensue, a Brahman or priest named Drona intervened, saying: "Our Buddha was a teacher of forbearance. Unfitting indeed is this clash of arms over the division of the [Buddha's] remains. May you all be united, sirs, reconciled; rejoicing together we shall make eight portions; relic monuments will be widespread in all directions."

This story provides a dramatic object lesson in both the great value accorded the Buddha's remains and in the dangers of selfish attachment. The resolution of the story suggests that the Buddha's relics are so precious that they should be widely distributed and thus made accessible to as many people as possible.

Whatever the historical legitimacy of any particular relic, the practice of relic veneration has been central to the spread and maintenance of Buddhist tradition for more than two millennia.

ART AND ARCHITECTURE *Michael Willis*

DEPICTING THE BUDDHA

The future Buddha's final birth as Prince Siddhartha was the culmination of the many existences recounted (and often illustrated) in collections of *jataka* stories (see p.191). After a life of ease as a young nobleman, Siddhartha turned his back on privilege and began his career as a wandering ascetic. His departure from the palace, years of spiritual searching, enlightenment at Bodh Gaya, first sermon at Sarnath, and final passing at Kushinagara were taken as the central events in the Buddha narrative, and they appear frequently in sculpture and painting throughout the Buddhist world. Some subjects, such as the *bodhisattva*'s princely life and departure from the palace, were especially common in early relief sculpture, while images of the Buddha meditating and teaching were favored from about the fifth century CE. The moment of enlightenment became a popular subject as a result of a growing interest in the Buddha as the embodiment of supreme wisdom. These images invariably depict the Buddha with his eyes lowered and his legs crossed in a yogic position (lotus or half-lotus), iconographic indications that his wisdom is entirely spiritual and derived from within (see illustrations on pp.44, 74, and 81).

This is a detail from a long scroll painted in Nepal in the early 18th century called Sakyasimha Buddha Jataka. Its subject is the life of the Buddha. The scene shows the bodhisattva's *groom, Chandaka, returning to the palace with the* bodhisattva's *horse and turban. He is reporting to the grief-stricken family that the prince has renounced the world in search of enlightenment.*

The emphasis on wisdom in the Mahayana traditions of Tibet, China, and Japan led to the representation of the Buddha as a monumental cosmic being, transcendent in essence, unmoveable by nature, and eternal by definition. This form of the Buddha was described as the Sambhogakaya ("Celestial Body"), a sublime form that resides only in the highest pure worlds. Despite the prevalence of this otherworldly vision of *buddha*hood, storytelling was never entirely abandoned and narrative vignettes often surround sculptures or paintings of the Buddha meditating or teaching. This is encountered from at least the twelfth century CE in relief carving from India and Burma. The ongoing popularity of the Buddha's life story in southeast Asia and Sri Lanka is also shown by the frequent occurrence of the Mahaparinirvana or Great Final Nirvana, in which the Buddha is shown reclining on his deathbed (see illustrations on p.40, and 69). The greatness of this historical event is accentuated by monumental size: for example, the nineteenth-century reclining Buddha at Wat Po in Bangkok is 150 feet (46 metres) in length.

The first Buddhist sculptures in India date to the second century BCE, at least two hundred years after the Buddha's time. Without exception, this art was used to decorate monuments in monasteries, typically the stone railings which surround and protect the *stupa*s built to contain sacred relics (see box, p.48 and pp.51–3). A peculiar feature of early sculpture is the apparent absence of the Buddha in human form, an issue which has recently been the subject of scholarly debate. Although Siddhartha before enlightenment is freely shown, the Buddha himself is generally absent or represented by symbols, such as his footprints or the tree under which he sat to meditate. This has been explained as a way of showing respect for the Buddha's spiritual achievement. Because he had attained *nirvana* and escaped the confines of both a human body and the material world, it would be contradictory and demeaning to show the Buddha in stone or any other mundane substance. The absence of Buddha images is confirmed by early texts such as the Milindapanha ("Questions of Menander;" see box, p.119), which makes no mention of carved images or other representations but makes clear that the Buddha is to be found and seen in shrines which contain his bodily relics. The importance of relics is reinforced by texts and inscriptions which record that the Buddha's remains have a "living presence" which allow them to emit marvelous rays and to assume or project the physical appearance of the Buddha himself. These kinds of religious visions, seen at places connected with the Buddha's life or at sites where his relics were later deposited, may have prompted the creation of commemorative images of the Buddha. The most common location of such images, in the few instances where their ancient context is preserved, is directly in front of *stupa*s. The placement of images in *stupa* niches remains customary in Nepal, Sri Lanka, and southeast Asia.

Hints about when and why Buddha images were first introduced are provided by the Ashokavadana ("Stories of Ashoka"), a narrative that is set in the time of the emperor Ashoka (see pp.50–53) but which was probably composed in the first or second century CE. The monk Upagupta, a key figure in the story, encounters Mara, the divinity who had tried to distract the

Stone head of the emaciated Buddha, brought close to death by fasting. Gandharan style, ca. 200CE.

THE FASTING BUDDHA

During his period as a wandering ascetic prior to his enlightenment (see p.31), Siddhartha fasted to such an extent that he reduced himself to a living skeleton. After six years he abandoned such excesses and resolved to follow the Middle Way, a path of moderation which rejected both sensory indulgence and extreme mortification. Depictions of the Buddha in the middle of his period of penance are found notably in Gandhara, an ancient region embracing northwest Pakistan and Afghanistan. Gandharan art reflects the strong Hellenistic cultural influences in the region.

Buddha during his final meditation at Bodh Gaya (see p.35). Like the Buddha before him, Upagupta is able to overcome the difficulties thrown in his way by Mara. Yet Mara is not destroyed—apart from the fact that his destruction would be a violent act and thus unacceptable to Buddhists, Mara is ever-present since he represents desire and hence death, rebirth, and the whole material world. Upagupta realizes that Mara was present at the time of the Buddha and thus had the opportunity of seeing the Master when he was alive. Upagupta asks Mara to call on his memory and magically transform his appearance into that of the Buddha. When Mara obliges, Upagupta is so overjoyed that he begins to worship the form that has appeared before him. When Mara castigates Upagupta for his unseemly behavior, Upagupta replies that it is not the actual substance of Mara which he is worshipping but the ideal behind the image. Upagupta draws a parallel with what people do when they worship terracotta images: "knowing that what they worship is the god and not the clay."

This story is important because it seems to embody the debates that were current in the first century CE about the acceptability and validity of Buddha images. At the time, *stupas* containing the bodily relics of the Buddha were well known. These relics were, of course, by their nature material remains, but they contained a "living presence" and had a capacity to act upon the world because the Buddha resolved that this should be so during his lifetime. Just like the monastic community and the Dharma, relics continued to function after the Buddha's passing. However, artistic representations of the Buddha, in whatever material, are unconnected with the Buddha personally and are part of the material world that is directly opposed to *nirvana*. To make Buddha images worthy objects of veneration, they had to be understood as symbolic rather than what might be described as idols. Whatever devotees might have thought about the matter in actual practice, sculptures were technically described as *uddesika dhatu* or "relics of indication or referral." This connection between relics and images was essential and has never been lost. Throughout the Buddhist world, sculptures are consecrated with a variety of deposits, sometimes inserted in a recess at the back or, in the case of hollow metal images, underneath a metal plaque in the bottom. These deposits could include a relic of some kind, a cosmic diagram (*mandala*), scrolls with Buddhist texts and, in the Tibetan world, small shafts of wood that were considered to be a "tree of life" which animated the casting. In India, stone carvings were consistently engraved with the teaching of Dependent Origination (see illustration on p.79, and pp.140 and 197). In Mahayana Buddhism, copying, reciting, and venerating the texts which contain the Buddha's wisdom was much emphasized, Mahayana followers believing that the Buddha was and is accessible primarily through his words. Since the verse about Dependent Origination was a condensed summary of these words, it was the essence of the Buddha's Dharmakaya ("Dharma Body;" see pp.91, 100, and 176–7). The presence of the text could thus be taken as a genuine part of the Buddha's body, a "relic" which could transform a mere piece of stone into something worthy of veneration.

A seated image of the Buddha, in the attitude of subduing Mara, in the ruins of the 14th-century main assembly hall at Wat Mahathat, the principal temple complex of Sukhothai, the ancient capital of Thailand.

PART 1 • CHAPTER 3 *Todd T. Lewis*

A NEW COMMUNITY

EXPANSION AND FRAGMENTATION

The Buddha's following steadily grew as he found interested audiences among the forest-dwelling ascetics as well as among Brahmans, urban house-holders, and "men of good family." He traveled almost continuously, except during the monsoon season when his monks (*bhikshu*s) remained in one place, partly because of the difficulties caused by the weather and partly to show compassion toward the profusion of living creatures which might be harmed by travelers walking about during the rains. This period of settled life helped to forge the group's identity and facilitated the establishment of relations between the religious community and local lay patrons. The monks probably used this time both to bond and to engage in intensive meditation.

As the Sangha expanded, it adjusted to new situations as they arose. In addition to his teaching, the Buddha also created an entirely new institu-tion—a community of renunciants whose extensive rules evolved with the emerging society of northeast India. After much urging (at least according to some legends), he also gave permission for the creation of a *bhikshuni sangha* of female renunciants (see pp.38–9).

The Buddha agreed that the Sangha could receive lands, buildings, and other communal resources, which were probably donated initially to make the monsoon retreat easier to manage. In doing so, he established the means by which the Sangha shifted its focus over time to a settled, cooper-ative, communal existence, a development that also gave householders a fixed focus for their meritorious patronage. Life in the Buddhist Sangha was a true refuge for those "noble sons and daughters of the Buddha" (as monks and nuns were called) who wished to leave behind their homes and seek enlightenment. The ideal was simple—material needs were provided by lay householders and the ordained would assist each other, so that renunciation and meditation could be practiced without encumbrances.

The Buddha was also sensitive to the state laws under which he lived and prohibited criminals, runaway slaves, or debtors from joining the Sangha; he also specified rules or principles by which the community should be governed (by seniority, as reckoned from the time of ordination) and insisted that a collective monastic ritual of reconfirmation, the Pratimoksha (see also pp.99, 106–7, and 189), should be observed each fortnight. The Buddha's genius as a community founder is also evident in his cultivation of a householder community that provided for the needs of the Sangha.

Following the Buddha's death, and in accordance with his instruction that no single person or institution be given authority over his community, the monks and nuns settled in widely separated monastic colonies which perpetuated the faith. Each settled Sangha evolved a distinctive form of communal life and those with the aptitude memorized the Buddha's teachings that they had heard.

Buddhist textual sources generally agree that one or more Buddhist councils met during the first two or three centuries following the Buddha's death, although they disagree on where and when these meetings occurred and who attended them. There is widespread agreement that a communal recitation of the Buddha's teaching was held at Rajagriha (modern Rajgir, Bihar) soon after his death. According to Theravada tradition, this council consisted of 500 *arhat*s, including Ananda (see p.41), who gained enlightenment on the eve of the meeting. There are also accounts of a second meeting roughly a century later, this time at Vaishali, when a division occurred within the Sangha, perhaps owing to a dispute over disciplinary issues, although disagreements over the status of *arhat*s are also attested. This resulted in the emergence of two lines of ordination: the Sthavira ("Elders") and the Mahasanghika ("Great Assembly") (see pp.54–5). These groups later divided further into a number of different communities or schools. Disciplinary issues, then, rather than doctrinal disagreements, were probably

A monastic ordination ceremony being conducted at Wat Bovornives, Bangkok. The communal setting of the early Sangha differs markedly from the environment to be found in the big cities of Asia today, and this has meant the Sangha has had to be responsive to the expectations of the lay community. In Thailand, and other Theravada countries in southeast Asia, it is the practice for young men to spend a short period of the year—a few weeks or months, often a rainy season retreat—once in their lives living as monks.

THE WORSHIP OF RELIC MEMORIALS

Worship at Buddhist shrines (*stupa*s or *chaitya*s) has been traced back to the Buddha himself in early texts such as the Mahaparinirvana ("Great Final Nirvana Sutra") and became a primary focus of Buddhist ritual activity. These shrines generally enclose sacred objects, including the corporeal remains of *buddha*s, saints, and revered teachers, objects used by them, or Buddhist texts, as well as a variety of other auspicious objects. The traditional accounts record that soon after the Buddha's death his remains were divided into eight collections (see box, p.41) and that each was enshrined under a *stupa*.

These relic burial shrines probably derived from those used to honor the *chakravartin* kings and were adopted by Buddhists to honor the Buddha who reigns supreme over all through his Dharma. It was at *stupa*s that his disciples could venerate his "sacred traces" to gain merit.

*Stupa*s are sites for remembering the Buddha through joyful devotional celebration, including in some cases musical accompaniment, a practice attested in early accounts of the Buddha's funeral. *Stupa*s were also "power places" where, according to some Buddhist traditions, a relic could impart the blessings of the Buddha's presence and healing power.

One of India's best-preserved stupas is to be found at Sanchi. These scenes from the Buddha's life and acts of stupa veneration were carved in the 1st century CE.

the primary cause of division within the early Sangha, with the communities sharing considerable common ground in the teachings that they collected in their respective scriptural canons (the Tripitakas, see pp.186–7).

Despite the aparent failure to reach consensus on matters of discipline, the Vinayas (monastic codes) of the early schools are remarkably similar; the disagreements that led to schisms seem to have originated over relatively minor points of monastic life. After the first two councils, it is not certain that all the monks and nuns in northern India ever gathered together again. The autonomous nature of the early Buddhist communities, and the divergent understandings of the Dharma which existed between them, contributed to the development of regional pluralism. These differences continue across the Buddhist world right up to the present.

Wherever Buddhism took root, monks, nuns, and devout lay followers established monasteries: independent, corporate institutions which influenced local societies and regional polities. India's early Sangha disregarded the *varna* (social class, see box, p.14) of its members. In Buddhism's subsequent missionary migrations, ordination into the Sangha offered citizens an opportunity for religious practice and educational advancement that was otherwise unavailable. Buddhism, in turn, depended upon the householders making donations to the Sangha in order to earn merit to improve their *karma* and to garner blessings for themselves, their families, and communities.

The typical Buddhist community had its center in a monastery (*vihara*), where monks or nuns would take their communal vows, meditate, and study. Over time, these institutions also supported monks who specialized in memorizing the teachings, preaching the Dharma, practicing medicine, and performing rituals essential to the Buddhist lifestyle of the locality. An important distinction soon developed within Buddhist monasticism between the forest monastery, where meditation and optional ascetic practices (*dhutanga*) could be undertaken (often under the leadership of a charismatic teacher), and the village monastery, where compassionate service to the community (ritual, medical, educational) could be blended with individual cultivation and study. Cave dwellings (*lenas*) were favored in some regions, notably, though somewhat later, in central Asia and China. Typically, a monk or nun moved between village and forest monasteries in the course of his or her career.

A 19th-century Burmese marble figure of a young Buddhist monk or novice holding an alms bowl in which to receive a lay donation to the Sangha.

In many areas, the focus and inspiration for followers was a monk whose charisma and teaching ability drew both ascetic disciples and meritorious donations from the laity. The biographies of such monks commonly resemble that of the Buddha: disillusionment followed by renunciation and retreat to the wilderness, enlightenment, then returning to teach.

Many formulations of proper Buddhist practice, from simple to advanced, were made in the course of early Buddhist history to guide the faithful. These were organized around the triad of moral practice (*shila*), meditation (*dhyana*), and insight cultivation (*prajna*).

Buddhist monasticism arose to provide refuge and support for renunciants seeking enlightenment, but the tradition survived by building multifaceted relationships with lay followers. As it spread, Buddhism adapted to myriad local traditions, from urban centers to villages, spreading outward to frontier regions and attracting devotees from all social classes, from kings and Brahmans to merchants and artisans. All became members of "the assembly" (*parishad*) of ordained monks, nuns, and dedicated householders.

The general ideals of Buddhist civilization were articulated very early. Monks and nuns served the world through their example of renunciation and meditation, and by performing rituals and healing. As preservers, transmitters, and exemplars of the Dharma, members of the Sangha were obligated to be spiritually worthy and, as the Buddha instructed, "show the householders the way to heaven." Householders could hope for rebirth in one of the heavenly realms (see pp.62–3) through earning merit by making donations to the Sangha. The early communities, then, came to share common traits: *stupas* ("relic shrines," see box, opposite) as centers of community ritual; *viharas* as refuges for meditation, study, and material resources; and Sangha members who assume leadership of the community's religious instruction and ritual life.

The Buddha's emphasis on practical spiritual endeavors adapted to each individual also contributed to the strength and diversity of the expanding tradition. He taught that there are very different kinds of people who are at different stages of spiritual development, and according to whether they are "ordinary persons, learners, or adepts," each is to be instructed differently. Regardless of the individual's ability, the rare opportunity of human birth should not be wasted and life should be lived with purpose.

THE BUDDHIST EMPEROR

After Alexander the Great's (355–323BCE) campaign of world conquest faltered in northwest India, the small states on the Indus River that had been weakened by his incursions were subsequently conquered and integrated into India's first large empire, that of Chandragupta Maurya (reigned ca. 321–297BCE), centred on the Ganges plain and extending to the Bay of Bengal in the east and the southern Deccan plateau in the center. When his grandson Ashoka (reigned 274–236BCE) assumed the throne, he followed the Indian royal norm of consolidating his frontier regions with brute force, directing an assault at Kalinga, a southeast coast region encompassing modern Orissa. However, Ashoka is said to have felt remorse at the widespread destruction and bloodshed that his army caused in securing victory.

At just that time, the emperor encountered a charismatic Buddhist monk and became a staunch devotee. Having extended the Mauryan empire across most of the Indian subcontinent, Ashoka sent ambassadors and scribes to explain the Dharma throughout his realm and beyond.

Ashoka's edicts were both general and specific in their explanation of the *dharma*, a term with many shades of meaning, not necessarily the Buddha's teachings specifically. He considered *dharma* to be the key to a just and compassionate society. On a pillar, he had this early edict inscribed: "*Dharma* is good. But what does *dharma* consist of? It consists of few sins and many good deeds, of kindness, liberality, truthfulness, and purity." Having stated these and other principles in prominent public places, Ashoka also sought to have his bureaucracy administer the empire in accordance with them: "My officials of all ranks—high, low, and intermediate—act in accordance with the precepts of my instruction. For these are the rules: to govern according to *dharma*, to administer justice according to *dharma*, to advance the people's

THE IDEAL BUDDHIST RULERS: *DHARMARAJA*S AND *CHAKRAVARTIN*S

Buddhist teachers in the centuries after Ashoka invoked his deeds as a model of leadership. Ashoka's chief concern was for Buddhism as a moralizing force: "One should obey one's father and mother. One should respect the supreme value and sacredness of life. One should speak the truth. One should practice these virtues of the Dharma." Charity, justice, concern with the common good, and generosity toward the Sangha became the norms by which a good Buddhist ruler was measured.

Since Ashoka, Buddhists have also depended on the assistance of rulers to realize their ideal of a moral and spiritual civilization. Leading members of the Sangha could offer those wielding political power the highest legitimation in the eyes of the faithful if they acted rightly. A good king could be called a *bodhisattva* ("future *buddha*") or a *dharmaraja* ("just king"). Merging both was the *chakravartin* monarch, who set the wheel of the Dharma in motion, and whose rule was marked by various supernatural signs (see pp.36–7). Engagement with political rulers also gave Buddhist societies a distinctive weakness: monasticism was dependent upon political leaders who had to "purify" the Sangha periodically; for example, by removing those not properly ordained or acting contrary to the Vinaya norms.

happiness according to *dharma*, and to protect them according to *dharma*." He had trees and wells planted to aid travelers, declared certain days when animal slaughter was prohibited, and worked to limit religious conflict.

His inscriptions also indicate that Ashoka went on pilgrimage to visit the places the Buddha had lived. Texts recount that he unearthed the Buddha's relics from their *chaitya*s in order to distribute them across his realm, building thousands of *stupa*s to enshrine them. Sri Lankan chronicle traditions also link Ashoka with the transmission of Buddhism to the island: his son Mahendra (Pali, Mahinda), a monk, introduced the monastic ordination lineage and his daughter Sanghamitra brought a cutting of the Bodhi tree.

Through his edicts, patronage of notable monks, and prestige, Ashoka helped spread Buddhism far and wide. Inscriptions indicate that he sent emissaries throughout the known world, including Greece, China, and some still uncertain destinations in southeast Asia. Ashoka immeasurably assisted Buddhism's emergence, and Buddhist shrines and monasteries soon dotted the major trade routes in every direction from the religion's northern Indian heartlands.

ART AND ARCHITECTURE *Michael Willis*

ASHOKA THE BUILDER

*One of four carved gateways (*toranas*) to the* stupa *at Sanchi, which was founded by Ashoka and much embellished in later centuries. Each* torana *marks a cardinal point and has three horizontal beams with spiral-decorated ends and surfaces carved with stories of the Buddha's lives and other Buddhist images. Also found at the site are the remains of a number of columns, monasteries, and temples.*

The emperor Ashoka's inscriptions (see sidebar, opposite) are spread widely across the subcontinent, from Bihar in the east to the Afghan frontier in the northwest, and almost as far south as the Tungabhadra River, near the Tamil country of south India. The distribution of these records gives some idea of the scale of the empire and the great power of its ruler. As well as describing Ashoka's personal concern for his subjects and for *dharma* (a term which in the context of his inscriptions primarily refers to public morality, orderly conduct, respect for elders, and religious tolerance; see also pp.50–51), they also describe his building of wells and rest-houses. Near an inscribed pillar in Nepal, set up to commemorate Ashoka's visit to the Buddha's birthplace at Lumbini, an inscription records that the king expanded the *stupa* of Kanakamuni, an earlier *buddha* who lived many eons before Siddhartha.

This picture of Ashoka as a builder with Buddhist sympathies is confirmed by other archaeological evidence. A number of third-century BCE

brick-built *stupa*s can be assigned with reasonable confidence to Ashoka, giving some color to the legend in the Ashokavadana ("Stories of Ashoka") that he built many *stupa*s. The most celebrated of these is at Sanchi, where there is also a pillar with an imperial edict and the remains of a hall, perhaps used for monastic assemblies. Sanchi was embellished in subsequent centuries and the original *stupa* was hidden by later enlargements. Other *stupa*s—for example that at Amaravati (see also p.51) on the banks of the Krishna River—have been reduced to little more than a circular mark on the ground, although parts of the first railing that surrounded the *stupa* have survived.

Before the third century BCE, wood was the preferred medium for building and carving. Due to the rigors of the climate, practically all ancient Indian woodwork has disappeared. Under Ashoka, or perhaps under his grandfather Chandragupta, carving in stone became widespread. Ashoka's free-standing stone pillars, crowned by animal capitals and incised with inscriptions, were thus a startling innovation, especially notable for their burnished surfaces which gave the sculptures a sparkling appearance in the bright sun. The pillars and capitals are made of the same sandstone, which was quarried and carved in eastern India and then transported over considerable distances. The technology for such undertakings was apparently brought to India by Persian craftsmen fleeing in the face of the advancing armies of Alexander the Great, who reached the frontiers of India in 326BCE.

The best preserved of Ashoka's animal capitals comes from Sarnath. It originally crowned a pillar, the stump of which can still be seen among the ruined monasteries and temples at the site. The capital has four lions and was originally surmounted by a large spoked wheel. This wheel, and the smaller ones around the base of the capital, is presumed to symbolize the *chakravartin*, or "wheel turner" (see p.26), a reference both to Ashoka, the ideal monarch, and to the Buddha, whose first sermon, or "turning of the wheel of the Dharma," took place at Sarnath. The lions are thus dual symbols (see also p.51), alluding simultaneously to the royal power of Ashoka and to the Buddha, who is frequently called the "lion of the Shakya clan."

Although scripts of some kind may have been used in India as early as the fifth century BCE, the first securely dated writing belongs to the Ashokan era. Termed *brahmi* by scholars, it was used for the inscriptions on prominent rocks and stone pillars in various parts of Ashoka's vast empire (see illustration, right). Probably invented at the royal court explicitly for Ashoka's edicts, the script appears to have drawn on Aramaic, a Semitic tongue widely used throughout the Near East as a bureaucratic language.

A reference to the Indian inscriptions is found in the writing of the Chinese pilgrim Xuanzang (see p.112). His comments on the contents of these texts suggest that by his time (the seventh century CE) the ability to read the scripts had been lost. It was not until 1834 that James Prinsep, who headed the British East India Company mint in Calcutta and took an interest in early coin inscriptions, deciphered one of Ashoka's edicts. In doing so he transformed Ashoka from a legendary figure into a tangible personality, and thus inaugurated a new era in the study of ancient Buddhism.

Carved into a stone pillar, this inscription forms part of Ashoka's edict from Sarnath, near Varanasi, which includes a warning of expulsion for any dissident monks.

DIVISIONS IN THE SANGHA

In the first centuries after the Buddha's death, the new movement spread out to many different regions and the earliest divisions within the Sangha appear to have been the result of varied local interpretations of the monastic code, the Vinaya, caused in part by the dispersion of communities. Traditional accounts refer to eighteen distinct "schools," although this number is merely convention and more than eighteen are listed in the various accounts.

Most scholars accept the historicity of a division within the Sangha between followers of the Sthavira (Thera in Pali), or "Elders," and those of the Mahasanghika, or "Great Assembly," though it is not clear if this was primarily occasioned by disagreement between those who favored stringent religious discipline and those who took a liberal view, or had to do with questions concerning the nature of the *arhat* (though this, too, had disciplinary implications). Dating is problematic, but most agree it was prior to Ashoka's reign. Both the inscriptional evidence and texts support the view that there was further division due to varying disciplinary and doctrinal perspectives, though it remained common practice for traveling monks to reside in any community and there seems to have been harmony within the larger Sangha.

THE DECLINE OF BUDDHISM IN INDIA

By the twelfth century CE, Buddhism in India was in decline, for several reasons, including anti-Buddhist polemics within a resurgent Hinduism, and Muslim invasions. The latter had destroyed the north Indian monasteries by 1200CE, several centuries after Muslim merchants had come to dominate the trade along the Silk Road that had once been largely controlled by Buddhists. Without patronage or state support, monks fled and the institutions of the Gangetic plain were left in ruins.

Were it not for Mahayana's successful expansion beyond northern India, this school of Buddhism may have remained a minor philosophical schism. However, the tradition attracted the peoples of central Asia and Nepal, and then by means of monks from those centers it spread onward to Tibet, China, and further afield. One reason advanced for Mahayana's appeal was the celestial *bodhisattva*s, and the uncompromising compassion they offered to all who requested it.

The torso of a stone statue of a bodhisattva *from Gandhara region, the region that served as a stepping stone for the spread of Mahayana Buddhism beyond the Indian heartland and into central Asia.*

A Tibetan thangka, *date unknown, showing the Buddha surrounded by* bodhisattvas *and famous* lamas. *Devotion to* bodhisattvas *is a central element of Mahayana Buddhism.*

It is out of this still largely obscure context that a Buddhist movement arose that came to be known as the Mahayana, or "Great Vehicle" (see pp. 132–49). Its followers accepted the Mahayana *sutra*s (see pp. 196–211) and the teachings to which they give written expression. In contrast to earlier theories that argued for the prominence of lay Buddhists in the rise of the Mahayana, scholars increasingly emphasize its monastic origins and the prominence of devotion to the *sutra*s themselves, or what some have called the "cult of the book." Not surprisingly, the first evidence for this is textual, with most scholars dating the earliest Mahayana texts to around the first century BCE. It is not until the fourth century CE that inscriptional evidence for the movement appears in India, and even this does not make direct use of the term "Mahayana," which first occurs in sixth-century inscriptions.

Although the emergence of the Mahayana literature clearly marks a major shift in doctrinal perspective, there is reason to believe that it did not at first cause a division within monastic communities which had Mahayana followers. Supporters of the Mahayana practiced the same Vinaya discipline as their co-residents who rejected the new teachings. Only later did divisions emerge, and these stemmed in part from the fact that the forms of Buddhism that spread to Tibet and east Asia were primarily Mahayana in character, though they too retained Vinaya traditions from the pre-Mahayana schools.

PART 2

PRINCIPLES AND PRACTICE

A Theravada monk at Aukana in Sri Lanka lays an offering of a garland of flowers at the feet of a colossal, 5th-century CE statue of the Buddha. Representations of the Buddha abound in Sri Lanka, attracting devoted worshippers.

PART 2 • CHAPTER 1 *Todd T. Lewis*

THE HUMAN CONDITION

SAMSARA AND THE SOUL

Buddhism shares with Hinduism the doctrine of *samsara*, whereby all beings pass through an unceasing cycle of birth, death, and rebirth until they find a means of liberation from the cycle. However, Buddhism differs from Hinduism in rejecting the assertion that every human being possesses a changeless soul which constitutes his or her ultimate identity, and which transmigrates from one incarnation to the next. The Buddhist perspective is that humans, like all phenomena, are constantly changing, in flux, impermanent. Therefore no fixed entity called "the soul" is possible.

The Buddha's teaching of *anatman* ("non-self") rejects any notion of an intrinsic, unchanging entity at the core of a person. What then did he regard as a human being? Seeking to see all reality as process, the Buddha analyzed a person as a collection of five components (*skandha*s): the physical body (*rupa*), which is made of combinations of the four elements (earth, water, fire, air); feelings (*vedana*), which arise from sensory contact in the

THE COMPASSION OF SUJATA

The hundreds of *jataka* ("birth") tales—accounts of the Buddha's previous lives—indicate the emphasis that Buddhists place on the reality of rebirth as the framework for all experience. In the following story, the future Buddha alleviates his father's grief by compassionately reminding him that his grandfather has passed on, literally, to another existence in a different form. "Grandfather," like the ox, existed only when all the five *skandha*s (see main text) were present, and hence the father's attachment to a few physical remains is pointless.

"In the past, when Brahmadatta [a king] was reigning in Benares, the future Buddha was born in the house of a landowner and called Sujata. When his grandfather died, his father, steeped in grief, brought the bones from the burning pyre, laid them out on a mound, and honored them with flowers, contemplating and lamenting,

and neglected to bathe, eat, or attend to his work. The future Buddha conceived a plan to make his father lose his excessive sorrow. He found a dead ox, then fetched some grass and water; laying them before the ox, he called out 'Eat! Drink!' Passers-by reported this to his father, who asked Sujata to explain his actions. The future Buddha replied:

'The head's yet there, the feet, / Front, hind, and tail / Are still the same—methinks / The ox may yet rise up. / But no more is seen of / Grandfather's hands, feet, or head! / Weeping beside the mound / You are alone, out of your mind!'

The father reflected and said, 'Dear wise Sujata, I know the saying, "all things are transient." Henceforth, I will not grieve further, thanks to my grief-dispelling son...' So in compassion work the very wise, turning us back from grief."

form of sight, sound, smell, taste, touch, or thought; perceptions (*samjna*), which attach the categories good, evil, or neutral to these sensory inputs; habitual mental dispositions (*samskaras*), which connect *karma*-producing will to mental action; and consciousness (*vijnana*), which arises when mind and body come in contact with the external world.

The spiritual purpose of breaking down any apparently unchanging locus of individuality is to demonstrate that there is "no thing" to be attached to or to direct one's desire toward. Attached to things, addicted to themselves, and in denial about their mortality, human beings misconstrue reality and bind themselves to suffering and inevitable rebirth in *samsara*. The *anatman* doctrine presented Buddhist exponents with the perpetual problem of explaining moral causality: how can the doctrine of *karma* (see pp.60–61), with its emphasis on moral retribution, operate without the mechanism of a metaphysical soul which connects the doer to moral results?

Early texts show that this question was clearly posed to the Buddha: if there is no soul, how can karmic "fruits" of any good or evil act pass into the future of this life or into an individual's later incarnation? The standard Buddhist response is that *karma* endures in habitual mental energy (*samskara*), which is impressed in the fifth *skandha*, consciousness. Although always evolving and thus impermanent, consciousness endures in this life and subsequently leaves the body at death, passing on to be reincarnated in the next life form.

This painting by the 18th-century artist Kim Hongdo in the temple of Yongju in Suwan, South Korea, shows a pivotal episode from the life of the Buddha: Prince Siddhartha's chariot journey and his encounter with death and a renunciant, two of the Four Sights, which first alerted him to the transience and impermanence of all existence.

KARMA

Buddhism is founded on the understanding that all life in the universe is subject to moral causality, a process that links present actions to future consequences, both in this life and in lives to come. This force is *karma*, a word meaning "deeds," but also their consequence, the individual's cumulative balance of *punya* ("merit," or what is familiarly called "good *karma*") and *papa* ("demerit," or "bad *karma*"). Buddhists regard all intentional acts of the body, speech, and mind as producing "karmic" consequences. *Karma* primarily determines the nature of every rebirth after death, ruling one's destiny until, and unless, one realizes *nirvana* and eliminates *karma*.

What makes humans differ from one another is *karma*, the key factor accounting for the variations in people's physical traits, mental abilities, and character. For this reason, Buddhism is not a "spiritual democracy," requiring the same religious practices of everyone. Some are suited for advanced meditation, while others are capable of comprehending only the most

A page from a 19th-century Burmese jataka *manuscript, illustrating the Buddha's previous existence as a tree spirit (right). In the Buddhist view, the right moral practice leads to a reduction in* papa *(literally "bad" or "evil," implying demerit), as a result of which the individual attains progressively higher forms of rebirth until the effects of* karma *are eliminated.*

THE BUDDHA'S SUFFERING AND THE INDETERMINACY OF *KARMA*

The Buddhist understanding of causality is that not all contingencies in life are *karma*-determined. The issue originally arose when sceptics questioned how it was that the Buddha himself, even though enlightened, suffered in old age and was injured when his enemy Devadatta attempted to assassinate him with a boulder, though only a shard from it injured his foot.

In one text, the Milindapanha ("Questions of Menander"), this issue is explained explicitly, as an enlightened monk teaches that in life there are eight causal contingencies that affect all beings: "It is not all suffering that has its root in *karma*. There are eight causes by which sufferings arise; the first three are wind, bile, and phlegm in superabundance; the union of these humours; variations in temperature; the avoiding of dissimilarities; external agency; and *karma*. So what arises as the fruit of *karma* is much less than that which arises from other causes; no one without a Buddha's insight [*prajna*] can fix the extent of the action of *karma*."

This influential text continues by noting that while only enlightened *buddhas* can ascertain whether *karma* or other contingencies are at work in life, most people are faced with uncertainty in evaluating the karmic consequences of their experiences.

elementary moral instructions. The Buddhist path rests on "gradual teaching" (*anupurvikatha*), whereby meritorious gift-giving (*punya dana*) is the foundation for Buddhist practice. An individual progresses through the following four stages of practice: *dana* ("self-less giving"), which aims to diminish desire (see pp.66–7 and 110–11) and earn merit; *shila* ("morality"), to avoid acquiring demerit; *svarga* ("heaven"), a goal of meritorious rebirth; and *dharma-deshana*, or "instruction on doctrine," especially that of the Four Noble Truths (see pp.64–71).

All Buddhists, irrespective of tradition, aim to act in such a way as to generate merit and eliminate "bad karma." For the laity, this is achieved primarily through the practice of *dana*, which can be translated as "charity" or "generosity" (see pp.110–111).

Buddhist philosophy emphasizes that certain actions have strong karmic effects, and that a person's circumstances at birth offer strong evidence for the moral quality of his or her past lives. However, this does not necessarily mean that the doctrine of *karma* is fatalistic, since Buddhist textual sources make it clear that one's balance of merit and demerit, like all phenomena, changes constantly, and hence one's destiny cannot be predetermined in any given instant.

To the average human being, his or her own *karma* is not fully knowable. Nor is *karma* the only force at work in life, for other natural cause-and-effect relationships are recognized and random chance is also an accepted part of reality (see box, above). However, a "general reading" of one's *karma* can be discerned from one's status at birth and from what has happened in one's life since. As far as the future is concerned, the logic of the *karma* doctrine has motivated Buddhists everywhere to endeavor to generate merit whenever possible—frequently likened to planting good seeds to guarantee a rich future harvest of karmic fruit. Living with *karma*, then, is one of the chief concerns of the typical Buddhist.

THE SIX REALMS OF BEING

Buddhist doctrine holds that until they realize *nirvana*, beings are bound to undergo rebirth and redeath due to their having acted out of ignorance and desire, thereby producing the "seeds" of *karma*. As long as one makes and carries this burden of *karma*, rebirth is inevitable. The most common formulation of *samsara* recognizes six domains, or "realms of being," into which one may be reborn, in accordance with one's *karma*.

The first realm is the domain of human beings. This is regarded as the best existential state, because only humans are capable of achieving *nirvana*. The Buddha's sermons encourage his listeners not to waste the rare and precious opportunity of human birth. Fortunate indeed are those blessed with human intelligence and good health, and who have heard the Buddha's teaching, the Dharma. However, owing to *karma*, humans have vastly different physical endowments, moral natures, and spiritual capacities.

To be born in the second realm as a deity (*deva*) in one of the heavens—often said to number twenty-six, although the total varies—is thought to be the result of very good *karma*, and in the Buddhist understanding heaven-born individuals enjoy a supremely sublime environment. In heaven, one is free from work, and can enjoy all the earthly pleasures. However, the problem with the heavens is that they are so satisfying to the senses that they can promote attachment and are thereby not conducive to advancing one's understanding or spiritual practice. It is still true, nonetheless, that the prospect of a heavenly rebirth motivated the devotions of the vast majority of Buddhist lay people in history. A human or heavenly rebirth is the only desirable destiny in *samsara*.

To be reborn as a demon (*ashura*) is to have some supernormal powers, but to be dominated by anger. Periodically the demons assault the heavens, another reason why life in these realms is less than perfect. Buddhists in Asia regard demons as capable of causing trouble for humans, for it is believed that certain forms of illness are caused by demonic possession.

The fourth realm is that of the restless spirits (*preta*s), who in previous lives were excessively attached to human life and so are reborn only with bodies of "subtle matter." The most frequently mentioned is the hungry ghost *preta*, who was not generous with family, friends, and especially when it came to supporting the Buddhist Sangha. Normally invisible, these *preta*s are born with large stomachs and very small throats, so they suffer with an extreme inability to satisfy their unrelenting thirst and hunger. Compassionate Buddhist lay people and monastics across the world set out food offerings before they eat and these are left outside their dwellings to feed any hungry ghosts residing nearby. Buddhist festivals in east Asia specifically seek to satisfy these unfortunate beings who must suffer the consequences of their bad *karma*.

Even more dramatic forms of suffering are endured by those whose negative *karma* results in rebirth in the realm of hell, or purgatory. There are

A Tibetan thangka *(devotional painting) of the Wheel of Life, which depicts the human cycle of death and rebirth.*

THE *KLESHAS*

At the center of the Tibetan Wheel of Life (left)—a map of *samsara*—are three animals that symbolize the hindrances or poisons (*klesha*s) that cause all beings to generate *karma* and suffer rebirth. The pig represents delusion; the rooster, lust; and the snake denotes hatred or anger. Until these are removed, individuals will be reborn in one of the six realms of existence. The hideous demon enclosing the wheel is Yama, the Lord of Death, who can be interpreted as symbolizing the tendency of human beings to cling to material existence. Originally an Indian deity, he appears—in person or through his henchmen—to claim the dead and, in the Buddhist imagination, oversees the process of karmic retribution. Yama is sometimes identified with Mara, who tempted the Buddha (see p.34) and who is thought to induce desire to divert those on the spiritual path.

numerous types of infernal region, including eight hot and eight cold hells. Each involves a distinctive form of suffering such as extreme heat, cold, laceration, or being eaten alive, repeating the retribution of bad karmic deeds again and again. Specific moral misdeeds have potentially dire consequences, especially lying, theft, and adultery. Buddhist teachers used the fear of hellish rebirths to inspire devotees to good moral behavior in their daily lives.

Rebirth in the animal realm is thought to be, in some instances, similar to rebirth in purgatory, because animals prey on one another, are driven solely by instinctual desires, and can only in rare instances generate good *karma* (as in a famous incident when a troop of monkeys is said to have offered a bowl of honey to the Buddha). The early texts regard some plants as having a primitive form of consciousness as well.

PART 2 • CHAPTER 2 *Todd T. Lewis*

THE "FOUR NOBLE TRUTHS"

SUFFERING AND UNSATISFACTORINESS

The Buddha's earliest and most enduring formulation of doctrine, the Four Noble Truths, diagnose the human condition and prescribe a treatment: the path toward *nirvana*. The biographies of the Buddha reveal that through his realization of these truths, he reached enlightenment. The Four Noble Truths were the subject of the Buddha's first sermon and are discussed often in the earliest texts.

The medical methodology of diagnosis, prescription, and treatment used in the presentation of the Four Noble Truths contributed to yet another epithet of the Buddha: the Great Physician. His medicine is the Dharma and it is the Sangha, the monastic community, that continues to administer this treatment in his absence.

The First Noble Truth (see sidebar, left)—that all life entails suffering (*duhkha*)—alerts the Buddhist to the inevitable experience of mortal existence: physical and mental disease, loss of loved ones, bodily degeneration in old age, and inescapable death. The reality of suffering was all too evident in the pre-modern world. The era in which the Buddha lived was one of warfare and disease, in which life expectancy was short, where roughly one-half of children died before the age of five, and epidemic illnesses swept through settlements, killing large sections of the population.

Even pleasure and good times, however enjoyable, have an unsatisfactory quality since they are only temporary. Humanity is trapped in the potentially endless cycle of *samsara* and must endure lifetime after lifetime of suffering and unsatisfactoriness (the broader sense of *duhkha*) in all their forms. The intention of this truth is not to induce pessimism, but to direct one's focus toward clear, realistic observation. The Buddha asserts that spiritual maturity is not possible if one remains in denial about one's inevitable degeneration and mortality, or ignores the suffering of others. Just as he himself was alerted to spiritual action when he encountered the Four Sights (see pp.28–9), so too must humans clearly see the reality of suffering for all mortals in order to reach enlightenment. The appropriate Buddhist response to the truth of suffering is to make the most of the spiritual opportunities of human birth and to show compassion (*karuna*) and loving-kindness (*maitri*) in order to alleviate the suffering affecting all other beings.

THE FIRST NOBLE TRUTH
"The Noble Truth of suffering is this: birth is suffering; old age is suffering; sickness is suffering; death is suffering; sorrow and lamentation, pain, grief, and despair are suffering; association with the unpleasant is suffering; dissociation from the pleasant is suffering; not to get what one wants is suffering. In brief, the five aggregates [*skandhas*] of attachment are suffering."

जोड़ों के दर्द की दवा

A modern wall painting depicting the pain of embodied existence, from a Buddhist monastery in Nepal. Only after the Buddha saw the reality of suffering, and realized that he and all his loved ones were doomed to succumb to it, did he decide to leave home and search for a means to escape samsara. *Recognizing the universality of suffering within* samsara *is a characteristic of a Buddhist's advanced spiritual understanding.*

Escape from *samsara* and suffering is through spiritual means. When, like the Buddha, individuals grow tired of the pain and bondage of life in *samsara*, they are ready to seek liberation, beginning by taking refuge in the Triple Gem of the Buddha, the Dharma, and the Sangha (see p.36–7). The seventh-century CE scholar Shantideva, in the Bodhicharyavatara ("Undertaking the Path to Enlightenment"), vividly expresses the alternative to seeking a way out of *samsara*: "Even one afraid of passing illness would not ignore the doctor's advice; how much more so one in the grip of the four hundred and four diseases, of which just one can wipe out all the people in India ...I stand with exceeding care even on an ordinary cliff. How much more so above a precipice of a thousand leagues through the great expanses of time?"

DESIRE AND ITS CESSATION

THE SECOND NOBLE TRUTH
"The Noble Truth on the Origin of Suffering is this: it is in this thirst which produces reexistence and rebecoming, bound up with passionate greed. It finds fresh delight now here and now there, namely, the thirst for sense pleasures; thirst for existence and becoming; and thirst for non-existence."

The Second Noble Truth states that the cause of suffering is desire. The term used is *trishna*, which is literally "thirst," and this usefully implies that all human beings yearn for food (in excess of biological need), possessions, power, and sex. The Buddha argued that all the world's troubles are rooted in desire. Like an addictive narcotic, desire warps our minds and distorts our understanding , leading us to act in desire-driven ways that insure the continuation of our own suffering and inevitable rebirth in *samsara*. In the early Buddhist texts, *samsara* is likened to a river in flood, sweeping away humanity to misery, death, and rebirth. This flood is caused by submitting to desire,

with the Buddha's teachings likened to the raft that one can take refuge in and overcome the current, reaching the "other shore," or *nirvana*.

One Pali text argues that desire is so integral to our world that its primal power shaped the early evolution of life on earth. The first beings born on earth, it says, were non-material beings, "made of mind," who enjoyed long and blissful lives. It was only after one of them tasted a sweet substance covering the earth that this being became consumed by desire and craved more of the substance. The others soon followed this example, and immediately their radiance disappeared, their bodies became solid, and plants and other edible life forms appeared. Eventually, desire grew so powerful that gender divided the creatures, they initiated sex, and then theft, lying, and other harmful actions appeared, all leading to the world as we know it.

While it may seem that Buddhism's emphasis on suffering and desire implies a certain pessimism about the human condition, the periodic appearance in the world of perfected *buddha*s to teach the means to liberation from suffering and desire offers optimism for human potential. Desire receives careful analysis in the early texts since the Buddha taught that the existence of any desire at all will prevent an individual from attaining *nirvana*. Desire's potential to overpower humans is conveyed in parables: just like insects attracted to the light of a wick lamp and thereby drawn to their deaths, humans likewise rush headlong, intent on their cravings, and miss what is worthwhile. Buddhist philosophers identified three main kinds of desire—for sensual pleasures, for rebirth, and for no further rebirth (a subtle form of final craving that must be renounced in the quest for *nirvana*). They also tracked subtle forms of desire, classifying them as arising with sights, sounds, smells, tastes, tactile stimuli, and thoughts.

Early Buddhists thus recognized the difficulty of following this ideal of ending desire. They sought a path somewhere between the sensuous life of the prince in the palace and the extreme asceticism of his forest-dwelling years. For Buddhists, the body has to sustain life and should be respected; it should be cared for but not loved; desire must be eliminated, yet without mutilating the body. Buddhists must act, yet cultivate equanimity

The focus on desire in the Second Noble Truth makes plain Buddhism's emphasis on renunciation and detachment. The advanced Buddhist lifestyle involves renunciation of the everyday world of desire in favor of the monastic community. The Sangha is considered a refuge for just this reason: it offers individuals the chance to live simply and to lose their desires. It is also a refuge in the sense that it administers in the name of the Buddha the "good medicine" of his Dharma to sick humanity. At the advanced stages of practice, the desire to learn the Buddha's teachings and even the desire to attain enlightenment, must also be renounced in order to reach the final goal.

For both monks and householders, for two millennia the ideal of human detachment, calm, and compassion has been conveyed by images of the Buddha. A proper image should have each part of the great teacher's body suggest to the viewer the antidote to humanity's deranged "thirsting" after desired things and its compulsive aggrandizement of the ego. The eyes should show detachment from visual stimuli, the mouth should suggest restraint of speech, the sage's hands convey absence of grasping, his face overall indicate desirelessness, and so on.

THE FIRE SERMON

The inevitability of suffering when one is unable to control desire is conveyed in one of the Buddha's most dramatic teachings, "The Fire Sermon": "Monks, everything is burning. And what is burning? Monks, the eye is burning, visible forms are burning, visual consciousness is burning, visual impression is burning... Burning with what? Burning with the fire of desire, the fire of aversion, the fire of delusion ...The ear is burning, sounds are burning... The tongue is burning, flavors are burning... The body is burning, tactile matter is burning...The mind is burning, ideas are burning, mental consciousness is burning... Burning with what? Burning with the fire of desire, the fire of aversion, the fire of delusion... Monks, the learned and noble disciple who sees things thus becomes dispassionate toward [all these] things...Being dispassionate, this disciple becomes detached; through detachment, one is liberated."

OPPOSITE *The wedding of Siddhartha's parents, Shuddhodana and Mahamaya, from the 18th-century murals depicting the life of the Buddha, which decorate the Buddhaisawan chapel in Bangkok.*

NIRVANA

THE THIRD NOBLE TRUTH
"The Noble Truth of the cessation of suffering is this: it is the complete cessation of that very thirst, giving it up, renouncing it, emancipating oneself from it, detaching oneself from it."

The Third Noble Truth—that the removal of desire in turn removes suffering—provides a terse reference to the central Buddhist focus on spiritual causation. The pattern of cyclical cause and effect by which desire leads to further suffering can also be reversed and eventually controlled to enable the possibility of enlightenment, or *nirvana*. Buddhism arose from the Buddha's own transformative experience of *nirvana* and then his compassionate wish to help others realize *nirvana* themselves.

The word *nirvana* itself derives from the Sanskrit verb meaning "to cool by blowing" and refers to one who has "cooled" the feverish *klesha*s ("hindrances" or "poisons") of greed, hatred, and delusion, which create *karma* and bind the individual into *samsara*, the world of rebirth and suffering (see pp.56–61). In Buddhist texts, the realization of *nirvana* is often compared with the extinction of a fire. As it was understood in ancient India, an extinguished flame was released to return to a diffuse, unagitated, and eternal state. *Nirvana* carries similar associations, although it is most often said to be beyond all states of existence.

Both men and women can realize *nirvana* through the cultivation of *prajna*, often translated as "wisdom" but perhaps better rendered as "insight," since it refers to the active capacity for spiritual discernment, "seeing into" the true nature of reality as something marked by suffering, impermanence, and non-self, the three characteristics of existence (see

EXPERIENCES OF ENLIGHTENMENT

Nirvana is famously indescribable, but practitioners across all the traditions have endeavored, often with great beauty and eloquence, to express their experience of enlightenment. In the early Therigatha (see p.132) the nun Patachara wrote: "After washing my feet, I watch the water, and follow it going down the drain; that makes me calm and control my mind as though it were a noble thoroughbred horse. / Taking a lamp, I then enter my cell; thinking of sleep, I sit on my bed; / With a needle, I put out the wick. The lamp goes out: *nirvana*. My mind is freed."

The famous Tibetan master Milarepa (1052–1135) put it thus: "Accustomed long to contemplating loving-kindness and compassion / I have forgotten all difference between myself and others... / Accustomed... to meditating on this life and the future life as one / I have forgotten the dread of birth and death. / Accustomed

long to keeping my mind on the body of the Dharma / I have forgotten conventional and artificial usages."

A striking more recent account comes from the Zen Master Sokei-an Sasaki (1882–1945): "One day I wiped out all the notions from my mind. I gave up all desire. I discarded all the words with which I thought and stayed in quietude. I felt a little queer—as if I were being carried into something, or as if I were touching some power unknown to me—and Ztt! I entered. I lost the boundary of my physical body. I had my skin, of course, but I felt I was standing in the center of the cosmos. I spoke, but my words had lost all their meaning. I saw people walk towards me, but all were the same person. All were myself! I had never known this world. I had believed I was created, but now I must change my opinion: I was never created; I was the cosmos; no individual Mr. Sasaki existed."

pp.64–5 and 74–5). The full development of *prajna* is essential to enlightenment, a view shared by all Buddhist schools. The Theravada schools have emphasized *vipashyana* (Pali, *vipassana*) meditation as the most important practice leading one to see "life as it is" (see pp.74–5). The Mahayana schools also define the path of the *bodhisattva* in reference to *prajna*, viewing it as the culminating *paramita* ("perfection"), realized only through meditation. The term "enlightenment" expresses how this fullness of *prajna* eliminates ignorance and enables the mind to see reality clearly.

The enlightened one at death enters *parinirvana* ("complete *nirvana*"), although the texts say that strictly speaking this after-death state is beyond description. *Nirvana* has been described in both negative and positive terms: a realm where there is neither sun nor moon, coming nor going; beyond causality; an impersonal state that transcends individuality. But stated in positive terms, *nirvana* is sometimes described as eternal, tranquil, pure, and deathless. Buddhist philosophers recognized *nirvana* as the only permanent reality in the cosmos. It is not, as erroneously depicted by early Western interpreters, "annihilation," an extreme position rejected by the Buddha. One influential definition of *nirvana* utilized in the Mahayana tradition is the famous dictum of the second-century CE philosopher Nagarjuna (see also pp.140–41), "There is not the merest difference between *samsara* and *nirvana*." Ultimately, *nirvana* is beyond all conditions, including even "otherness."

A colossal statue of the Buddha reclining as he awaits his complete, or final, nirvana. Known as Manuha Paya, this immense work is to be found among the Buddhist buildings of Pagan, Burma (Myanmar), founded in 849CE along the banks of the Irrawaddy River.

THE "NOBLE EIGHTFOLD PATH"

THE FOURTH NOBLE TRUTH
"The Noble Truth of the path leading to the cessation of suffering: it is simply the Noble Eightfold Path, namely right view, right thought, right speech, right action, right livelihood, right effort, right mindfulness, right concentration."

The Fourth Noble Truth provides the formula for removing desire: the Noble Eightfold Path. The eight ideals outlined in this concept offer a "cure" for the continuous cycle of rebirth, suffering, and death.

The ideals of the Eightfold Path are traditionally divided into three categories (see pp.72–9) that mark the progressive path to *nirvana*: morality (right speech, right action, right livelihood); meditation (right effort, right mindfulness, right concentration); and the cultivation of *prajna*, wisdom or insight (right view, right thought).

In defining the Eightfold Path, the Buddha rejected two ideas that are central to other world religions. First, there is no belief in or relationship with a transcendent creator God who sustains the world and on whom one depends for security or salvation. Second, the belief in an immortal soul is rejected as another false consolation, similarly unsupported by critical analysis. "Soul," like "God," is regarded as a projection of the desire-driven human mind in its search for security and immortality.

The Buddha emphasized the Eightfold Path as a practical goal-directed guide and urged his disciples not to engage in idle speculation or mere intellectualism. In one famous parable, "The Poison Arrow," he describes the problem facing a man who is hit by a poison-tipped arrow. The Buddha asks if the man should inquire about who shot the arrow? Or what kind of wood the arrow is made of? Or whether the shot that hit him was aimed high or low? After going through many other similar scenarios, the Buddha points out that only if the man quickly and practically addresses the mortal danger immediately before him—removing the poison that will kill him—can he survive. The Buddha cautions his disciples that if they waste their time on pointless philosophical inquiry, they will squander their own spiritual opportunity (see also p.191).

For this reason, the Buddha taught his disciples to be pragmatic teachers and to recognize that there are very different kinds of persons, each of whom has a different status determined by their *karma*. According to whether they are "ordinary persons," "learners," or "adepts," each is to be instructed differently and led along the Buddha's path. Regardless of the individual's level, the tradition emphasizes that the opportunity of human birth should not be wasted and that life should therefore be lived with purpose. All Buddhists hope to attain *nirvana*, if not in this life then in a future rebirth.

The Buddha said that "as long as my vision of true knowledge was not fully clear...regarding the Four Noble Truths, I did not claim to have realized the perfect enlightenment." As the Buddhist progresses toward enlightenment, understanding the Four Noble Truths deepens through meditation and critical reflection. Mere knowledge of the elements of the path, however intellectually sophisticated, is not sufficient. Only following the path and perfecting one's understanding of each element will lead to *nirvana*.

STAGES ON THE PATH

There are several stages for classing "adepts" on the path to *nirvana*. The first is that of the "stream-enterers," who will realize the illusion of the self and have no doubts about the Buddha's path; consequently, they will expect no more than seven more human rebirths before attaining *nirvana*. At a more advanced stage, the devotee will be a "once-returner"—one whose highly developed *prajna* means that he or she will experience only one further human life.

In both Theravada and Mahayana Buddhism the highest form of being is a *buddha*. In the Theravada tradition, both the *buddha* and the *arhat* (the enlightened disciple) have fully developed *prajna*, share the same realization of *nirvana*, and pass at death into the *parinirvana* state (that is, cessation of rebirth). However, a *buddha*, unlike most *arhat*s, is endowed with a host of supernormal powers and a commitment to teach. In contrast to the Theravada, the Mahayana views the *nirvana* of an *arhat* as only a preliminary awakening, and regards the *nirvana* of a *buddha* as the proper final goal of all Buddhists. The Mahayana also lays great emphasis on the *bodhisattva*, the compassionate being on the verge of *buddha*hood. (See also pp.88–93.)

A 17th- or 18th-century Chinese silk devotional banner depicting a group of Buddhist lohan (arhats), the enlightened disciples of the Buddha who await the birth of the next buddha, *Maitreya (Mile Fo, in China). The figure of the* arhat *became very popular in China, associated by some with the popular Daoist figures known as the Eight Immortals, a group of "perfected persons".*

PART 2 • CHAPTER 3 *Todd T. Lewis*

THE PATH
OF THE BUDDHA

MORALITY

The Noble Eightfold Path is the most important summary of Buddhist practice, outlining the necessary and progressive means for the realization of *nirvana*. The Eightfold Path is usually understood as the cultivation of morality (*shila*), meditation (*samadhi*), and insight or wisdom (*prajna*) (see p.70). It emphasizes that moral progress is the foundation for successful meditation and that the measure of successful meditation is the development and perfection of insight or wisdom. In the Visuddhimagga ("Path of Purity"), the fifth-century CE Theravada commentator Buddhaghosa calls morality and meditation the two "legs" of Buddhism, upon which the "body" of liberating insight stands.

The constituent stages of the Eightfold Path underscore Buddhism's practical emphasis, whether in the foundational goal of improving moral standards, good conduct, and the material welfare of society, or the more advanced ideal of eliminating desire-driven behavior, restructuring cognition, and, finally, realizing enlightenment.

Shila or moral practice (right speech, right action, right livelihood) is the starting point of the Buddhist path. One cannot advance toward *nirvana* without ethical integrity; or, in terms of *karma*, one cannot accumulate the positive balance of *karma* needed to reach advanced stages on the path while behaving immorally. Stated positively, Buddhist morality emphasizes the wisdom of cultivating detachment, discernment, and compassion (*karuna*).

Buddhist morality hinges on attending to three areas of human behavior: actions, speech, and livelihood. "Right action" is defined negatively, as not killing, stealing, or harming other beings. Each of these leads to negative karmic consequences, poisons the mind, and predisposes an individual to future immoral actions (see pp.60–61). However, only intentional actions lead to karmic effects. For example, if one steps on a worm without realizing it, in Buddhist moral terms one has not committed an action that entails the acquisition of *papa* (demerit). If one does it on purpose, it is an immoral act.

One aspect of right action that has divided Buddhists for centuries is the question of diet. Monks in the Theravada school are permitted to eat meat placed in their alms bowl as long as the animal was not killed for them. However, monastics in the Mahayana schools of east Asia (but not in Nepal or Tibet) concluded that all meat-eating entailed animal suffering at some point, and that therefore vegetarianism was the only dietary practice consistent with compassionate behavior.

THE "FIVE PRECEPTS"
The Five Precepts constitute the earliest Buddhist moral code to be derived from the Eightfold Path. They are chanted regularly in rituals by both monks and laity, and regarded as general ideals applicable to everyone. The precepts are:
1. No intentional destruction of life
2. No stealing
3. No sexual misconduct
4. No lying
5. No intoxication.

Discussions of right speech in the Buddhist texts decry the effects on the mind resulting from harsh and frivolous speaking. The content of our spoken words is important. Silence is preferable to gossip and other potentially harmful "speech acts" that can lead to human suffering, while further addicting the mind to false understandings and desires.

Right livelihood refers most obviously to occupations that are not conducive to the spiritual progress either of oneself or of others. Selling poisons or intoxicants has the negative karmic effect of habitually leading others into immorality. Above all, Buddhists should not pursue careers involving killing—they are forbidden to be butchers, hunters, or executioners.

Taking their example from the life of the Buddha himself, who abandoned his princely wealth as a precondition for embarking on his spiritual quest, Buddhist monks and nuns undertake to live simple lives with few material possessions (see pp.98–9). But Buddhism does not necessarily display a negative attitude to lay occupations that generate great personal wealth. On the contrary, the acquisition of wealth may represent the karmic fruits of one's meritorious actions in past lives, and affluence provides the opportunity for further charitable actions during one's present lifetime. On the other hand, of course, the wealthy must be aware that their material prosperity may encourage excessive attachment and desire and divert them from the spiritual path.

A couple make an offering of incense in a Buddhist temple in Ho Chi Minh City, Vietnam. Such offerings are considered an act of generosity, which, together with the Five Precepts (see sidebar, opposite), form the basis of good moral practice.

MEDITATION

In the Noble Eightfold Path, right effort, right mindfulness, and right concentration refer to meditation, a term encompassing various techniques and traditions of working with the mind. The practice of meditation is essential for the development of mental clarity, insight into conditioned reality, freedom from negative states, and, ultimately, *nirvana*.

Buddhist meditation has its roots in the practices of ancient India and stems from the experience of the Buddha himself, who was instructed in meditation by the itinerant holy men who were his first teachers. Following the Buddha's example, the practitioner may require years of effort, guided by an experienced mentor, in order to learn advanced meditation.

Meditation rests on the development of mindfulness (see pp.82–3) and on the two key elements of "concentration" and "insight." In the Eightfold Path, "right concentration" refers to the practice of trance meditation (*samadhi*). This is the type of meditation that the Buddha learned from his teachers, involving an intense focus on a particular object of meditation, leading to a state of "one-pointedness" in which the duality of "self" and "other" dissolve. However, there is a risk that the practitioner may become attached to the blissful mental states (*dhyana*s) experienced in *samadhi* (see p.80) and so be diverted from the realization of *nirvana*.

The most important form of mind practice is "insight meditation" (*vipashyana*), developed by the Buddha, which aims to discipline the mind while fostering a profound clarity about the nature of reality. "Right mindfulness" entails careful attentiveness to the "three marks of existence" as they relate to one's own physical experience: suffering (*duhkha*), impermanence (*anitya*), and non-self (*anatman*). Attention to, and comprehension of, the latter has a twofold effect—it promotes non-attachment (for if there is no "soul," then there is no locus for clinging), which stills desire, and it cultivates spiritual insight (*prajna*), which dispels ignorance (*avidya*).

In all forms of *vipashyana* meditation, the meditator moves from a simple awareness of a focal object (such as the breathing), a stage called "bare attention" (see box, opposite), to a higher level called "clear comprehension." Here one scrutinizes the phenomenon in the chain of causality and sees exactly how the process occurs that binds the individual to desire and ignorance. The meditator moves on to contemplate feelings, noting their existence, how they arise from causes and condition our experience. The meditator's focus progressively turns to the contemplation of how perceptions and emotions can determine, in turn, our states of mind.

This gilt statue of the Buddha, eyes closed and in contemplation, is in the 14th–15th-century Shwedagon pagoda in Rangoon, Burma's holiest shrine. The assumption in Buddhist meditation is that practice can slow down one's "experience of experience." The ultimate stage in this training is contemplation of "mental contents," leading to an acute awareness of the specific terms of the Buddha's analysis: attachment, patterns of causality in the consciousness, and the means of liberation.

VIPASHYANA BREATH MEDITATION

Throughout the modern Buddhist world, the main form of meditation is known as *vipashyana* (Pali, *vipassana*), commonly translated as "insight meditation." Its earliest exercise stages center on the contemplation of the body, beginning with breathing, bodily postures, parts of the body, the four elements found within it, and ending with "cemetery contemplations," which involves observing human bodies decaying after death (see sidebar, p.83).

Vipashyana meditation begins with the meditator assuming a comfortable seated posture: perhaps seated on a cushion on the floor, and with the legs crossed in either the lotus position (with legs crossed and each foot resting on the opposite thigh), or the half-lotus (with just one foot on the opposite thigh). However, comfort is most important and beginners can start by sitting in a straight-backed chair.

With the eyes closed, one begins by focusing the mind on the phenomenon of breathing. Most teachers suggest focusing on the sensation of the in-breath and out-breath just below the nostrils as the "anchor experience" to return to when the mind inevitably strays.

This practice makes one aware of the "three marks of existence" (see main text). The meditator quickly observes any uncomfortable bodily sensation. The reality of impermanence is seen directly in the continuous movement of the diaphragm and in the ever-changing stream of distracting thoughts. Non-self is conveyed when one discovers that there is no center from which to keep focused on the breath, despite one's will to do so.

A Tibetan nun meditating. Living outdoors as a monastic is thought to help to achieve sublime states of consciousness.

WISDOM

The Buddha's Eightfold Path culminates in the means to *nirvana* realization: right view and right thought. Right view is traditionally understood to be a thorough understanding of the Four Noble Truths (see pp.64–71); right thought refers to detachment from hatred and cruelty. Both of these qualities lead to enlightenment.

The means to realize them is unique to the Buddha's teachings. As one moves from morality to meditation, success is measured by the development of something that the early texts call *prajna*. This term is often translated as "wisdom," in the sense of existential knowledge that is the result of meditative experience. But it is also important to capture the active characteristic of Buddhist *prajna*, that is, as a kind of faculty that enables one unfailingly to see reality clearly amid the constant flow of human experience. Hence, another translation is "insight," emphasizing the ability to "see into" the fundamental truth of any situation, for example in terms of the "three marks of existence." These three "marks" or "characteristics"—suffering, impermanence, and non-self—are true at all times and in all places. *Prajna* enables one to see reality and not to be thrown into greed, lust, or anger—no matter what situation one finds oneself in. Looking at each of these characteristics of existence from the viewpoint of *prajna* helps to clarify the Buddhist vision of the highest truth.

Seeing the world clearly means not being in denial about one's own mortality, or about the suffering that afflicts all beings in *samsara*. Seeing the universality of this existential fact opens the trained mind to see the necessity for compassion, both to succor the afflicted and to undermine attachment for one's own inevitably mortal body.

Perceiving impermanence means to see reality in a fundamentally different manner from the commonsense perceptions that develop as humans reach maturity. From a Buddhist point of view, humans are conditioned from birth to perceive the world in an illusory framework. Having been taught from infancy to separate the self from the world and then to distinguish myriad objects as entities completely separate from ourselves, humans focus on gratifying this self using all the five senses. However, in both the ancient world and from the perspective of modern atomic physics, close observation establishes the physical world as being always and every moment in flux. Solid objects are merely atoms in constant motion and themselves consist mostly of empty space; the substances that make up the human body are completely replaced every seven years. What seem to be enduring entities, seen dispassionately in meditation and through *prajna*

Manjushri, the bodhisattva *of wisdom, is depicted in his most common form— holding a book and a sword—in this 12th-century bronze figure from Tibet, inlaid with copper, silver, and turquoise. The sword enables him to overcome those obstacles, such as delusion, which stand in the way of enlightenment.*

REDEFINING THE HUMAN "BEING"

Rejecting the notion of an immortal soul, Buddhists were compelled to explain what a human being then is. (To avoid the presupposition of permanence that the term "being" inherits from Western philosophy, Buddhists might refer to individuals as "human becomings," so as to suggest the incessant transformations inherent in embodied life.) There are two formulas used in mindfulness meditation. First is one that focuses on the body. A list of the body's "thirty-two constituents" is used during mindfulness meditation on the human "being." The meditator is taught to review the presence of each of these constituents as part of "oneself": the head hair, body hair, nails, teeth, flesh, sinews, bones, bone marrow, kidneys, heart, liver, pleura (the membrane enveloping the lungs), spleen, lungs, intestines, mesentery (the sac covering the abdominal viscera), stomach, feces, bile, phlegm, pus, blood, sweat, tears, serum, saliva, mucus, lubricant, urine, and brain. The purpose of reviewing this listing is not to dwell on the repellent parts of a living being, but to drive the mind to understand the full, interdependent nature of ourselves.

The second listing is the five *skandhas* ("heaps"): the physical body (*rupa*) that is made of combinations of the four elements (earth, water, fire, air); feelings (*vedana*) that arise from sensory contact; perceptions (*samjna*) that attach the categories good, evil, or neutral to these sensory inputs; habitual mental dispositions (*samskaras*) that connect *karma*-producing will to mental action; and the consciousness (*vijnana*) that arises when mind and body come in contact with the external world. Mindfulness meditation works progressively through each of the five, intending to investigate, understand, and ultimately transform human consciousness.

analysis, are constantly changing. Reality is a process, not "thing-based," but always in flux. "Things" arise and pass away, but only as matter and energy in endless interchange and interdependency.

Seeing that our embodied world is in flux makes it clear that there is no reason for desire or attachment: no "thing" actually exists. Language, by trying to "fix" reality into unchanging thought units, only serves to confuse us further; here, again, the meditative experience allows one to see beyond the surface illusion—cultivating *prajna*.

The third "mark" of existence, *anatman*, has several meanings. As stated previously, the term indicates Buddhism's rejection of the immortal soul posited in brahmanic/Hindu tradition. Rejecting an unchanging soul is of course consistent with the doctrine of impermanence. As has been suggested, mindfulness meditation shows the individual that there is no permanent entity "within." In this sense, *anatman* can also be understood as meaning "no ego." Letting go of this falsely posited center of the self (or "self-centeredness"), the basis of self-attachment, is liberating. Mindfulness meditation, which cultivates *prajna* and undermines the reality of the ego, enables individuals to reconstruct fundamentally their own experience. That is, the enormous energy that individuals habitually use to form fixed boundaries of their "self", "bolster their egos", arm themselves with "defense mechanisms," obsess over their self-image, and so on, can now be freed for other purposes. From the perspective of Buddhist doctrine, this liberated energy provides the power to renounce worldly desires, push on toward enlightenment, and explains the boundless compassion of the saints. How do meditation and *prajna* development relate to *karma* production and the mechanism of *nirvana* realization? As long as there is *karma* (see pp.60–61), *karma* must "ripen;" accumulated karmic consequences produce inevitable rebirth. And if there is future rebirth, there is no realization of *nirvana*. Buddhist philosophers and saints have stated that practicing meditation and developing *prajna* overcome this problem. In the lower rungs on the path to *nirvana*, meditation serves to make good *karma* for the practitioner. Meditation is in itself a merit-producing act. To the extent that it weakens the individual's *kleshas*—greed, delusion, and anger—meditation also motivates a person to act rightfully while also diminishing the negativity of one's subsequent *karma*. But for advanced practitioners, meditation and *prajna* cultivation are also capable of "burning up" the "seeds" of past *karma*.

The "good news" of the Buddha's Dharma is that it is possible for humans to be transformed and liberated by meditation. When they reach a quantum point of developing *prajna* in a thoroughgoing way, this leads to a breakthrough as full detachment occurs, *karma* is cut off, and one experiences an extraordinarily clear mental state. The texts call this *samyaksambodhi* ("utterly complete" or "perfect" enlightenment); it cannot be described in words, except inadequately as bliss and the experience of true freedom. The term for this employed in the Japanese Zen tradition may be more familiar to Westerners: *satori*.

Thus, *prajna* is a faculty necessary for enlightenment and central to all the Buddhist schools. The Theravadins have seen *vipashyana* meditation as the essential practice that cultivates it (see box, p.75). The Mahayana tradition characteristically developed rich symbolic imagery to express the cultivation of *prajna*: the celestial *bodhisattva* Manjushri, for example (see illustration, p.76), is commonly depicted as wielding a sword that cuts through delusion and detachment. His sword symbolizes *prajna*; he wields it bravely to cut through what deters us from enlightenment. Other celestial

This Tibetan funerary ritual painting of unknown date represents the five celestial buddhas, who together embody the supreme wisdom of the Buddha and his teaching. Each buddha is associated with a specific color, with one of the five skandhas (see box, p.77), and with a personality trait that he helps one to overcome on the path to wisdom. Yellow is Ratnasambhava ("Born from a Jewel"), representing feeling and ill-will; white is Vairochana ("Resplendent"), representing form and delusion; blue is Akshobhya ("Imperturbable"), representing perception and anger; red is Amitabha ("Infinite Light"), representing consciousness and greed; and green is Amoghasiddha ("Infallible Power"), representing mental dispositions and envy.

*bodhisattva*s are often depicted with a "third eye" on the forehead, representing their extraordinarily powerful spiritual insight.

The Mahayana school describes the path of the *bodhisattva* with reference to *prajna*, as it is the culminating perfection (*paramita*) on the path to *buddha*hood. Mahayana philosophers argue that it is *prajna* that allows one to see the world, calmly and clearly, as empty—having no-thing-ness, and so there is "no thing" to be attached to. The Mahayana path to enlightenment, and life beyond it, has been evocatively expressed in a traditional sequence of paintings produced for centuries by Chan/Zen artists and known as the "Ox-herding." This compares the Buddhist practitioner's quest for enlightenment to a herder's search to find his ox:

1. "Seeking the Ox": lost in *samsara*, but pulled toward a higher truth.
2. "Finding the Tracks": listening, studying, seeing the path
3. "First Glimpse of the Ox": meditation gives the beginnings of *prajna*.
4. "Catching the Ox": a deeper grasping of the *klesha*s; recognition of the hindrances of selfhood.
5. "Taming the Ox": beginning of breakthrough *satori* experiences
6. "Riding the Ox Home": complete *satori*.
7. "Ox Forgotten, Self Alone": experiencing the freedom of *satori*.
8. "Both Ox and Self Forgotten": experience of ultimate emptiness, even of tradition itself (see illustration, p.141).
9. "Returning to the Source": seeing the natural world as a sphere of innate enlightenment.
10. "Entering the Market with Helping Hands": the *bodhisattva* ideal as the final vocation after enlightenment.

A clay votive plaque (ca. 9th century CE) *from the Mahabodhi temple, Bodh Gaya, impressed with an image of the Buddha on the verge of enlightenment. The inscription cites a verse summarizing his teaching of Dependent Origination (see pp.140, 197).*

MENTAL CULTIVATION

MEDITATIVE TRANCE

The word "meditation" has been used to cover the many forms of sustained concentration and attentiveness that are central to almost all notions of Buddhist practice (see pp.74–5). From the earliest stage of the religion, such forms of meditation not only often led to trancelike states of mind, but these states were explicitly extolled as goals of meditation. However, an important difference between the cultivation of meditative practice and the attainment of trance states is that the latter is only possible when there is an accompanying advancement in physical and ethical discipline. Physically, one must be trained to sit comfortably in a meditative posture for a sustained period of time, and to regulate breathing, and so on. Ethically, one must first remove all impure, egotistic and destructive thoughts. In addition, five habitual categories of thought must also be suppressed totally: sensual desire; resentment or ill-will; indolence or lethargy; guilt and agitation about lapses in concentration; and indecision or doubt. Conceived of as "mental hindrances" to the attainment of trance, these thoughts and urges are seen as too disrupting of the advanced concentration needed to reach what are extremely unusual and easily lost states of mind.

The Buddhist tradition generally categorizes meditation practice under three headings: mindfulness (see pp.82–3), concentration, and wisdom. All of these are vital to spiritual progress, but it is generally under the discussions of concentration that we find reference to what one would call trance. Although the tradition typically claims that its meditation is achieved without the need to disengage the senses from the outside world, the discussion of trance meditation in Buddhist literature makes frequent reference to transforming sensory functionality to reveal that it is ultimately unreliable, and the advanced forms of trance are described as transcending perception. Indeed, the most exalted state is said to be a trance of total mental cessation (*nirodha-samapatti*), described as neither cognition nor non-cognition, where the operations of sensation and conceptualization have shut down. There is in Buddhism an *a priori* conviction that, for the person who is ethically prepared, turning the mind away from the objects of sensory perception naturally brings the individual closer to *nirvana*.

Since these trance states function as concrete goals of meditative practice, their attainment has always been associated with the goal of individual liberation. In the early Nikaya (Pali) and Agama (Sanskrit) *sutras* (Pali, *suttas*) the word *dhyana*, usually translated simply as "meditation," frequently denotes four specific states of trance (see sidebar, left). In Buddhist doctrine, the successful practice of these *dhyana*s leads to a highly

THE FOUR *DHYANAS*

The initial four trance states that represent the world of desirelessness are described in the Maha Satipatthana Sutta ("Great Discourse on Establishing Mindfulness"), the Bhayabherava Sutta ("Middle Length Sayings of the Buddha"), and elsewhere. These may be summarized as follows: In the first *dhyana* (Pali, *jhana*) one is detached from all desires of the senses and detached from the other four states that give rise to unwholesome *karma*. This state is characterized by applied and discursive thinking, detachment, rapture, and joy.

In the second *dhyana*, normal discursive thinking and deliberation have both ceased, and have been replaced by a "one-pointedness" of thought. One feels serene yet uplifted. There are also feelings of delight and elation from a sense of conviction, or faith, in something which cannot yet be grasped discursively.

In the third *dhyana*, the distaste for the elation that characterized the previous trance leads to its abandonment. This stage is accompanied by equanimity and mindfulness, pervaded with a calm happiness.

In the fourth *dhyana*, all affect has been dropped and the mind dwells in a pure mindfulness characterized by a complete equanimity unperturbed by any thought of happiness or sadness.

advanced spiritual condition in which all sensory desires have been eliminated and further progress toward the final goal of *nirvana* is relatively easy.
The fourth and highest *dhyana* is the stage from which *arhat*s and *bodhisattva*s (see pp.90–93) enter *nirvana*, and this process is itself described in
terms of progressing through another four types of trance called the "four
*dhyana*s of formlessness," because they are characterized by a state of mind
in which form as we know it does not exist.

In the Mahayana, trance is usually termed *samadhi*. Often the trance
has a name and may appear in the title of a *sutra* as the ultimate aim of the
Buddha's sermon: Samadhi-raja Sutra, for example. Many include supernatural visions, such as "the pure color *samadhi*" or the "*samadhi* of the direct
encounter with the *buddha*s of the present." As with the four *dhyana*s, their
descriptions generally include the negative mental qualities that have been
dropped and the positive qualities that have been acquired, but it is in the
visionary aspect that the salvational message is now located. That is, in
Mahayana, where the sense of a religious path is usually more detailed, one
looks for these trance experiences of extrasensory perception as confirmation of having reached a particular stage in one's progress to emancipation.

*The Buddha depicted in seated meditation,
one of four large statues carved in the 12th
century from the rock-face at Polonnaruwa,
Sri Lanka. His experience of enlightenment
is said to have included ascension through
each of the four* dhyanas *(trance states).*

MINDFULNESS

A central part of all Buddhist systems of practice is the cultivation of what is called "mindfulness." This word translates various practices that come under the headings of *samadhi*, *smrti* (see sidebar, opposite), *manasikara* (or *manasikaroti*), *anupashyana*, and so on (see pp.74–5). They all refer to "mental application" in the sense of attentiveness to a particular object of concentration, denoting precisely where the mind is directed, or what it is paying attention to, at any given moment. Since the Buddhist view of consciousness presumes a rapid series of discrete thoughts, the exercise of maintaining an object in one's mind over a period of time, from a few minutes to a few hours, requires constant concentration to keep one's senses directed at that object, whether it lie outside the self, or inside in the case of mindfulness of something conjured up from the past.

The Buddhist theory of causality—in which volition is conditioned by spiritual ignorance, and consciousness in turn conditioned by this volition, and so on (see pp.60–61)—is wrongly understood by many people to mean that there is no possibility of free will in Buddhism. However, the impor-

Monks of the Eiheiji, the head temple of Japan's Soto Zen school, sit cross-legged at their hour-long morning service, reciting the Heart Sutra in unison. Known as zazen, *serene meditative concentration has primacy in the lives of Zen monks.*

tance that Buddhism places on the practice of mindfulness should dispel this misunderstanding. It is a subtle point, perhaps, but an important one: although the way in which one processes information may be affected by previous thoughts, decisions, and opinions, there is still a decision at every moment of consciousness regarding what the mind will be concerned with or focused on. One purpose of mindfulness practice, therefore, is gradually to free oneself from habitual ways of responding to the world and to the self. Without progress in mindfulness, then, one cannot proceed to the more difficult meditations characterized by trance and wisdom.

A classic early treatise from the fifth century CE, Buddhaghosa's Visuddhimagga ("Path of Purity"), devotes hundreds of pages to various forms of mindfulness meditation (see also pp.194–5). The two most basic categories of mindfulness are called "calming" (shamatha) and "insight" (vipashyana), and both are categorized as samadhi practice (see pp.74–5). Calming practice is the first stage of any form of meditation—the mind's usual busy activity of jumping from one idea to another must be brought to a halt. This can be extremely difficult and is often pursued with simple objectives, such as fixing the mind on bodily movements (for example, walking) or, as in the Zen school, on a particular work activity such as hoeing the ground. Concentrating on one's breathing while seated in a meditative position may be the most widely practiced form of mindfulness. In the Zen tradition, this usually takes the form of counting breaths, with the number slowly brought to mind upon each exhalation. When ten is reached, the meditator abandons the count and returns to zero, lest his attention wander to the meaning of the count. In the Theravada tradition, there are sixteen ways in which breathing mindfulness can be practiced, including focusing on the length of the inhalation and exhalation, taking the breath to different places in the body, and so on.

After attaining a degree of stability in calming mindfulness, one then moves to insight meditation (see p.75), for this is the basis of wisdom (prajna) and is imperative for attaining more advanced states of spirituality. The relationship between calming and insight meditation somewhat resembles the philosopher Hegel's distinction between understanding and reason: the former is essential for creating the proper perspective, but the latter is the means by which one utilizes the composure gained to grasp the higher principles of truth. The three principles into which one seeks to gain insight are: impermanence in all phenomena (see also sidebar, right); the lack of substantiality in all knowable things; and the pervasiveness of duhkha (suffering or unsatisfactoriness) in human experience (see pp.76–9). Universal principles such as these derive their significance in Buddhism not from what they tell us about the laws operating in the natural world, but because they lead to penetrating insights into the construction and maintenance of one's personal identity or notion of self. To paraphrase an early sutra, "the effort to change one's external world is the way of a worldly man; the effort to change one's internal world is the way of a bodhisattva."

Mindfulness practice is so prevalent throughout Buddhism that one could even say it is characteristic of Buddhist culture as a whole. Such practices need not be introspective: Zen monks, for example, practice both silent meditation and group recitation of sutras in which their collective voice is used to focus the mind (see illustration, left).

CONTEMPLATING THE DEAD
The Maha Satipatthana Sutta ("Great Discourse on Establishing Mindfulness") contains detailed discussions about the topic of smrti (Pali, sati), and it includes the famous charnel-ground mindfulness practice, where, for the purpose of grasping the truth of their own mortality, monks visit cremation sites to fix their attention on corpses. This practice continues today, and has been augmented in some cases by the observation of autopsies.

CHANT

A Tibetan manuscript, date unknown, recording a ritual chant notation, indicating the patterns of rising and falling intonation in the chant melody. The thickness of the lines indicates when the voice should swell, the red letters represent the syllables in the prayer, and a description of its religious significance is written across the center in black.

Despite the Buddha's admonition against attachments to rites, the oral ritual recitation of liturgical texts, or chanting, is found in all schools of Buddhism. Its effect derives not only from the presumed sacredness of the canonical words themselves, but also from the power emanating from the practitioner, whose mind is focused as a result of his or her participation in the ritual. Even the iconoclastic Zen schools all have their chanted texts, especially the Heart Sutra. In schools where ritual plays a more prominent role, such as Tantra or Pure Land, a service may be chiefly occupied with chant and last for hours. The continuous repetition of a *mantra*, a sacred syllable or series of syllables, and a *dharani*, a somewhat longer phrase of sacred text, are well known as meditation techniques. Both derive their power from the Buddhist belief that human lives are shape through our bodily actions, speech, and mental activities. This form of mental cultivation, valued as much for focusing the mind as for its role in providing protection from unseen forces, is so central to tantric practice that many refer to this approach as Mantrayana, or "the *mantra* vehicle" (see also pp.162–73). A typical Buddhist service will always contain some form of liturgical chanting, usually drawn from the scriptures that a school views as definitive of its doctrines.

Chanting has a long history in Buddhism, and reflects a widespread belief in the special power of the spoken true word. In Mahayana countries outside of India, the canonical language was Sanskrit (see pp.178–9), despite the fact that few spoke it. *Sutra* chanting today in east Asia is mostly done in the Chinese form of the scripture, a language that, while archaic, can still be understood. The chant of *mantra*s and *dharani*s continues in Sanskrit.

The Mahayana tradition also gave rise to a class of scriptures called "*buddha*-name *sutra*s," which contain little more than lists of the names of past, present, and future *buddha*s. Specifically written for ritual chanting, these texts when recited were thought to produce great merit, which was usually transferred to someone recently deceased. The production of merit is an important part of all *sutra* recitation, and when a person dies his or her family will typically ask a Buddhist priest to recite *sutra*s in the hope that this act will help to secure a favorable rebirth for the deceased. Reciting *sutra* passages for the dead not only generates merit but has the effect of preaching: it is believed, particularly in Tibet, that the spiritual content of scriptures recited in rituals for the recently deceased has a good chance of being perceived by the dead person's subtle consciousness in the intermediate state (Tibetan, *bardö*) between death and rebirth. This may lead to a religious awakening, altering the deceased's karmic status and potentially improving the state of his or her imminent rebirth (see box, p.209).

Another purpose of ritual chanting is the use of ritual language as a "speech act," where the spoken words have the power to change a situation for the living. *Mantra*s and *dharani*s are "speech acts," as is the Triple Refuge chant that marks conversion or commitment to Buddhism (see p.103). A third purpose for *sutra* chanting is as mindfulness meditation, when each participant simultaneously focuses on the sound of his or her own voice and on the message being recited. As the texts become memorized, recalling them is another exercise in mindfulness.

Short texts, pithy passages, and symbolic phrases are popular subjects for ritual chanting because of the sense of power generated by multiple repetition. The Heart Sutra (in Xuanzang's translation into Chinese) is an extremely popular vehicle for ritual chanting: it is short, its message is enigmatic ("All form is just emptiness, all emptiness is none other than form"), and it is contains a *mantra* to avert misfortune. The Heart Sutra is recited in Zen meditation halls before *zazen* (see p.82), at Buddhist funerals, and even at weddings. Followers of the Pure Land tradition (see pp.144–7) repeatedly recite phrases (referred to as *nianfo* in Chinese and *nembutsu* in Japanese) which may invoke the holy name of Amitabha Buddha or describe his qualities (see box, p.144).

PARITTA

The most widespread form of ritualized chanting in Theravada Buddhist communities is the Paritta (Sinhala, *pirit*) ceremony. The term *paritta* means "protection," and it generally refers to a special form of ritualized chant performed by monks, although *paritta* verses can also be recited by lay people. In Sri Lanka, a formal *pirit* ceremony may last all night or as long as seven days, with monks working in shifts to keep up a more or less continuous flow of chanted Pali, which is read from a special book of *pirit* texts collected from the Pali scriptures. These formal ceremonies also commonly employ a specially constructed pavilion where the monks sit while they chant, and the use of a special *pirit* string and vases of water which are believed to absorb the powerful protective force of the chanted words and which are used to make amulets. Paritta is generally believed to bring both religious and mundane benefits, including mental cultivation, protection from harm, and healing.

Zen monks at Eiheiji temple, Japan, engaged in the daily chanting of holy phrases as part of their rigidly disciplined routine.

VISUALIZATION

A rock-painted mural of the bodhisattva Padmapani ("Bearer of the Lotus", an iconographical form of Avalokiteshvara, from one of the 7th-century cave temples of Ajanta, western India. A simple gift such as a flower is believed to cultivate positive mental attitudes (see also pp.110-11), particularly when the giver has become fully mentally aware of the flower's transient beauty. A verse of offering makes the point well: "With this flower I make an offering to the Buddha, and by this merit may I gain release [nirvana]; even as this flower withers, so my body tends toward destruction."

Visualization, often linked with visionary experiences, is an important meditative practice that characterizes later developments in Mahayana thought, particularly in the Vajrayana (Tantric) schools, although there are traces of it in the early Theravada tradition as well. The term "visualization" refers to the concentrated imagining of a particular sacred image or icon, such as the physical form of a *buddha* or *bodhisattva*, the features of a Pure Land (see pp.144–9), or simply a physical object or color. Given that "imagination" is usually a code word for delusional thinking in much of Buddhist doctrine, the persistent popularity of a meditation practice that requires imagination confirms how effective it has been.

Although in principle humans are capable of recalling any sensory experience, visual memory has played the largest role in Buddhism in coupling imagination with mindfulness (see pp.82–3). Even the early literature describes how the Buddha could project an image of himself into a devotee's mind to aid him or her in crisis. Such events, however, are probably best understood as part of the Buddha's arsenal of teaching techniques, in that the practitioner perceives these sudden apparitions passively rather than as the result of conscious imagining. In one narrative, the demon Mara appears to a monk in the form of a *buddha*, but the monk is nonetheless overjoyed.

Prior to the rise of Tantric Buddhism, the Mahayana's most systematic use of *buddha* and *bodhisattva* visualization is drawn from six *sutra*s without known Sanskrit antecedents that appeared in Chinese in the late fourth and early fifth centuries CE, and proved deeply influential in Chinese Buddhism in the Tang period. Probably written in central Asia, they describe practices involving the visualization of the physical form of the *buddha*s Shakyamuni and Amitayus (Amitabha), and the *bodhisattva*s Samantabhadra, Maitreya, Akashagarbha, and two unidentified figures translated as "Medicine King" and "Superior Medicine." Among these works, the *sutra* known as the Guan Wuliangshou Fo Jing ("Visualizing the Buddha of Limitless Life Sutra," or "Contemplation Sutra"), devoted to the cult of Amitabha Buddha and his Pure Land, is certainly the best known, for it generated enormous interest from the sixth century CE onward and became the subject of much debate and numerous commentaries. This work

VISUALIZING THE DIVINE WISDOM

In an example of a visualization practice from the eleventh-century text Sadanamala ("Garland of Meditative Techniques"), the practitioner attempts to acquire deeper religious insight through an identification with what is visualized. The object is an imagined female deity representing the spiritual goal of the "perfection of wisdom," or *prajnaparamita* (see p.79 and pp.196–7):

"One should envisage in one's own heart the syllable *dhi* set upon a lunar disk, and with the rays that emerge from it one should arouse all *gurus* and *bodhisattvas* and *buddhas*, and drawing them in before oneself, one should imagine them as sitting there in their various positions... Then with these words one should meditate on Emptiness: 'I possess in my essence the adamantine nature which is knowledge of Emptiness.' Next one should imagine this same syllable on the lunar disk as transformed into the Lady Prajnaparamita. She bears a headdress of twisted hair; she has four arms and one face. With two of her hands she makes the gesture of expounding the Dharma, and she is adorned with various jeweled ornaments. She blazes like the color of gold and in her [second] left hand she holds a blue lotus with a *prajnaparamita* book upon it... Visualizing her thus, one should perform the act of identification: 'Such as is the Lady Prajnaparamita, even so am I. Such as am I, even so is the Lady Prajnaparamita.' Next one should set out the *mantras*, at the throat [that is, chant] *om dhih*, on the tongue [that is, say] *om gih*."

A sandstone-carved figure absorbed in meditation, from Angkor, ca. 12th–13th century. Often identified as Prajnaparamita, the exact identity of the female is not known for certain.

describes thirteen different forms of visualization practice, beginning with a simple visualization of the sun after it has set and progressing to ever more complex images (see pp.148–9). In addition to its promise of eliminating previous *karma* that has been produced over countless ages and lifetimes, the practice has a significance for personal salvation that is made clear when the object is the Buddha himself: "when you perceive a *buddha* in your mind, it is your mind that possesses the thirty-two prominent and eighty-four secondary marks [of a *buddha*]; your mind becomes a *buddha*, your mind is a *buddha*; and the wisdom of the *buddhas* arises from this mind."

It is in the Vajrayana tradition that visualization has played the most prominent role in meditative discipline. Here, visualization is used for a variety of different purposes, such as the cultivation of mindfulness; spiritual empowerment through identification with ideas expressed in the form of powerful deities; freeing the mind from habitual errors of thought; and so on. All require imagination and concentration. For example, the many Tantric initiation rituals (see pp.172–5) usually involve standing within a *mandala*, a cosmic diagram that symbolizes the sacred or spiritual realm and includes representations of deities and other Buddhist figures (see pp.88–9). The initiate experiences the *mandala* by imaging being "within" it and it "within" him or her, and also memorizes the form so that he or she can in turn project it upon the world again in future rituals as a kind of visualization practice.

ART AND ARCHITECTURE *Michael Willis*

MANDALAS

Links between the Buddhist meditator, the visualization process, and cosmic symbolism are elaborated in the Tibetan tradition of the *mandala*. The core meaning of the word *mandala* is simply "circle" or "enclosure," but due to cosmological and mystic associations, *mandala*s are generally understood as maps of the cosmos which visually guide the devotee toward realization.

Although there are a great variety of *mandala*s for different Buddhist deities and for different forms of initiation and meditation, all tend to share a number of basic features. In one instance, the outer edge consists of concentric circles symbolizing the succession of oceans and mountains that make up the external world. Inside these circles is a square with T-shaped gates on each side. These face the four cardinal directions and display a characteristic color—usually white for the east, red for the west, green for the north, and yellow for the south. Beyond the gates is the sacred precinct of the *mandala*, often blue or green in color. In the center is a special meditation deity or some form of the Buddha, at times with his "wisdom partner" (*prajna*). The central image is set in a lotus and on each of the surrounding lotus petals there can be celestial *buddha*s, *bodhisattva*s, or protective gods and goddesses. These can be represented in pictorial form, by symbols or by single "seed" letters, the sounding of which is meant to bring forth the appropriate image in the devotee's mind (see illustration p.16 and pp.86–7).

In their most basic form, *mandala*s are simple line drawings. One of the oldest examples of this type comes from Dunhuang in central Asia and dates to about the ninth century CE. The lotus in the middle carries the Chinese character Fo (for "Buddha"). Elaborate *mandala*s painted on cloth scrolls or on temple walls were once common in many parts of the Himalayas, the best preserved examples being found in Bhutan, Nepal (see illustration, right), and those parts of India which are culturally Tibetan, such as Ladakh. Many parts of a *mandala* are inherently architectural and thus it is common for *mandala*s to be conceived and built three-dimensionally, either as entire temple buildings, such as the magnificent ninth-century structure at Borobudur in Java, or as architectural models, of which the Chinese produced many particularly finely crafted examples (see illustration, left).

The oldest surviving objects which give the appearance of *mandala*s are the votive slabs found at Mathura in north India. Termed *ayagapatta* in inscriptions, they date to the second or third century CE. Although they lack the four gates of later *mandala*s, the *ayagapatta* have a circular format with a sacred image surrounded by auspicious emblems and assorted celestial beings. Circular devices for

A three-dimensional Qing dynasty period mandala *made of precious metals and* cloisonné *enamel, produced during the reign of the Chinese emperor Qianlong (ruled 1736–95). This miniature shrine has all the key features of the traditional Buddhist* mandala: *an outer circle, four elaborate gates marked with flights of stairs and an inner sanctum with a lotus at the center. The pagoda-style roof, edged with victory-banners and parasols, is surmounted with the sun and moon, elements that emphasize the all-inclusive cosmology of the* mandala.

A four-part mandala *from Tibet which depicts four forms of Hevajra, the protector deity of the Sakyapa school, one in each of the four circles, surrounded by eight mystic consorts. The lower circles contain simpler forms of the deity, the upper ones more complex manifestations. At the center are two Sakyapa monks. Nepalese style image, ca. 1480.*

worship and meditation were thus well established by the fifth century CE when Buddhaghosa (see p.83) composed his widely read classic, the Visuddhimagga ("Path of Purity"). This lists ten meditation aids or *kasina*: earth, air, water, fire, blue, yellow, red, white, space, and light. The aids are traditionally arranged in a circle: for example, the earth *kasina* consists of a circle of brown clay. Buddhaghosa's devices represent the essential constituents of the devotee and of the world: the elements, the cardinal directions (represented by colors), and intellectual discrimination (represented by light).

Most *mandala*s on paper are ephemeral objects, intended to be used in specific rituals. The most celebrated temporary *mandala*s are painstakingly made of colored sand; after the initiation rites for which they are made are finished, the sand is swept up and deposited in a river or lake. This emphasizes that the process of visualizing, building, and consecrating the *mandala* is a temporary affair. The permanent and real effect is found only in the devotee's consciousness.

PART 2 • CHAPTER 5 *John Peacock*

THE BUDDHIST COMMUNITY

BUDDHAS AND BODHISATTVAS

Although the historical figure whose personal name was Siddhartha Gautama is commonly known as the Buddha, the term "*buddha*" does not refer to any single individual. All the various Buddhist traditions claim that other *buddha*s existed before Siddhartha, and will do so in the future.

The title *buddha* is also descriptive, in that it means "enlightened one" or "one who has woken up." The young prince Siddhartha Gautama awoke to the true nature of existence: suffering (*duhkha*), impermanence (*anitya*), and non-self (*anatman*). In the Pali canon the Buddha is referred to, and refers to himself, as the Tathagata—one who is both "thus come" and "thus gone." It specifically refers to the Buddha's having arrived at his penetrating insight into the nature of existence, and his ultimate transcendence of suffering and rebirth. If a *buddha* is one who has "woken up" to the way things are, then ordinary humans are stumbling around in an unawakened state, trapped within *samsara* and acting out of ignorance, greed, and

A Tibetan thangka *(votive hanging) depicting the celestial* buddha *Amoghasiddha ("Infallible Power") surrounded by various other* buddhas, bodhisattvas, lamas, *and protector deities.*

PAST AND FUTURE *BUDDHAS*

An important *jataka* tale relates the story of how the Buddha, in his previous life as Sumedha, encounters an earlier *buddha* called Dipankara. Sumedha is so impressed by Dipankara's infinite wisdom and compassion that he resolves to cultivate these qualities. Inspired by this encounter, Sumedha eventually gains the status of a *bodhisattva* and thus becomes a being who dedicates lifetime after lifetime to the achievement of perfect *buddha*hood for the sake of all sentient beings. Many of the *jataka* tales recount the *bodhisattva*'s development of the "perfections" of generosity, morality, patience, vigor, meditation, wisdom, skill in means, conviction, strength and knowledge.

If Dipankara is a past *buddha* and Shakyamuni a *buddha* of the present epoch, then the *bodhisattva* Maitreya is the *buddha* who is yet to come. Stories about Maitreya have become the foundation of messianic cults in China and the story is also to be found in Theravada countries where it is quite common to aspire to be reborn in Maitreya's time. Maitreya is said to dwell in Tushita heaven, whence he will descend into the world at the appointed time.

In art, Maitreya is often shown seated not in the traditional lotus position but on a chair with his feet on the ground, indicating his readiness to descend into the world, many eons in the future.

A 19th-century gilt bronze statuette of the bodhisattva Maitreya *("Loving One"), the* buddha *of the future who will reestablish the truth of the Dharma.*

hatred. It is said that a *buddha*, having eradicated these root defilements, acts solely from the virtues of wisdom, generosity, and friendliness.

Given the profound insight that the Buddha had into the nature of reality it is perhaps worth asking whether the Buddha is a man or a god. The early Buddhist scriptures are tautological in that they merely state that the Buddha is a *buddha*. However, in his previous existences the being that was to become the Buddha undoubtedly dwelt in the human and divine realms, as many of the *jataka* tales attest. In Buddhist cosmology both humans and deities (*deva*s) are irrevocably rooted in cyclic existence (*samsara*) and the important point is that, in becoming a *buddha*, Siddhartha Gautama transcended the categories of both the human and the divine.

Although a *buddha* is outside the categories of the human and the divine, he—traditionally, *buddha*s are male—does, paradoxically, possess three bodies (*trikaya*). These bodies are known technically as *dharmakaya* ("truth body"), *nirmanakaya* ("emanation body"), and *sambhogakaya* ("enjoyment body"). The *trikaya* doctrine and its sophisticated interpretation became particularly important with the development of the complex theories of the Mahayana. However, all forms of Buddhism possess some conception of the bodies of the Buddha. The main distinction that is being drawn is between the Buddha's physical form and his spiritual qualities. In early Buddhism, the Buddha was seen as literally "embodying" the qualities that constitute the Dharma, his teaching. Thus the Buddha embodies the virtues of

BODHICHITTA

The first step on the path of the *bodhisattva* is the development of *bodhichitta* or "awakening mind." What the development of *bodhichitta* marks is a fundamental shift in focus from self-concern to concern for the suffering of others, which manifests itself as compassion (*karuna*). Shantideva, in a passage from the Bodhicharyavatara ("A Guide to the Bodhisattva's Path to Awakening"), highlights the enormity of this transformation when he says, "may I be medicine for the sick and weary. May I be their doctor and their nurse until disease appears no more. May I quell the pains of hunger and thirst with rains of food and drink... May I be a torch for those in need of light, a bed for those in need of a bed, and a servant for those in need of service for all beings."

The development of *bodhichitta* and its accompanying compassion provides the motivating force behind Mahayana Buddhism. It is only with the awakening of *bodhichitta* that the aspirant is said to have truly entered the path of the *bodhisattva*. Until the awakening of *bodhichitta* occurs, the practitioner is considered to possess the motivation of the non-Mahayana paths. For example, one is concerned with one's own liberation from the cycle of rebirth, with its attendant suffering (*duhkha*).

compassion, wisdom, non-violence, friendliness, and generosity. However, it is not merely the physical body of the Buddha that makes him a *buddha* but the perfection of his spiritual qualities. This is made very clear in a passage from the Pali canon in which a monk called Vakkali, who is incapacitated by illness, criticizes the Buddha for not visiting him sooner. The Buddha explains: "What good is the sight of this putrid body to you? Vakkali, the one who sees the Dharma sees me; the one who sees me sees the Dharma."

The later developments of the theories of the bodies of the Buddha reflect a general change in the way in which the Buddha is conceived. In early Buddhism the Buddha is seen as a figure who attains *nirvana*, teaches, and finally enters *parinirvana*, thus exiting *samsara* forever. While there are some questions surrounding the status of the Buddha after his death, it is clear in the earlier beliefs that he no longer has any direct influence in the world. In the fully developed Mahayana theory, the Buddha becomes more sublime in that he exists on three different planes: earthly, supramundane, and transcendent. The earthly form that ordinary human beings can see is his "emanation body" (*nirmanakaya*). While the Buddha appears to be born, this physical form is merely created by the Buddha out of his compassion for suffering beings. *Sambhogakaya*, on the other hand, is the idealized or supramundane form of the Buddha that possesses the marks of the fully perfected one (see box, p.27). As such, this body appears in different realms according to the different needs of sentient beings and may be closer to what the Buddha really is. Although this body is a physical body it is not the gross physical form of the *nirmanakaya*. According to some traditional views, the

sambhogakaya only teaches *bodhisattva*s whose attainments are sufficient enough to enter a Pure Land. It is this body which is extremely important in east Asian countries as it is the body of Buddhist devotion. The *dharmakaya* is synonymous with ultimate truth and is seen as being totally transcendent and unchanging (see pp.45 and 176–7).

The seminal figure of the Mahayana is the *bodhisattva* (see also pp.132–9). As the figure of the *bodhisattva* gained prominence in the emerging Mahayana, the figure of the Buddha faded more into the background, becoming more sublime and god-like as he did so. However, although the *bodhisattva* is of such importance in the Mahayana, this is not to say that he or she is absent in the non-Mahayanist Buddhist movements. The *jataka* tales testify to the importance of the *bodhisattva* in these movements.

The *bodhisattva* is a being who vows to achieve perfect and complete *buddha*hood for the benefit of all sentient beings. As such, the *bodhisattva* sets out on an arduous path which involves the cultivation of six (or ten) perfections (*paramita*) (see pp.136–7) and the development of five paths (*marga*) and ten grounds (*bhumi*). It is motivation that is said to distinguish the path of the *bodhisattva* from other forms of Buddhism. In early non-Mahayanist Buddhism, the goal was outlined in terms of the *shravakayana* ("the path of the disciple") and the *pratyekabuddha* ("solitary *buddha*"). Although admitted as being some kind of awakening by the Mahayana schools, these paths were viewed as inferior (*hina*). The path of the *bodhisattva*, however, was viewed as the path to the attainment of *samyak-sambuddha*, that is, "complete and perfect *buddha*hood" for the benefit of all beings (see pp.136–7).

In Mahayana Buddhism cults have developed around specific bodhisattvas *which were considered to be enormously powerful, with very little distinction between them and buddhas. This serene face is thought by many to represent the* bodhisattva Avalokiteshvara. *It was carved at Bayon temple in the ruined 13th-century complex of Angkor Thom, Cambodia. It is also possible that the portrait is that of the site's creator, the Khmer god-king Jayavarman VII (1181–1219), who identified himself with the heavenly deities (see pp.126–7).*

OVERLEAF *The gilded face of a statue of Maitreya, the* buddha *of the future, in Tikse monastery, Ladakh. The coming of such a supremely enlightened being is predicted by both Theravada and Mahayana schools of Buddhism, but only after the Dharma has been forgotten.*

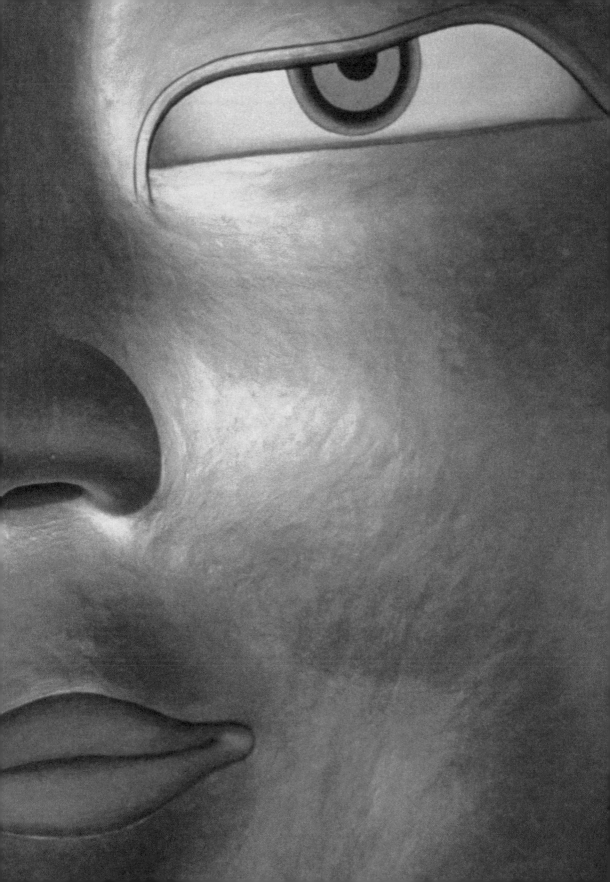

SAINTS AND TEACHERS

The Buddha himself has been the principal model of the Buddhist holy individual, or saint, since the early years of Buddhism. The exemplary nature of his life is held out as a paradigm for his followers, and his holiness is indicated by his "great wisdom" (*mahaprajna*) and "great compassion" (*mahakaruna*). It is to his life that reference must be made for any understanding of "saintliness" in the Buddhist context.

After the Buddha, the earliest Buddhist saints were his closest disciples, who each attained the enlightened status of *arhat* ("worthy one"), the foremost among them being Ananda, Shariputra, Maudgalyayana, and Kashyapa (or Mahakashyapa, "Great Kashyapa"). Such was their level of spiritual attainment that, according to the *sutra*s of the Pali canon, some of them were authorized by the Buddha to deliver whole discourses. An examination of the lives and legends surrounding some of these close disciples reveals that they are identified by certain virtues. For example, Kashyapa is called "foremost among those who follow the *dhuta*s," the *dhutavada* being the code that describes the solitary forest renunciant and meditator. Shariputra, on the other hand, is portrayed as having attained enlightenment by living a flawless life in a settled monastic community.

The earliest records that we possess of the lives of *arhat*s are the poems found in the Khuddaka Nikaya ("Group of Small Texts") section of the Pali canon. These collections are known as the Theragatha ("Poems of the Male Elders") and Therigatha ("Poems of the Female Elders") and were composed by those who lived the wandering lifestyle of the mendicant, probably during the Buddha's lifetime. Both collections were transmitted orally for centuries prior to being written down toward the end of the first century BCE. The poems are ecstatic songs which detail both the hardships of that particular way of life and also the bliss that arises with the attainment of enlightenment. Within the poems there is much evidence of the virtues associated with Buddhist sainthood: for example, the renunciation both of sensory pleasure and of the way of life of the householder (lay person), together with the release from the cycle of rebirth. It is clear within both collections that the Buddha is the paradigm of the saintly life: "I saw the light of the world. I paid homage to him and sat down. Out of great compassion the one with vision taught me the Dharma." (See also sidebar, opposite.)

While the *arhat* is the source of inspiration in Theravada Buddhism, the same role in the Mahayana is taken on by the figure of the *bodhisattva* (see pp.91, 93 and 136–7). In Tibetan Buddhism, for example, *bodhisattva*hood is not considered simply as a distant ideal but as a living presence in the form of *tulku*s, or reincarnated *lama*s, who populate Tibet's religious landscape (see pp.170–1). The most famous *tulku* is the

An 18th-century gilt bronze image of Padmasambhava, the great saint credited with the establishment of Buddhism in Tibet through the building of Samye monastery in the 8th century CE. It is believed that the tantric master used his mystic powers to subdue the Tibetan demons opposed to the new religion. He holds a vase containing the elixir of immortality and a diamond thunderbolt (vajra) (see pp.162–3).

Dalai Lama, who is the reincarnation of his predecessor and of the *bodhisattva* Avalokiteshvara, Tibet's patron deity (see box, p.171). While of immense significance for all Tibetan Buddhists, he is just one of hundreds, perhaps thousands, of reincarnate *lama*s and *bodhisattva*s.

The Dalai Lama ("Ocean [of Wisdom] Teacher"] is a famous example not simply of a Buddhist leader but also of a great teacher (Sanskrit *guru*, Tibetan *lama*). The ideal of holiness has always gone hand in hand with a supreme ability to transmit the Dharma to others. Again, the teacher *par excellence* is the Buddha himself, who appeared in the world to communicate, through his boundless wisdom and compassion, his timeless insights. The teacher is a conduit for the Dharma, so much so that in Tibetan Buddhism, when the *lama* assumes his teaching role he is deemed to acquire the status of a *buddha* for the period that the instruction lasts. In most Buddhist traditions the relationship between student and teacher is an extremely close one. Historically, many teachers have founded new schools and assumed the mantle of sainthood: a celebrated example is Bodhidharma, the Indian Buddhist teacher who is traditionally said to have founded the Chan (Zen) school (see p.150).

"POEMS OF THE ELDERS"

The Theragatha and the Therigatha (see main text) are remarkable collections that bring us face to face with the lives and aspirations of the early Buddhist saints. One brief example from the Therigatha captures the essence of these works beautifully:

> Free, free, ecstatically free,
> Of the three crooked things,
> The pestle, the mortar, and my
>   crook-backed husband.
> I have found release from the cycle
>   of rebirth,
> And every thing that would lead to
>   further births,
> Has been severed.

THE IMPORTANCE OF THE BUDDHIST MASTER

As the ones who transmit the Dharma directly to the next generation, teachers have always played a central role in the history of Buddhism. Long, unbroken lineages of great teachers are characteristic of several traditions, such as Tantra and Zen. Within the contemporary Buddhist world some teachers have gained significant reputations for the quality of their teachings. While the personalities of these teachers are of obvious importance, it is their ability to communicate the Dharma to people of differing capabilities that is considered to be paramount. Highly qualified teachers from all Buddhist traditions regularly travel and dispense teachings to both lay and monastic communities in both the East and the West.

Notable figures in today's world are the Dalai Lama (born 1935), the temporal and spiritual head of Tibetan Buddhists, and Thich Nhat Hanh (born 1936), a Vietnamese monk who moved to the West in the 1960s during the Vietnam War. Both of these figures travel continuously, spreading the Buddha's message of wisdom and compassion.

The first and greatest teacher in the Buddhist tradition was the Buddha himself. Here, Theravada monks venerate a rock-cut figure of the Buddha (although it is sometimes identified as his disciple Ananda), near Gal Vihara temple, Polonnaruwa, northeast Sri Lanka.

MONKS, NUNS, AND MONASTERIES

The Buddhist monastic tradition arose out of that of the Shramanas (see box, p.21), who were to be found in India during the Buddha's lifetime. Both traditions rejected conventional ways of living, based on the home and social duties, in favor of a lifestyle devoted to spiritual goals. At its inception, the Sangha, the monastic community founded by the Buddha, was essentially a wandering mendicant order (see pp.46–7), which exhibited many of the same traits as the earlier tradition, including a dependency on the goodwill of the community for donations of alms in the form of food and clothing. That Buddhism was so successful early on was in part due to these already established practices. However, as a result of the Sangha's growing popularity, it also received gifts of land and property. One effect of this was that the renunciants started to establish more settled lifestyles, which eventually evolved into communities of monks living together to study and teach the Dharma.

Buddhist monks are known as *bhikshu*s, and to enter the religious order the Theravada Vinaya states that the candidate must be old enough to "scare crows away." This is usually interpreted to mean that the candidate

Nuns in Seoul, South Korea, engaged in religious devotion during the annual festivities for the Buddha's birthday. This event is observed on the full-moon day of the lunar month Vesak, which falls around April-May, and is a public holiday in many Asian countries. South Korea and Taiwan are notable for their significant female monastic communities.

THE ORDER OF NUNS

According to tradition, the Buddha had to be requested by one of his disciples, Ananda, to found the order of nuns (*bhikshuni*s) and was initially reluctant to do so. When pressed on his reluctance, he claimed that the ordination of women would hasten the downfall of the Dharma, although his reasons for this opinion are unclear. It is possible that he simply considered it unwise to place communities of celibate male and female renunciants together. The Buddha certainly believed that women were entirely capable of attaining *arhat* status, and indeed there is a collection of poems composed by female *arhat*s known as the Therigatha (see pp.96–7). It is noteworthy though that the Pratimoksha for nuns is even more stringent than that for monks, and there are 311 for nuns compared to 227 for monks (see sidebar, right).

The ordination of nuns died out in the Theravada tradition some time ago, as far back as the eleventh century in Sri Lanka, for example. In terms of contemporary Buddhism this means that fully ordained Buddhist nuns are to be found only in east Asian Mahayana tradition.

must be between the ages of seven and eight. In entering the Buddhist monastic order the *bhikshu* embarks on a life of "depending on little" for his existence. This phrase was emphasized by the Buddha so that Buddhist monasticism could be seen as removed from the extreme ascetic austerities practiced by other Shramana orders. At the conclusion of full ordination into the Sangha, a monk is told of "four resources" (*nishreya*) that he can always depend on for the "four requisites" (*parishkara*) of accommodation, clothing, food, and medicine. These resources are: the foot of a tree, robes made out of rags, food offered as alms, and fermented cow's urine. In addition, a monk is allowed eight possessions—three robes, a water strainer, an alms bowl, a needle, a razor, and a belt. As signs of his renunciation of the worldly life, a monk must shave his head and live a celibate life.

Buddhist monasteries vary both in scale and in function, some being large-scale teaching institutions, such as those found around Lhasa in Tibet, and others being small village-based temples inhabited by just a few monks. In general, the religious heart of a monastery is centered on a *stupa* (a reliquary mound containing relics of a saint or the Buddha), a Bodhi tree (the species under which the Buddha gained his enlightenment), and an image house or shrine room. In addition, most monasteries contain a library, residential quarters for the monks, toilets, and cooking and bathing areas. Some of the monasteries in ancient India and Sri Lanka would have been very large indeed. Faxian, a fifth-century Chinese pilgrim, recorded that the Abhayagiri monastery at Anuradhapura (the capital of Sri Lanka) contained as many as five thousand monks. As recently as 1959, prior to the Chinese invasion, Drepung monastery in Tibet was estimated to house ten thousand monks.

MONASTIC DISCIPLINE
In the Theravada tradition monks must abide by 227 rules known as the Pratimoksha. Within the different Buddhist traditions the number of rules varies: for example, Tibetan monks follow 258 rules, and Japanese monks 250. The penalties for the infringement of these rules vary in severity. The most serious transgressions are having sexual intercourse, stealing, killing, and claiming false spiritual attainments—these four are literally known as "defeat" (*parajika*) and call for expulsion from the Sangha. In most Buddhist traditions, once a fortnight, on the new moon and full moon, the whole monastic assembly gathers to chant the Pratimoksha and to confess any breaches of discipline (see p.46).

ART AND ARCHITECTURE *Michael Willis*

MONASTIC ARCHITECTURE

Anathapindaka, a merchant of great wealth and influence, invited the Buddha and his retinue of monks to spend the rainy season in his native town of Shravasti (Savatthi), at the time one of the leading cities in north India. After the Buddha accepted the invitation, Anathapindaka began the search for a suitable location to house the monks. He settled on a beautiful park outside the city belonging to a prince called Jeta and consequently known as Jetavana, the "Forest of Jeta." The prince was not inclined to sell the park but was finally convinced when Anathapindaka paid for it by completely covering the ground with coins. As he knew the park was to be given to the Buddha and wanted to make a donation of his own, Jeta retained some of the land and built an impressive gateway on it using Anathapindaka's money. Inside the grounds, Anathapindaka constructed cloisters, dwellings, halls, wells, and other buildings, all of which are elaborately and poetically described in textual sources. The Buddha eventually spent nineteen rainy seasons at the monastery and it remained an important center of Buddhism for many centuries. There are Burmese, Tibetan, and Chinese temples at the site today, not far from the extensive ruins of the ancient monastery.

Accounts of the founding and subsequent support of Jetavana provided a model which lay followers in Sri Lanka, China, Korea, and Japan emulated in varying degrees. Economically and politically this ideal involved

DHARMAKAYA
Just as *stupa*s became integral elements of the Buddhist monastic center (see box, p.48), so too did the noble qualities of knowledge, concentration, and wisdom considered to form the Buddha's "Dharma Body." Since this was most clearly articulated in the texts, these became substitutes for the Buddha and were revered as actual physical relics, thus accounting for Buddhist practices such as the deposition of texts inside images and *stupa*s. At Haein-sa monastery in Korea, the most elevated part of the large complex is not a temple or *stupa*, but an extensive library containing printing blocks for the entire Tipitaka (see pp.186–7).

The painted eaves of the Haein-sa temple, Mount Kayasan, South Korea.

the financial influence of a great merchant and the patronage of a powerful prince. The setting also articulated a number of geographical features of the ideal Buddhist retreat: the monastery was to be outside the city, but not completely isolated; it was to be set on a hill and filled with lovely trees; it was to have a good supply of water; it was to have properly built and maintained structures for both monks and visitors. All this was meant to provide an appropriate setting for the community to develop a regulated life, bound by rules laid down in the relevant monastic code (Vinaya, see pp.188–9), and thus to facilitate progress on the path to enlightenment.

In every part of Asia, Buddhist monasteries can be found which follow this general pattern. The celebrated complex at Sanchi, established in the third century BCE and active until about the thirteenth century CE, is set on a hill a few miles from the ancient city of Vidisha (see p.52). Mihintale, perhaps the oldest Buddhist retreat in Sri Lanka (see illustration, p.102), is a similar distance from Anuradhapura. The famous temples at Famen in China (see p.103) and Nara in Japan (see p.135) were similarly removed from the capital and royal palace.

In architectural terms, a *sangha*'s needs were met by residential buildings (monks and nuns had separate establishments), bath chambers, refectories, and clinics. The residential areas generally consisted of single cells ranged in cloisters around a central court. In Sri Lanka great care was taken in matters of hygiene and a particular feature of the monasteries are well-designed and well-drained bath chambers and toilets.

Tibet's Ganden monastery—named after the paradise of Maitreya—was founded in 1409 by Tsongkhapa and is situated on the ridge of Mount Wangkur, overlooking the valley of the Phenyul River. A great deal of destruction took place during the Cultural Revolution, when its population of 3,000 monks was reduced to no more than 300, but in recent years much work has been undertaken to try and restore it to its former glory.

It was, and is, the role of monastics to apply the Dharma within the walls of their monasteries and to ensure that it is preserved for the coming generation. While the Dharma touches every aspect of Buddhist spiritual, ritual, and physical life, in architectural terms it is most clearly embodied in the meeting halls where residents assemble to chant sacred scriptures. As texts and commentaries were written down, edited, and translated, monastic communities began to accumulate great collections of books. Monastic libraries were not just book repositories and places of study, but active centers from which all manner of knowledge was disseminated. Buddhist monasteries, such as the famous Indian "university" of Nalanda, became the principal centers of learning throughout southern and eastern Asia, a development further facilitated in China and Korea by the advent of woodblock printing (see pp.182–5).

The Milindapanha ("Questions of Menander") records a series of questions addressed to the monk Nagasena by Menander (Milinda), a Greek king who ruled in northwest India in the second century BCE. At one point the king asked the monk to define the Buddha's "general shop," the use of a commercial metaphor being indicative of the mercantile patronage Buddhism enjoyed from its very beginnings. In reply, Nagasena tells the king that the Buddha's "general shop" consists of three things: his monastic community, his teachings, and "shrines for his relics." This makes clear that after his final passing, the presence of the Buddha was perpetuated by relics, generally fragments of cremated bone. These relics were always kept in monasteries, where they were enshrined in buildings called *stupa*s. The great *stupa* at Sanchi, which contains relics of the Buddha, is set in the middle of a large monastic complex. A similar arrangement is found in Sri Lanka, where some of the relics finally came to rest, the most celebrated being the tooth relic at Kandy. In China, a finger bone of the Buddha was discovered in the 1980s in a forgotten crypt in the Famen temple (Famensi) in Shaanxi province. Renowned as one of the four places in China with Buddha relics, the Famen temple enjoyed direct imperial patronage, especially in the ninth century CE. The relic was placed in a series of containers and, according to a Chinese inscription, set inside a white marble "Ashoka *stupa*." This reference to Ashoka linked the monastery and its relics with the celebrated Indian monarch who did so much to promote the Buddhist cause (see pp.50–53). It was in China that the original dome-like *stupa* developed into the distinctive multi-tiered form generally referred to as a pagoda, which was also adopted in regions under Chinese cultural influence, such as Korea and Japan.

Before the first century CE, relics were a key instrument in the spread of Buddhism, helping to establish new centers of religious significance. When images were introduced they were technically described as "relics of indication or referral" (see p.45) and the principal Buddha image in a monastery was typically housed in a shrine room known as the *gandhakuti* ("perfumed chamber"). This referred initially to the apartment where the Buddha stayed at Jetavana but it was also applied to any place where he resided and where his image was later installed.

OPPOSITE *Standing near the Buddha statue at Mihintale, Sri Lanka, the stupa of the Ambasthale Dagoba is characteristically Sinhala in style, with its undecorated white plaster. Mihintale, 8 miles (13km) from Anuradhapura, is where the monk Mahinda, who according to tradition brought Buddhism to Sri Lanka in the 3rd century BCE, first preached on the island. The stupa was once covered by a protective wooden dome, but all that remains of this are the stone columns that once supported the roof.*

THE LAITY

THE DAILY ALMS ROUND
In many countries where the monastically centered Theravada tradition is a dominant influence, the practice of going for alms defines relations between monks and the laity. In Thailand and elsewhere, for example, it is still common for the monks to engage in the traditional daily alms round and for lay people to place food directly into the alms bowl of the monk. Such occasions for material and spiritual exchange exemplify the clearly differentiated core values and practices of the monastic and lay communities. While members of the Sangha have a high social status by virtue of their fidelity to the renunciant ideal, they nevertheless are materially dependent on the laity who advance along the Buddha's path by fulfilling the religious ideal of generosity (see main text and pp.110–11). Monks walking on alms rounds are expected to exemplify, through their physical deportment, an inner attitude of detachment. Lay donors, in turn, enact their lower status through gestures of respect and gratitude toward those who embody the possibility of following the path that leads to *nirvana*. In return for their freely given donations, the laity acquire merit which advances them toward better rebirths and the possibility of becoming renunciants themselves.

At the heart of traditional Buddhism is the relationship between the laity and the Sangha. In founding his monastic order the Buddha initiated a social contract between monk and lay person that is still as important today as it was when the Sangha was established. Traditionally male and female lay people who committed themselves both to the Buddhist Dharma and Sangha were known respectively as *upasaka*s and *upasika*s. They made their commitment by formally reciting the Triple Refuge (see pp.106–7) and by this act they defined themselves as Buddhists.

The Buddhist path can be seen in terms of the progressive development of generosity (through donation, *dana*), morality (*shila*), and meditation. In traditional Buddhist societies it is still relatively uncommon for lay people to engage in meditation, and lay practice centers very much on the development of generosity and morality. It is perhaps true to say that without the generosity of the laity the Theravada Sangha would not have survived, as the monks have traditionally depended on lay donations for their most basic requirements of food, clothing, and so on

In Theravada countries the most frequently seen act of *dana* is the offering of food to mendicant monks (see sidebar, left). However, in Sri Lanka lay people, particularly women, tend to take prepared food directly to the monastery. In countries dominated by the Mahayana tradition, the situation is a little more complex. In Tibetan communities lay people often make what is known as a "tea offering," whereby enough money is donated to offer the traditional Tibetan drink of hot butter tea to all the monks in the monastery. On occasion the laity also sponsors the recitation of particular texts or *mantra*s by the monks. In east Asian Buddhism it is more common for the laity to make offerings of flowers, incense, and money. The form that *dana* takes is reflective of the varying cultural contexts and the size of monastic institutions.

The act of giving is seen as a lessening of the bonds of attachment and a reorientation of the mind away from egotistical concerns. This act is also viewed as an opening out to others, and is seen as the development of the virtues of non-attachment and friendliness. Many of the *jataka* tales recount stories of the Buddha's supreme acts of generosity in his previous lives. One famous tale tells how the he offered his flesh to a hungry tigress so that she should have the strength to feed her young. Such stories demonstrate the Buddha's perfection of generosity and are meant to inspire faith in the Buddhist practitioner. On a day to day level, in addition to the offering of food and clothing, lay generosity is demonstrated by the donation of money for the building and maintenance of monasteries, and the sponsorship of the publication of Buddhist literature. In return for their generosity, lay supporters of the Sangha gain merit (*punya*), or "good *karma*" (see also pp.60–61 and 110–11).

Also important to lay life are the Five Precepts (see also p.72). Often recited by lay practitioners after the Triple Refuge, they are commitments to refrain from: harming living beings; taking that which is not offered; sexual misconduct; lying; and taking intoxicants which may cause heedlessness. In addition, on important occasions such as full-moon days (see box, p.108), the practitioner may undertake to abide by a further three Precepts, usually described as a commitment to refrain from: solid food after midday; dancing, singing, music, improper shows, and ornamenting the body with garlands, scents, or unguents; and high and luxurious beds and seats.

Lay devotional practice focuses on activities that are conducive to the production of faith (*shraddha*). The primary form of religious expression open to the lay community is in the practice of "good conduct," or morality (*shila*), as set out in the Noble Eightfold Path (see pp.70–71). Another important lay practice is pilgrimage to the holy sites associated with the Buddha's life or to important temples and shrines (see pp.108–9 and 112–13). In Tibet lay people express their devotion by prostrating themselves hundreds of times at holy places (see illustration p.113), by turning prayer wheels filled with *mantras*, or by hanging up prayer flags).

A monk from Thiripyitsaya, near Pagan, Burma (Myanmar), on his daily alms round proffers his begging bowl to a cart driver.

PART 2 • CHAPTER 6 *Kevin Trainor*

BUDDHISM IN PRACTICE

❁❁❁❁❁❁❁❁❁❁❁❁❁❁❁❁❁❁❁❁❁❁❁❁❁

ENTERING THE PATH

How does one become a Buddhist? This question has taken on new significance as Buddhism has become more widely known and practiced outside the Asian cultures where it has long been a dominant force. For example, the question may be posed by someone who knows of Buddhism only through reading a book or browsing an internet site, and this person may think of Buddhism as a set of ideas that one either simply affirms or rejects. The question takes on a different meaning when asked in communities where Buddhist teachings and practices have long exercised a deep and pervasive influence on the dominant culture and where children are customarily brought up within the tradition.

One answer to this question is the following: to take the Triple Refuge (see sidebar, opposite). What, however, does "refuge" mean in this context, and what is meant by taking refuge in these three entities, often characterized in Buddhist texts as the Triple Gem? Clearly it is impossible to generalize about what this rite means to any given Buddhist who may think about it differently at various points in his or her life. Nevertheless, it is clear that the ritual potentially marks a significant reorientation in the lives of those who by means of it place themselves in a relationship of dependence upon the perfectly enlightened Buddha (or *buddha*s), the Dharma (the transforming truth that he realized and taught), and the Sangha (the community of Buddhists—this is a term that can refer both to the monastic community as a whole and to the élite group of Buddhists who have reached a high level of realization). Seen within the context of countless past and future lives, the taking of the Triple Refuge can mark the point at which one fundamentally redirects one's life course from ceaseless wandering and onto the Middle Path leading to *nirvana*. To use a common Buddhist metaphor, it places one upon the raft that ferries one safely across the vast ocean of *samsara*.

In Theravada Buddhist communities, where membership of the monastic community has traditionally been regarded as a necessary condition for the effective practice of meditation and for rapid progress along the Middle Path, there has been a clear distinction between what "taking refuge" means for lay people and for monks and nuns. For this latter group, ordination into the Sangha represents a more advanced taking of refuge, one accompanied by a dramatic severing of conventional social ties and close adherence to the code of monastic discipline established by the Buddha.

In Mahayana Buddhist communities, the Triple Refuge takes on related but nevertheless distinct associations. The "jewel" of the Buddha

Two young monks chanting during a festival at Pang Mu, Thailand. In countries where the Theravada tradition is predominant, as it is in Thailand, the members of the Sangha represent in principle the highest embodiment of the Buddha's teaching and thus the best field of merit, that is, the source of greatest karmic benefit for those who, with proper intention, make offerings of material support.

may mean not Gautama Buddha but one or more of a great number of other *buddha*s who are accessible to those following the Middle Path. Refuge in the Dharma in this context includes reliance upon expanded collections of authoritative teachings that differ from those accepted by the followers of the Theravada. Also numbered among the membership of the Sangha are great *bodhisattva*s, upon whom followers of the Mahayana rely for assistance in their own progress toward perfect enlightenment.

Among the followers of the Vajrayana, the form of Buddhism most commonly associated with Tibet, progress toward enlightenment includes a succession of esoteric initiations that mark special relationships with particular teachers, *bodhisattva*s, and *buddha*s (see pp.164–5).

Whatever the distinctive variations that characterize the great diversity of Buddhist communities, all have in common a recognition that individuals embark upon the path to enlightenment by establishing a relationship of dependence upon those compassionate and perfectly enlightened beings who have gone before them, upon their teachings, and upon the community of beings who embody higher levels of spiritual progress along the Middle Path.

THE TRIPLE REFUGE RITUAL

If there is anything that resembles a universal rite of passage into the Buddhist community, it is the taking of the Triple Refuge. In Theravada Buddhist communities this means performing a particular ritual in which one recites aloud three times the following lines in the Pali language: "To the Buddha I go for refuge; to the Dharma I go for refuge; to the Sangha I go for refuge." This is commonly recited in an antiphonal fashion, with each "refuge" first recited by a Buddhist monk and then repeated by a group of lay Buddhists, and the vast majority of public ceremonies within the Buddhist community begin with this public affirmation. In many cases this verbal recitation is accompanied by bodily prostration, a physical enactment of the relationship of dependence and gratitude that the ritual initiates and deepens. Other Buddhist communities have their own variations on this basic rite.

DEVOTION

The subject of devotion in Buddhism has been a vexed one for Western scholars. While it has long been acknowledged that some Buddhist traditions have strong devotional elements, these have usually been interpreted as relatively late historical developments—often in response to the needs of the laity. The earliest tradition, so this line of analysis goes, was largely free from devotion and rituals of worship. The Buddha was a human being, not a god, and his early monastic followers regarded him as nothing more than a revered teacher. In this light, even the traditional practice of "going for refuge" to the departed Buddha appears problematic, for he has disappeared from the cycle of rebirth and thus cannot provide his followers with refuge. What sense is there, then, in making offerings to the Buddha, and what value could this have in a religion that so strongly emphasizes self-reliance and personal realization of the truth?

While it is impossible to know what the Buddha's earliest followers thought of him, both textual and archaeological evidence shows that devotion has long been a part of Buddhism. The practice of venerating relics and images has played a central role even in Buddhist traditions that strongly emphasize that Gautama Buddha was a human being who died and is no longer able to aid his followers. In Mahayana Buddhist traditions, which allow for continuing interaction with a virtually infinite number of coexisting *buddha*s and *bodhisattva*s, the importance of devotion is even more pronounced. *Buddha*s such as Amitabha have the power to intervene directly in the lives of their devoted followers in order to free them from the woes of *samsara* when they die. In this latter case, the devotees' complete reliance on the power of the Buddha to deliver them serves the same function that striving to overcome attachment and the illusion of self plays in those Buddhist

UPOSATHA DAYS

Keyed in to the four phases of the lunar cycle, the tradition of observing special days of fasting and religious observance known as Uposatha days predates the rise of Buddhism in India. The full-moon day, considered the most auspicious of the four, is the day that Theravada Buddhists are most likely to visit a Buddhist temple, perhaps bringing flowers, incense, or oil for lamps as an offering. Some of the Uposatha days are marked by special celebrations, such as Vaishakha (see illustration, opposite).

The day begins with a ritualized taking of the Eight Precepts (see pp.104–5), which commit lay people to a higher form of moral discipline and resemble the rules adopted by novice monks. During the course of the day, those in attendance, many of whom may have donned white clothing for the day, listen to sermons, make offerings to the Buddha, and spend time seated on the ground reading devotional literature. Such activities are regarded as highly meritorious.

These days of special observance also allow the laity to move away from the distractions and anxieties of life in the world and approximate, for a limited time, the higher ideals of Buddhist practice that characterize the Sangha.

A Sri Lankan woman offers a flower at a stupa at the Kelaniya temple during the festival of Vesak (Sanskrit, Vaishakha; Pali, Vesakha). This is one of the most important Theravada Buddhist festivals, commemorating the birth, enlightenment, and death of the Buddha. In Sri Lanka this special day is marked by visiting Buddhist temples, devotional singing, and meritorious deeds such as setting up booths that offer hospitality to strangers.

traditions which stress one's own efforts. Although the strategies differ, the goal is the same—transcending egotistical self-regard.

Central to Buddhist devotion is the ideal of accumulating merit by cultivating proper mental states and performing good deeds, such as those exemplified in the rites associated with Uposatha days (see box, opposite). Even Buddhist traditions that regard the departed Buddha as unable either to receive offerings or intervene in his followers' lives cultivate a sense of obligation and gratitude for what the Buddha did for them in the past. By reflecting on the Buddha's virtuous deeds, the devotee's mind is directed toward a proper sense of dependence upon the one who, through countless lifetimes of self-sacrifice, perfected himself and made it possible for others to follow in his footsteps along the Middle Path.

DONATION

THE OFFERING OF MUSIC
Buddhist tradition reflects some ambivalence toward the pleasures associated with music. Members of the Sangha are prohibited from enjoying displays of music and dance, and the monastic discipline emphasizes the virtues of restraint of the senses. In spite of this, a tradition developed in Sri Lanka of making musical offerings, especially drumming, to the Buddha, as befits a great king. This role is traditionally performed by members of a particular caste who receive the right to farm monastic land in return for the service of drumming.

Drummers accompanying one of the many daily rituals of veneration at the Temple of the Tooth in Kandy, Sri Lanka. This relic has long been considered a source of political authority for the island's rulers.

One of the most widely practiced ideals throughout the Buddhist world is that of *dana* ("donation") and its attendant virtue, generosity. The highest paragon of this virtue is the Buddha who, during his many previous lives as a *bodhisattva*, sacrificed his possessions and even his own flesh to benefit other beings while simultaneously perfecting himself in the ideal of non-attachment. *Dana* is thus tied to two more fundamental Buddhist ideals—compassion for other beings and insight into the truth of non-self (*anatman*).

Given the importance of religious renunciation in the history of Buddhism, the great emphasis placed on the value of lay donations is not surprising, for without them the Sangha could not survive. In return for their various forms of provision, supporters of the Sangha gain merit. While there is a potential conflict between the ideal of selflessness and the goal of accumulating merit which leads to better rebirths, Buddhist tradition repeatedly stresses the value of giving freely with a sense of serene joy.

A consequence of this emphasis on intentionality is the value placed on rejoicing at the benefit that others will gain from being generous. In other words, an individual can gain merit simply by feeling glad when others gain merit—a great advantage for those who have little to give themselves.

An extension of this idea can be found in the practice of "merit transfer." Conventional Buddhist teaching emphasizes that one's intentional deeds determine the future course of one's rebirth and that each individual is thus responsible for his or her own progress along the Middle Path. However, the practice of transferring accumulated merit to benefit others became well established throughout a diversity of Buddhist communities. It is thus common to dedicate the benefit of an act of donation to all beings. Merit transfer is also especially identified with rites for deceased relatives. Since it is believed that departed loved ones may be reborn as *preta*s, restless and malevolent spirits who suffer constantly from hunger and thirst, Buddhist funeral ceremonies and commemorative rituals commonly include rites that transfer merit to the deceased to help them gain a better rebirth. Such rituals are also believed to benefit the living by placating malevolent spirits thought to cause misfortune and illness.

The ideal of generosity has also been a guiding principle for Buddhist kings. Royal patronage has been a major factor in the maintenance and expansion of Buddhist institutions. Given the assumed congruence between accumulated merit and worldly success, royal legitimacy has often been closely linked with such patronage. Thus those individuals who are worthy of kingship have, by the logic of karmic consequences, invariably performed many good deeds in the past and will continue to do so in the future. Some Sri Lankan kings were even said to have compiled "merit books" which recorded their many donations to the Sangha and these were read to them on their deathbeds to ease their minds as death approached.

KING SIRISANGHABODHI

One of the more dramatic examples of the ideal of generosity can be found in the Sri Lankan tale of the historical King Sirisanghabodhi, a king who lived in the fourth century CE. After ruling Sri Lanka as a paragon of royal virtue, he learned that his evil treasurer had gathered an army to overthrow him, so he abdicated his throne and became a wandering recluse. The ex-treasurer, who was now king, feared that Sirisanghabodhi's continuing popularity would cause the people to rise up and he put a price upon the former monarch's head. Not long after this, a poor man wandering in the forest encountered Sirisanghabodhi. He insisted on sharing his food with the former king, who rejoiced when he heard about the price on his head, for it meant that he would be able both to fulfil the perfection of generosity and to repay the man for sharing his lunch. He insisted that the man should take his head to the king and receive the bounty. When the man hesitated, Sirisanghabodhi decapitated himself. A famous Buddhist temple was later constructed at the reputed site of this event, and the story of Sirisanghabodhi, the king who was willing to donate even his own head, became a popular ideal of Buddhist generosity.

A sculpture at Atanagalla temple, Sri Lanka, depicting the dramatic moment when, in an act of selfless generosity, King Sirisanghabodhi is poised to decapitate himself.

PILGRIMAGE

However much the Buddha's teachings seem to focus on the cultivation of inner states of consciousness, Buddhism has also highlighted the importance of place. It is noteworthy that the scriptural accounts of the Buddha's last days include explicit instructions for the construction of monuments to house his relics and a recommendation that his followers undertake pilgrimages to four places associated with key events in his life (see p.41). According to the account of the Buddha's final days, he described the places associated with his birth, enlightenment, first teaching, and death, as sites worthy of being seen by monks, nuns, and lay people because they evoked powerful emotion in those who visited them. Moreover, he stated that those who die with a serenely joyful heart while traveling to these places are assured rebirth in a blissful heavenly realm. These texts thus explicitly link the inner experience of Buddhists with an exterior sacred geography. And if the initial list of sacred sites was limited to just a few places marked by the Buddha's presence during his lifetime, the outward dissemination of his relics made possible an expanding network of sacred centers throughout the Buddhist world. At the same time, the number of important sites associated with the life of the Buddha in north India also expanded, thus facilitating the development of a detailed Buddha biography.

The earliest documented Buddhist pilgrim was the third-century BCE Indian emperor Ashoka who memorialized his pilgrimage to Lumbini, the Buddha's birthplace, with an inscribed pillar. Legendary accounts of Ashoka's life also record that he divided up the Buddha's relics and enshrined them in 84,000 *stupa*s throughout his realm (see pp.50–53). These accounts greatly influenced later generations of Buddhist kings who sought to emulate Ashoka by building *stupa*s and visiting sacred sites.

There are also written accounts detailing the heroic journeys of Chinese Buddhist monks to the motherland of their adopted religion. The earliest of these, Faxian, left China in 399CE and traveled the southern branch of the Silk Road through central Asia to northern India. His account describes his visits to the many sacred sites then associated with the life of the Buddha, and the numerous *stupa*s that local traditions traced back to the emperor Ashoka. Faxian made his way back to China by ship, with visits to Sri Lanka and Java, finally reaching his homeland fifteen years after he had left it. He returned with a precious cargo—authentic Buddhist texts, including a complete Vinaya (the code of monastic discipline). Later pilgrims continued this practice by journeying to India and returning with sacred scriptures and relics, helping to establish the foundations of an increasingly vigorous Chinese Buddhist tradition.

As Buddhism spread throughout Asia, new pilgrimage sites were identified and became the focus of popular devotion, including sacred mountains (see sidebar, left). Whatever the particulars of the individual destinations, a number of common ideals and practices are shared by pilgrims throughout the Buddhist world. Pilgrimage is widely regarded as highly meritorious,

SACRED MOUNTAINS

As Buddhism became deeply rooted throughout Asia, the sacred abodes of indigenous spirits and gods were often incorporated into the Buddhist cosmology and became important pilgrimage destinations. In Sri Lanka, for example, ancient chronicles record that the Buddha visited the island on three occasions during his lifetime and stopped at a succession of places that were later sanctified by the enshrinement of important relics. A list of sixteen pilgrimage sites developed, including the mountain known as Sripada or "Adam's Peak" (see illustration p.194), the home of the god Mahasumana, where the Buddha was reputed to have left behind a giant footprint. This same peak was eventually assimilated into other Sri Lankan religious traditions, becoming a pilgrimage destination for Hindus and Muslims as well. Although it never became a major Christian pilgrimage site, a tradition also developed among some Christians that the mountain preserved the footprint of St Thomas. Other mountains throughout Asia also became important Buddhist pilgrimage centers, including Mount Wutai in China, Mount Fuji in Japan, and Mount Kailash in Tibet.

A female pilgrim prostrates herself in prayer outside Tibet's most sacred temple, the 7th-century Jokhang in Lhasa. The building, which houses the famous sculpture of the Buddha known as Jowo Rinpoche, is an important pilgrimage site all the year round, but especially at New Year. Some devotees prostrate themselves for hundreds of kilometres from their home village to their intended site, journeys which may take years to complete. Such pilgrims often protect their bodies by wearing leather aprons and hand and knee pads, similar to those seen here.

provided that one participates with the proper intention and mental disposition. Buddhist pilgrims often wear special clothing and observe distinctive conventions of speech and behavior along the route. Fasting or special attention to maintaining mental and physical purity is often undertaken. Pilgrims sometimes make special vows to the local gods and spirits residing at pilgrimage sites in the hope of a wide variety of mundane benefits. Clockwise circumambulation, in which the pilgrim keeps his or her right side facing the object of veneration, is also commonly practiced. Some Tibetan pilgrims undertake lengthy circumambulations in which they cover the entire route with consecutive full-body prostrations (see illustration, above).

Basic to the practice of Buddhist pilgrimage is a recognition that mental cultivation can be enhanced by a break from the mundane habits of everyday life. Whether the pilgrim travels a great distance to reach a site or instead visits a local shrine a few hours away from home, both the journey and the destination draw pilgrims out of their ordinary routines and engender a sense of heightened expectation. The importance of pilgrimage for Buddhists is perhaps especially fitting given the Buddha's choice of foundational metaphors—he and all who follow in his footsteps traverse the Middle Path that leads from the arising of suffering to its cessation.

ART AND ARCHITECTURE *Michael Willis*

BODH GAYA

ABOVE AND OPPOSITE The ancient Mahabodhi temple has been subject to repair and restoration for centuries. The Burmese were active at the site before the late 19th century when extensive rebuilding took place under British supervision (above), and work to restore the structure is still in progress today (opposite).

Bodh Gaya is the site where the Buddha became enlightened more than two millennia ago and it holds a special place in the sacred geography of Buddhism. It is located in the center of the *madhyadesha* ("middle country"), the ground made holy by the Buddha's presence. In the Mahaparinirvana ("Great Final Nirvana Sutra," see pp.206–7), the Buddha tells his followers that after he has passed away they can attain merit and a noble rebirth by going on pilgrimage to the places where he was born, gained enlightenment, first taught, and finally passed away.

Since then, countless pilgrims have made their way to Bodh Gaya to see the Bodhi tree, which is believed to be directly descended from the very one under which the Buddha attained enlightenment, making it the one living link between the Buddha and our own time. Like the Buddha's begging bowl and monastic robe, it is understood as a "relic of use" (*paribhogika dhatu*), something which is holy because the Buddha used it during his lifetime. In the early days of Buddhism, a cutting from the tree was taken to Sri Lanka as part of Ashoka's effort to transplant Buddhism to the island. Subsequent cuttings have been used to establish new tree shrines elsewhere.

The first building at Bodh Gaya dates to the third century BCE, when Ashoka set up a platform next to the tree. A large, decorated stone slab was placed directly on the spot where the Buddha sat in meditation. In the first century BCE the site was enclosed by a stone railing, similar to those at other early Buddhist monuments. Among the numerous additions in later times, the most important was a large brick temple constructed adjacent to the tree in the sixth century CE on the orders of Mahanama, a monk from Sri Lanka with royal connections. The temple, known as the Mahabodhi, was subject to repair, notably under the Pala kings of eastern India between the eighth and eleventh centuries CE, and later by pious Buddhists from other countries. Inscriptions in Chinese and Burmese have been found at the site and Tibetan texts mention pilgrims who came down to visit and study.

Pilgrims supported the temple in many ways. The wealthy endowed monasteries or set up images in subsidiary shrines, while more humble visitors left mass-produced votive plaques (see illustration, p.79). Monks and pilgrims also erected small *stupa*s in the temple precinct. Many of these seem to have contained the ashes of Buddhists who had died at Bodh Gaya.

The Bodhi tree stands at the center of what is known as the *bodhimanda*, the "place of supreme knowledge." The Buddha's seat under the tree is known as the *vajrasana* or "diamond throne." In Mahayana, the *vajra*, or "diamond thunderbolt," is emblematic of the indestructible nature of absolute emptiness (*shunyata*; see pp.140–41). The *vajrasana* is therefore a place of preeminent spiritual power, for it marks the spot where the Buddha transformed the abstract concept of wisdom and emptiness into reality.

BUDDHIST ETHICS

Fundamental to Buddhist teaching is the notion of intentional action (*karma*) and its consequences (see pp.60–61). Deeds have future consequences for the doer primarily because of the mental and emotional conditions that motivate them. If one is ignorant about the true nature of reality and driven by desire and attachment, then one's actions will necessarily reflect those conditions.

While Buddhist teaching includes many rules and prohibitions (for example, the Five Precepts that define the basic lay Buddhist ethic—see pp.104–5—and the Pratimoksha—see p.46 and 99), this moral discipline is consistently linked, at least ideally, with the cultivation of mental discipline and understanding. The question of vegetarianism provides an interesting case in point. Vegetarianism is highly valued in many Buddhist societies because of the first precept which prohibits the taking of any life. In spite of this ideal, however, most Buddhists customarily eat meat or fish, although a vegetarian diet may be adopted on days of special observance. Theravada Buddhist monastic codes do not prohibit members of the Sangha from eating meat. Monks and nuns are instructed to avoid eating the meat of animals specifically slaughtered for them, but they are generally exhorted to eat dispassionately whatever food they receive. Here the ideal of overcoming desire and attachment has priority over avoiding the ingestion of meat.

Although the principle of *karma* provides the fundamental Buddhist rationale for deeming some acts "skillful" and others "unskillful" in terms

JIZO AND BUDDHIST ETHICS

The *bodhisattva* Kshitigarbha is a popular figure in Japan, where he is known as Jizo Bosatsu. Jizo helps those in need of guidance in determining where they should be going, thus he has a long association with children and travelers. But he also assists the recently deceased, who are confused in the state between death and rebirth, and he is the *bodhisattva* of choice when children die. A more recent phenomenon is the role that Jizo plays to assuage the psychological pain for parents of stillborn babies, dead infants, and aborted foetuses. With the *bodhisattva* Avalokitesvara (Kannon Bosatsu in Japan), Jizo is prominent in a new genre of ritual known as *mizuko kuyo*, where offerings are made and *sutra*s chanted to send aid to a dead child (*mizuko*, or "water child"). Jizo is a popular choice for this rite, not only because of his traditional role as protector of dead children, but also for the reason that his shaven head evokes a child's appearance.

A small statue of Jizo, with a customary bib around its neck, which has been placed in the grounds of a temple in Kyoto to become a conduit for sending karmic merit to a dead child by way of the offerings presented. Over time, the statue comes to represent the deceased, and relatives will bring food, toys, and the like on the anniversary of the death.

of their effects on one's progress along the Middle Path, *karma* has its limits as a guide to ideal behavior. In Buddhist terms, it is because we believe, at least unconsciously, that we have an enduring self that we form desires and attachments even for "good" things such as attaining *nirvana*. Since *buddha*s, *arhat*s, and very advanced *bodhisattva*s have fully realized the truth of non-self (and the "emptiness" of the *dharma*s), they do not act with intention in the conventional sense and consequently have stopped accumulating the karmic consequences that lead to rebirth. When placed in this context, some actions that appear to violate conventional Buddhist moral teachings may be valued positively, if they are motivated by compassion for others and are grounded in a deeper realization of the Dharma.

A well-known example of selflessness is that provided by Prince Vessantara, the Buddha's last human rebirth before his life as Siddhartha Gautama, and the subject of a highly popular Buddhist story. Vessantara was famous for his generosity, which was most dramatically illustrated when he gave away his children to the grotesque Brahman Jujaka while their mother was away gathering food. The tale lends itself to multiple readings. It may, for example, resonate one way for women who can identify with the mother's anguish when she learns that her children have gone, and another way for Buddhist monks who have renounced familial and social obligations. The story clearly highlights the exceptional character of the future Buddha's action rather than its value as an ethical precedent. What is fundamental is not so much the deed itself as the intentionality behind it. The moral value of the action centers not on the consequences, but on the detached and selfless mental state of the donor who is willing to part with everything, no matter how dear.

A corollary to the emphasis on overcoming the illusion of self, and in Mahayana circles, on gaining insight into the emptiness of the *dharma*s (see p.140), is the notion of the interdependence of all things. This is connected to the ideal of compassion for all beings and also to the positive valuation of the natural world that characterizes some forms of Buddhism. Seen in this light, any mundane activity can be deeply imbued with spiritual significance.

While it is not difficult to sketch in broad strokes some of the basic teachings that inform Buddhist ethical reflection, it is impossible to generalize on this basis about the actual behavior of Buddhists or to predict what any society influenced by Buddhist teaching might legislate. It does seem likely, however, that Buddhist ethical discourses will become increasingly globalized and that the growing influence of "engaged Buddhists" committed to the transformation of society in accordance with Buddhist values (see p.234–7) will play an important role in shaping the future of Buddhist ethics.

This detail from the Burmese folding manuscript (parabaik) *Vessantara Jataka, dating from about 1800, shows King Vessantara seated in his forest abode. He is pouring water onto the hands of the Brahman Jujaka, prior to giving away his children to him.*

MONKS AND MONARCHS

The Dhamekha stupa at Sarnath marks the traditional site of the Buddha's first sermon. The existing structure is built over an earlier stupa that dates to the time of Ashoka.

As a social renunciant, the Buddha was in some respects fundamentally indifferent to the rise and fall of rulers and their court politics. In other respects, however, he appears to have recognized that the support or enmity of the local political order could greatly affect the well-being of the Sangha. Based on the evidence provided by early Buddhist sources, the Buddha was a skilled politician when he had occasion to deal with the rulers of his day. Some of his teachings warn of the sufferings that tyrannical kings can impose on their subjects, and the Vinaya accounts of the early years of the Sangha show that he was willing to adjust the community's rules to avoid conflict with local kings as, for example, when he prohibited the ordination of army deserters and instructed the community to adjust the dates for the rainy season retreat to accommodate royal preferences. While visiting kings seeking his teaching were expected to enact their religious inferiority through rituals of obeisance, he does not appear to have questioned their political authority.

THE "QUESTIONS OF MENANDER"

One of the most interesting early Buddhist texts from outside the canon of Buddhist scriptures (the Tipitaka) is the Milinda-panha ("Questions of Menander"), which survives in Pali and Chinese versions. The text records a series of dialogues between King Menander I (Milinda in Pali) and a Buddhist monk called Nagasena. Menander lived in the second century BCE and ruled one of the Indo-Greek kingdoms that had arisen in the wake of the conquests of Alexander the Great two centuries earlier. Nagasena traveled to Menander's kingdom—which lay in what is now Afghanistan and northern Pakistan—and the king interrogated him on various doctrinal issues by presenting him with a series of dilemmas based on quotations from Buddhist scriptures. Nagasena's answers skillfully demonstrated the coherence and persuasiveness of the Buddha's teaching.

The resulting text sheds light on a number of doctrinal issues of early Buddhism, such as the extent of the Buddha's omniscience, the character of *nirvana*, and the nature and experience of *arhat*s (enlightened followers of the Buddha). At the conclusion of the text, it is said that Menander abdicated in favor of his son to become a Buddhist monk, and later attained *nirvana*.

A silver 4-drachma coin of Hellenistic design with a portrait of King Menander I wielding a spear, ca. 150BCE. The Greek inscription says "Menander, King, Savior."

When we turn to the legendary accounts of the emperor Ashoka, we again see a model of cooperation between Sangha and state. Ashoka is converted to Buddhism by a charismatic monk, and actively supports the Sangha with lavish donations and *stupa* construction. Equally important, he purifies the Sangha by expelling members who have violated its disciplinary rules. While different versions of the Ashokan legend depict him as an advocate for one or another Buddhist sect, the inscriptional evidence suggests that his overriding concern was with maintaining the internal discipline of the order, not with resolving doctrinal disputes.

The Ashokan model was to prove highly influential for Buddhist kings throughout south and southeast Asia (see also pp.126–31). The Sri Lankan chronicles, for example, emphasize the close connections that existed between the Ashokan court in Pataliputra and King Devanampiyatissa in Anuradhapura, who is said to have been converted to Buddhism by Ashoka's son Mahinda. Ashoka came to be seen as the exemplary patron and protector of Buddhism, and later Sri Lankan monarchs constructed monastic residences, built new *stupa*s and enlarged old ones, and held great religious festivals all in conformity with the model bequeathed by Ashoka. Monks, for their part, were sometimes called to serve as advisors to kings, and since literacy and education were closely tied to the Sangha, kings frequently had monastic tutors. What emerges is a relationship of complementary responsibilities and benefits. In general, the Sangha has prospered during periods of strong royal patronage and sunk into decline when that support has been absent.

AN IDEAL BUDDHIST KING?

The story of King Kirti Sri Rajasinha, one of the last monarchs to rule over the Kandyan kingdom in Sri Lanka before it was conquered by the British in 1815, illustrates the complex forces shaping relations between Buddhist monks and kings. Kirti Sri is remembered as an exemplary ruler, despite his personal practice of Shaivitic Hinduism. He is chiefly celebrated for his role in reviving the Sangha by bringing a delegation of monks from Siam (Thailand) to reestablish a valid higher ordination lineage in Sri Lanka, and for his patronage of Buddhist temples and religious art. He also faced an assassination plot supported by the monk Valvita Saranamkara, the Sangha head with whom the king had cooperated in reviving it seven years earlier. After punishing the leaders of the rebellion, he kept Saranamkara on as the head of the Sangha.

PART 2 ● CHAPTER 7 *Kevin Trainor*

THERAVADA BUDDHISM

THE DOCTRINE OF THE ELDERS

HINAYANA BUDDHISM
The Theravada is sometimes referred to as the Hinayana or "Lesser Vehicle." The term Hinayana is still sometimes used by scholars to refer collectively to the various Buddhist schools that preceded the rise of the Mahayana or "Greater Vehicle" (see pp.46–9), but the basic meaning of the term has pejorative connotations and it should be avoided as a way of characterizing the followers of the Theravada.

Of the many distinctive schools of Buddhism that formed in the first centuries after the death of the Buddha (see pp.40–41), only one has survived into the present day—the Theravada or "Doctrine of the Elders." The followers of this tradition trace its origins back to Gautama Buddha himself. They maintain that the Buddha's teaching has been handed down in an unbroken succession within the Sangha or monastic community, hence the reference to "elders" or venerable members of the Sangha who have protected the tradition's integrity. The Theravada is also called "Southern Buddhism," reflecting the parts of Asia where it has had a dominant influence, including the regions presently defined by the nations of Sri Lanka, Thailand, Burma (Myanmar), Cambodia, and Laos (see map, opposite).

The centrality of the Sangha and its primary responsibility for preserving and embodying the Buddha's teachings are defining features of Theravada tradition in its diverse cultural and historical forms. Although there is a danger of exaggerating the continuity of Theravada teaching, the basically conservative character of the school is nevertheless striking. In contrast to the Mahayana, the Theravada has tended to emphasize the centrality of the historical Gautama Buddha and has resisted the expansion of its canon of authoritative scriptures. Yet Theravada tradition, comprised of both doctrines and practices, has also taken on a diversity of cultural forms throughout its long existence. The history of Theravada Buddhist literature, which has repeatedly been translated back and forth between Pali and vernacular languages, illustrates this basic dynamic. While this is overwhelmingly a literature produced within Theravada monastic communities with a primary focus on the teachings of Gautama Buddha as they have been defined by the Pali canon and its authoritative commentaries, these texts also bear witness to an ongoing process of adaptation as general Buddhist teachings have been selectively appropriated and made relevant to individuals and groups living in very different times and places. Thus the relatively conservative Theravada approach to doctrine has not left the tradition frozen in time.

Another general feature of the nations and cultures that have been deeply shaped by Theravada Buddhist teaching is the close alliance commonly forged between the Sangha and the state. The classical model for this has been the legendary patronage provided by the third-century BCE Indian emperor Ashoka (see pp.50–53 and 119). This basic ideal of reciprocal

support between Buddhist monastic institutions and the institutions of government has exerted a powerful influence on the history of Theravada Buddhism and of the peoples that have embraced it.

In addition, however central the Sangha remains to the organization and practice of Theravada, the modern age has witnessed a dramatic growth in the power and influence of the laity. For example, Theravada tradition has long reserved the practice of meditation to members of the Sangha and, in contrast, has encouraged lay people to engage in merit-making activities to improve their future rebirth status. Nevertheless, an increasingly influential group of lay people has taken up meditation and it aspires to more dramatic progress along the path to *nirvana*. Others have embraced meditation as a means of gaining worldly benefits. As a result, the clear distinction traditionally maintained between the respective ideals and practices of Sangha and laity has been eroded. Such changes are likely to become even more pronounced as Theravada communities become more deeply rooted in Western nations lacking a long history of Buddhist monastic institutions.

This map illustrates the broad transmission patterns of Theravada tradition from north India into south and southeast Asia. Sri Lanka became a center of the Theravada beginning in the 3rd century BCE *and Buddhist missions may have reached southeast Asia then as well. A diverse blend of Theravada, Mahayana, and Brahmanic/Hindu religious influences predominated in southeast Asia until a broad-based Theravada reform movement swept through the region in the 11th–15th centuries* CE.

THE BUDDHA AND THE GODS

After performing the "Miracle of the Double" (see p.193) at Shravasti in his ministry's sixth year, the Buddha used Yugandhara mountain (left, represented by a pillar) and Mount Meru as climbing stones to ascend to the Heaven of the Thirty-three. There he sat on Shakra's (Indra's) throne and preached the Abhidharma to his mother, attended by the gods of the ten thousand worlds. This 19th-century Burmese manuscript illustration captures the moment when the Buddha descended along the triple stairway of gold, silver, and jewels, accompanied by the many deities, and arrived at the city of Samkashya. This event is marked by Burma's festival of lights (Thadingyut) at the end of the rainy season.

Those who think of Buddhism as atheistic may be surprised to learn that worship of various gods has been thoroughly integrated into the practice of Theravada Buddhism. The Theravada Buddhist scriptures portray the Buddha interacting with numerous *deva*s who were part of the hierarchy of superhuman beings widely accepted within the north Indian cultural milieu of his day. What is distinctive about the Buddha's teaching about the *deva*s, in contrast to the brahmanical religious views of the time, is his rejection of a divine creator and his assertion that even the highest *deva*s are trapped in the cycle of rebirth (see pp.28–35). These brahmanical deities, as well as a wide range of supernatural agents such as demons and ghosts, were accepted into the broader Buddhist worldview in a manner consistent with the basic principle of *karma*—those in the higher reaches of the celestial pantheon are there by virtue of their previous good deeds, while those exhibiting greed and hostility occupy lower positions in keeping with the ethical values embedded in the Buddhist understanding of the workings of *karma*.

Thus the *deva*s are regarded as fully real and possess superhuman powers, though they are subservient to the Buddha. During his lifetime the

Buddha stood at the apex of this hierarchy, and after his final passing away he continues a symbolic hegemony over the *deva*s and lower superhuman beings. In general, the *deva*s are relatively distant figures (see sidebar, right).

More relevant, and also demanding of fearful respect, are the lower-level superhuman beings whose jurisdiction and cult are strongly regionally defined. In addition, there are a great number of locally identified demons and ghosts believed to cause personal illness and misfortune. Because these beings are largely known through local oral tradition, there is considerable fluidity in their names and attributes, though the broader structure of the hierarchy remains relatively constant. Each level of superhuman beings has its respective forms of offering and class of religious specialists, organized along a continuum of relative purity. All of these have the power to harm or benefit people in their daily lives, and it is these beings, not the Buddha, whom Theravadins invoke and propitiate to avert misfortune and gain worldly benefits.

This general outline of the structure and dynamics of the hierarchy of superhuman beings also applies to other Theravada Buddhist cultures. In Thailand, the group of superhuman beings below the *deva* realm are called *phii*, while in Burma (Myanmar) they are referred to as *nat*s. As in Sri Lanka, these beings range greatly in their relative purity and style of behavior. What remains consistent is organization of the pantheon according to the principle of *karma*, and the symbolic supremacy of the Buddha and his Middle Path over these powerful beings and their cults.

GUARDIAN DEITIES

According to the ancient Sri Lankan chronicles, the Buddha explicitly commissioned Shakra, king of the gods (another name for Indra), to protect the island of Sri Lanka, and he in turn delegated this authority to the god Upulvan (Vishnu), one of the four guardian deities of Sri Lanka, each of whom rules over his or her quarter of the island. The number is fixed at four, though the specific names included in the group have varied with time and place. These figures are all relatively remote by virtue of their celestial altitude and moral virtue; they are not much concerned with the passionate and misguided affairs of the world, and thus Sri Lankan Buddhists seldom resort to them for direct assistance in their daily affairs. The major exception is the god Skanda or Kataragama, who is generally counted among the four guardian deities, but whose behavior and cult are much less consistent with Buddhist ethical norms (see box, below).

KATARAGAMA WORSHIP

The Kataragama religious complex, located in the southeastern corner of Sri Lanka, is probably the island's most popular devotional center, attracting vast numbers of worshippers drawn from all the major religious communities. The primary religious focus of the complex is the god Kataragama, more commonly known among Hindus as Skanda, the warlike offspring of Shiva and Parvati. Although the Sri Lankan cult of Kataragama has for centuries attracted Tamil Hindus, his popularity among Sinhala Buddhists rose dramatically in the latter half of the twentieth century and they now represent the majority of visitors to the site.

Many of Kataragama's worshippers seek the god's favor by engaging in various austere physical practices, including rolling in scorching sand, piercing their cheeks, tongue, and other body parts with skewers or hooks, and walking across burning coals. More than half a million visitors flock to the complex each year, with the greatest number congregating during the god's festival in the month of Esala (July or August). Although Kataragama is regarded by many Buddhists as a *bodhisattva*, he is also associated with sensual passion and acts of retribution. Unlike the more remote guardian deities who are regarded as largely benevolent and rational (see sidebar, above), Kataragama is known for using any means to help those whom he chooses to favor.

The rise in popularity of Kataragama is explained by many factors. The complex is more accessible because of road improvements and greater access to transportation. Anthropologist Gananath Obeyesekere, who has studied devotion to Kataragama for many years, highlights the importance of social changes in Sri Lanka, including population increases, urbanization and the breakdown of traditional village culture, and economic uncertainties. In part, he suggests, Buddhists are drawn to Kataragama because the dramatic religious practices associated with devotion to him, many of which were brought to Sri Lankan by Hindu Tamils, offer a kind of emotional gratification that stands in sharp contrast to the ideals of sensual and emotional restraint that have traditionally characterized Sri Lankan Buddhism.

SRI LANKAN BUDDHISM

AVALOKITESHVARA IN SRI LANKA
However much Sri Lanka is presently identified exclusively with the Theravada tradition, this was not always the case. There is considerable textual and archaeological evidence attesting to the presence of Mahayana Buddhism on the island. A striking example of this is the cult of Avalokiteshvara, one of the most popular Mahayana Buddhist *bodhisattvas*, which was well-established in Sri Lanka by the eighth century CE, particularly among coastal seafaring communities. The figure of Avalokiteshvara later became associated with Natha, one of the four Sri Lankan guardian deities, and he, in turn, became identified with Maitreya (Metteyya in Pali), the next Buddha expected by Theravadins. Mahayana influence diminished after King Parakramabahu I united the Sri Lankan Sangha under Mahavihara leadership in the twelfth century CE.

From the time of its arrival in the third century BCE up to the present day, Theravada Buddhism has been inextricably linked with the history of Sri Lanka. The story of Mahinda's conversion of the king to the Buddha's Dharma (see box, below) and the king's subsequent construction of monasteries and relic monuments (thus establishing the Dharma, Sangha and Buddha—all three elements of the Triple Refuge; see sidebar, p.107) highlights the enduring connection between Sangha and state that has characterized the history of Buddhism in Sri Lanka. While the fortunes of Buddhism have risen and fallen during alternating periods of royal patronage and neglect and the effects of waves of foreign invasion, Sri Lankan Buddhists have long regarded their island as a special preserve of the Buddha's teaching.

Our knowledge of the history of Buddhism in Sri Lanka owes much to the ancient monastic chronicles composed and preserved within the Mahavihara monastic community, which traces its roots back to Mahinda's and King Devanampiyatissa's original monastic foundation in the ancient capital of Anuradhapura. According to the chronicles, the first major split in the Sri Lankan Sangha arose in the first century BCE when royal patronage shifted to a group of dissident monks who had founded the Abhayagiri monastery. The Abhayagiri community appears to have been more open to Mahayana teachings coming from India (see sidebar, opposite). A second split occurred in the fourth century CE with the establishment of the Jetavana

POSON FESTIVAL

One of the most widely celebrated Buddhist festivals in Sri Lanka is Poson, the full-moon day falling in May or June that commemorates the coming of Buddhism to Sri Lanka from India in the third century BCE. Hundreds of thousands of pilgrims from all over Sri Lanka travel to the ancient capital of Anuradhapura and nearby Mihintale to mark the day upon which the monk Mahinda (Sanskrit, Mahendra), son of the great Indian emperor Ashoka, is believed to have converted Devanampiyatissa, the king of Sri Lanka.

The site of Mahinda's first teaching of the Dharma to the king on a mountaintop at Mihintale is the same spot, according to tradition, visited by the Buddha on his legendary third visit to Sri Lanka, and is included among the sixteen primary pilgrimage sites on the island (see pp.112–13). Archaeological excavations have also uncovered numerous relic monuments and the ruins of an extensive complex of monastic structures. Since the 1950s, the festival has drawn considerable media attention as well as the interest of politicians, and has served to integrate popular Buddhist devotion and Sinhala Buddhist nationalist sentiment.

community in Anuradhapura, again under royal patronage. The Sri Lankan Sangha remained divided into these three distinct fraternities, at least in Anuradhapura, until the twelfth century CE when King Parakramabahu I sponsored a major purification of the monastic community and reunited the three groups under a single monastic leader from the Mahavihara lineage.

Three successive periods of European colonization exerted a profound effect on the history of Sri Lankan Buddhism, beginning with the Portuguese at the start of the sixteenth century. The Dutch subsequently seized control of the island in the middle of the seventeenth century and the British gained control at the end of the 1700s. With the British conquest of the Kandyan kingdom in 1815, the whole of Sri Lanka was for the first time under the centralized control of a foreign power. Although Christian missionary efforts under the various European powers failed to convert more than a small percentage of the population, official indifference, and at times hostility, hastened the decline of the Sangha. Following independence in 1948, a powerful wave of Sinhala Buddhist nationalism emerged, centered on the elections of 1956 and the 2,500th anniversary of the Buddha's final passing away. The current ethnic conflict between the Sinhala-dominated government of Sri Lanka and the Tamil independence movement, though not fundamentally about religious differences, is nevertheless shaped by a popular ideal of restoring and protecting a distinctive Buddhist heritage in a post-colonial setting.

The festival of Esala Perahera held each year in Kandy is the occasion for a parade of ornately dressed elephants in honor of one of Sri Lanka's most venerated relics of the Buddha—his tooth, which is said to have been brought to the island in the 4th century CE.

SOUTHEAST ASIA I

The vast region now referred to as southeast Asia, bounded by the Indian subcontinent on the west and China to the north, and stretching southeastward across the islands of Indonesia, has been deeply shaped by the interplay of Indian influences within the region's great diversity of indigenous cultures. Although the modern nations of mainland southeast Asia are, with the exception of Vietnam, predominantly Theravada Buddhist, forms of Brahmanic/Hindu religion and Mahayana Buddhism, including Vajrayana, exercised powerful influences in the region at least as early as the first century CE. Spread along the great maritime trading routes that linked Sri Lanka and the eastern coast of India with mainland and insular southeast Asia, Indian religious ideas and rituals were probably initially embraced by local rulers throughout southeast Asia as a means of strengthening their political authority. The magnificent ruins of Angkor in Cambodia, Pagan in Burma (Myanmar), and Borobudur in Java attest to the influence of Indian conceptions of kingship, both Brahmanic/Hindu and Buddhist, and to the depth of artistic and economic resources dedicated to the material embodiment of these ideas. Whether drawing upon the *devaraja* ideal, the "divine king" modeled on the

THE EMERALD BUDDHA

The long history of cultural links between south and southeast Asia and the close ties between Buddhism and political authority are both illustrated by the traditions surrounding the Emerald Buddha, the most prominent Thai Buddha image. According to Thai chronicles, the figure is said to have originated in India when the monk Nagasena (see box, p.119), assisted by the great god Shakra, obtained a powerful jewel associated with *chakravartin* kingship. The divine architect Vishvakarma then sculpted the image and Nagasena installed Buddha relics within it. From India, it traveled to Sri Lanka and then on to various locations throughout southeast Asia. This tradition was subsequently associated with an image that first appeared in northern Thailand in the fifteenth century and was later taken to Laos. In the eighteenth century, King Chakri, who founded the current Thai dynasty, captured the image during a military campaign in Laos and returned it to Thailand. When he established his capital in Ratanakosin (modern Bangkok), he built for it a magnificent image house next to his palace. The Buddha figure (in actuality carved from jade rather than emerald) became identified with the well-being of the dynasty and the Thai nation, and three times a year with the changing seasons the king performs an elaborate robe-changing ceremony in its honor.

The small figure of the Emerald Buddha (right), flanked by a gilded bodhisattva, *in the highly ornate* bot *of Wat Phra Kaew ("Temple of the Emerald Buddha") in Bangkok.*

figure of Shakra/Indra, or the Buddhist *chakravartin-bodhisattva* model of kingship (see p.50), rulers throughout southeast Asia consolidated their political legitimacy through ambitious building projects, attempting to mirror within their kingdoms the cosmic hierarchy of celestial beings dwelling upon sacred Mount Meru situated at the center of the universe.

According to ancient Sri Lankan chronicle tradition, the Buddha's teaching first came to southeast Asia through Buddhist missions sent out by King Ashoka in the third century BCE. The earliest archaeological evidence of Theravada Buddhism in this region, however, comes from a series of Pali inscriptions from the Mon Dvaravati kingdom in Thailand and the lower Irrawaddy Valley of Burma (Myanmar) dating roughly from the fifth to the eighth centuries CE. The Mon people were early inhabitants of extensive regions of Thailand and Burma who came under the influence of Indian culture, including Theravada Buddhism. It appears from this evidence that the Theravada enjoyed the patronage of political and social élites in these regions, though not necessarily to the exclusion of other forms of Buddhism. The broad-based dominance of Theravada tradition in mainland southeast Asia comes much later as a result of an extensive Theravada reform movement that spread throughout the region from the eleventh to the fifteenth centuries. Beginning with the eleventh-century conversion of King Anawrahta in Pagan by a Mon Theravada monk, Theravada-centered forms of Buddhism gradually spread across the region and were embraced within

An enormous buddha *figure at Wat Tham Sua, created in the Ratanakosin style (late 18th century onward). The ornate Thai architectural detail in both foreground and baxkground is known as a* cho fa, *or "tassle of air," and is thought to be derived from a stylized form of Garuda, the bird figure from Hindu mythology who protects against malevolent forces.*

both the élite and popular levels of society. Relations between Anawrahta's kingdom, centered in Pagan, and the Sri Lankan king Vijayabahu I, included reciprocal exchange of Buddhist relics, texts, and monks. For example, following a period of south Indian invasions of Sri Lanka, the Sri Lanka Sangha declined so precipitously that it was necessary to reestablish the Theravada ordination lineage by bringing monks to Sri Lanka from Pagan. In return, Vijayabahu sent a copy of the Buddha's tooth relic to Pagan. The influence of Burmese monks who had studied in Sri Lanka eventually led the Sri Lankan Mahavihara Theravada lineage to gain ascendence in Burma.

The influence of the Theravada in Thailand, already present in the Mon Dvaravati kingdom, was gradually consolidated with the migration of the Tai people into the region from China and their absorption of Mon cultural influences, including Theravada Buddhism. With the establishment of the Sukhothai and Chiangmai kingdoms in the southern and central parts of Thailand during the thirteenth and fourteenth centuries, Theravada tradition provided the religious inspiration for the construction of extensive temple complexes. In the fourteenth century, the influence of Sri Lankan Theravada spread throughout much of Thailand resulting from the efforts of Thai monks ordained in a Sri Lankan lineage and under the patronage of Sukhothai kings. It was during these periods of Theravada reform in Burma and Thailand that Buddhism came to define popular religious practice.

Given the pervasive cultural connections between Sri Lanka and Burma and Thailand, the similarities among the regional traditions of Theravada Buddhism currently practiced throughout these countries should not be surprising. There are, however, some important differences as well. Although the Buddhist Sangha occupies a central place in Theravada practice in all of its regional forms, it has been institutionalized somewhat differently in Sri Lanka and southeast Asia. For example, it has long been a common practice among most Thai and Burmese males to spend a period of time as members of the Sangha. As a consequence, a far greater proportion of the Thai and Burmese populations have personal experience of Buddhist monastic life than is the case in Sri Lanka, where only those seriously intending to remain in the Sangha for life are encouraged to seek ordination.

Another important difference is the extent to which the Sangha has been subject to a centralized bureaucratic organization. Although there have been periods of greater and lesser centralization in the history of the Sri Lankan Sangha, it has for the most part remained free of strong centralized authority. In contrast, the Theravada Sangha in southeast Asia has tended toward greater centralization under royal authority. In particular, the nineteenth- and early twentieth-century reform of the Sangha in Thailand led to a state-supervised monastic bureaucracy with an elaborate system of uniform education for monks.

Theravada tradition in Burma (Myanmar) and Thailand, as in Sri Lanka, experienced revival movements in the nineteenth and twentieth centuries. In both Sri Lanka and Burma, which were under British colonial rule, the Buddhist revival was closely linked with the independence movement. In Thailand, which retained its independence, the reform movement was initiated under royal auspices, most notably during the reign of King Rama IV (reigned 1851–68), who had been a monk for twenty-seven years.

THE BUDDHA AND THE *NATS*
Begun by King Anawrahta and completed by his son King Kyanzittha in the eleventh century CE, the Shwezigon pagoda is the most important relic shrine in Pagan and it remains a popular pilgrimage site for Burmese Buddhists, especially during the annual festival held in November-December. The shrine has served as a prototype for later Burmese *stupa* construction, and tradition holds that it enshrines several important relics, including the Buddha's collarbone, frontal bone, and a replica of the tooth relic that King Anawrahta obtained from Sri Lanka (see main text). The shrine owes its popularity, in part, to images of the thirty-seven *nats*, superhuman spirits venerated for worldly benefits (see pp.122–3), that were originally displayed on the pagoda's terraces but that now reside in a nearby shrine.

A ruined temple at the Burmese city of Pagan, dating from 1000–1200CE. Construction was supported by Mon royalty, carried out by Mon artisans, and executed in a synthesis of Burmese and Mon styles based on Indian architectural models. Pagan had been founded in the mid-ninth century CE and served as Burma's capital for 250 years.

SOUTHEAST ASIA II

Buddhism was first established in the lower reaches of the Mekong Valley—a region now included within Cambodia and Vietnam—during the Funan empire, whose origins date back to the first century CE. Funan, as it is known in Chinese sources, was the first of the "Indianized" kingdoms in this region. Its surviving sculptural remains suggest that a range of Indic religious beliefs and practices were well established there, including forms of Hinduism and Buddhism. Beginning in the sixth century, the Funan court migrated northward along the Mekong River into what is now Laos, and this became the kingdom known in Chinese records as Chenla (Zenla), which flourished until the close of the eighth century.

The same region saw the rise of another empire that became one of the most extensive and powerful in southeast Asia—the Khmer kingdom (see box, below). Around the year 800CE, Jayavarman II established his capital in a range of hills known as Phnom Kulen, north of the Great Lake in modern-day Cambodia. Nearly a century later, Indravarman I laid the groundwork for his capital at nearby Angkor. As the extraordinary architectural remains at Angkor testify, Khmer rulers drew primarily upon Hinduism as a basis for political authority, though some Khmer rulers embraced Mahayana Buddhism as well. In the thirteenth and fourteenth centuries, Theravada became established as the dominant religious force in what is

JAYAVARMAN VII AND ANGKOR THOM

Angkor Thom, founded by King Jayavarman VII in the twelfth century, is one of the largest city complexes at Angkor, the great city that was at the heart of the Khmer empire for more than four hundred years (except for a twenty-year period in the tenth century) until the Thai conquered it in 1431.

During King Jayavarman VII's more than thirty-year reign, the Khmer kingdom reached its widest expanse, incorporating Burma (Myanmar), southern Laos, central Vietnam, and parts of the Malay peninsula. The king, a committed follower of Mahayana Buddhism, built more than a hundred hospitals dedicated to the healing *buddha* Bhaishajyaguru, the "Medicine Teacher." He also undertook an ambitious building campaign which drew heavily upon forced labor. The Angkor Thom complex, centered around the Bayon temple, exemplifies his merging of Hindu *devaraja* symbolism with Mahayana Buddhist *bodhisattva* ideals (see illustration, p.93). The

temple complex represents a microcosm of the universe with the celestial Mount Meru, abode of Indra, situated at its center. The walls of the temple are lined with bas-relief carvings that depict religious figures, scenes of daily life, and battles between the Khmers and Chams. An image of the Buddha sheltered by a serpent-deity (*naga*) originally stood at the center of the temple. Archaeologists discovered its broken remains at the bottom of the central well where it was probably thrown at the order of Jayavarman VIII who, repudiating the earlier ruler's Buddhist sympathies, destroyed many of the Buddha images.

One of the most striking features of the Angkor Thom complex, and in particular the Bayon temple at its center, are the numerous towers adorned with sublimely smiling faces. While various theories have been put forward explaining the significance of these figures and their relationship to the overall symbolism of the complex, their precise identity remains elusive.

now Cambodia and Laos, largely under the growing influence of the Thai kingdom of Sukhothai (see pp.126–9).

The general character of Theravada Buddhist belief and practice remains largely consistent throughout southeast Asia, and nineteenth-century reforms within the Thai Sangha (see pp.126–9) influenced the Sangha in Cambodia and Laos, as well. What sets Cambodia and Laos apart in the modern era, however, are the devastating effects of the war in Vietnam and the political destabilization that followed. With the Khmer Rouge's rise to power in Cambodia in 1975, the traditional and central role of Theravada Buddhism in Cambodian society was destroyed. Of the 65,000 monks in the Cambodian Sangha prior to 1970, it is estimated that only 3,000 survived the horrors of the Pol Pot regime, and roughly two-thirds of Buddhist temples were destroyed. Efforts to revive the Sangha met with resistance from the Vietnamese-controlled government until the late 1980s. Since then, however, there has been a major resurgence in Sangha membership, and over 95 per cent of the population remains Theravada Buddhist.

In Laos, a large percentage of the Sangha leadership fled the country in the wake of government-enforced Sangha "reforms" initiated by the Communist regime which took power in 1975. Despite constitutional guarantees of religious freedom, religious communities have been under strict government control. Recently, however, there has been more contact between the Laotian Sangha and Laotian Buddhist refugee communities abroad, and a move to declare Theravada Buddhism the state religion.

The Hindu temple complex of Angkor Wat was begun in the 12th century during the reign of King Suryavarman II. It was built as a microcosm of the universe with Mount Meru at its center and was dedicated to the Hindu god Vishnu. In 1431 the city of Angkor was abandoned after it was sacked by a Thai army. The adoption of Theravada Buddhism brought with it a more restrained artistic style and a shift from monumental stone construction to wooden buildings.

PART 2 • CHAPTER 8 *Mark L. Blum*

MAHAYANA BUDDHISM

THE TWO TRUTHS

The Mahayana doctrine of the Two Truths, postulated by Nagarjuna, refers to "conventional truth," in the sense of measurable facts, and "ultimate truth," in the sense of the higher, absolute nature of things beyond normal linguistic description. When a *bodhisattva* progresses to where he or she sees things in a non-dualistic way, realizing that good and bad are not wholly different, this reflects the higher nature of things. This is the point of the statement in the Diamond Sutra, that in order to practice the perfection of charity one should give without any sign of giving. That is, charity in which all accompanying identities are empty of any inherent reality produces merit that is "immeasurable," but charity that presumes the reality of giver, gift, beneficiary, or reward reflects a worldly understanding of things and produces minimal merit. The doctrine is also a critique of language as embodying a set of cultural presumptions that unavoidably conditions our understanding of the world. For this reason even the Dharma itself can only be considered as a collection of provisional statements and in the final analysis must be recognized only as "conventional truth."

THE GREAT VEHICLE

After the Buddha's death, Buddhism began to take shape as a multi-ethnic religion, spreading throughout south Asia (see pp.47–9). During the first century CE, a new movement arose that opposed many of the prevailing orthodoxies. It became known to its followers as the Mahayana, or "Great Vehicle" (a term first recorded in the sixth century CE), as opposed to other schools of Buddhism, which were disparagingly referred to by Mahayanists as the Hinayana, the "Lesser" or "Inferior Vehicle."

The Mahayana offered a new path to a newly defined goal and some strikingly new philosophical and psychological assertions. It presented a number of very different understandings of the Buddha's message, based on a body of scriptures which, it was claimed, had been uttered by the Buddha, but had lain undiscovered for centuries. The Mahayana became prominent in northern India, and as a consequence, when Buddhism spread from the subcontinent into central Asia and beyond, it was almost exclusively Mahayana missionaries that penetrated Tibet, Mongolia, China, and Japan.

When a disciple of the Buddha had attained enlightenment he received the title of *arhat* ("worthy one"). In the Mahayana *sutras*, monks who devote their lives solely to the pursuit of *nirvana* for themselves are referred to as *shravakas* ("listeners"), because they only pursue the letter, rather than the spirit, of what they have been taught. In the Mahayana, such individuals are criticized for self-centeredness in ignoring the sufferings of others in their withdrawal from the world, which in turn means that they are striving for what, at best, can only be an illusory liberation. In the Mahayana, everyone—monastic and lay person alike—is encouraged to strive for the ultimate goal of becoming not an *arhat*, but a *buddha*.

Thus *buddha*hood is expounded as the actual goal of Shakyamuni's message, and one pursuing it is called a *bodhisattva*, meaning "enlightenment being" or "future *buddha*." Prior to the emergence of the Mahayana, the word *bodhisattva* was used mainly to refer to the Buddha before his attainment of *buddha*hood. In the Mahayana view, the path to *nirvana* was impossible without the inclusion of the perfection of others as well, an ideal expressed in the twin virtues of wisdom and compassion, which *bodhisattva*s need in equal measure to attain their goal. Liberation in the Mahayana is thus *buddha*hood, and the Mahayana is also called Buddhayana or Bodhisattvayana (words which may be rendered as "*buddha* path" and "*bodhisattva* path"). It is commonly believed that *bodhisattva*s, embodiments of compassion, vow to postpone their own final emancipation until all other sentient beings have been emancipated.

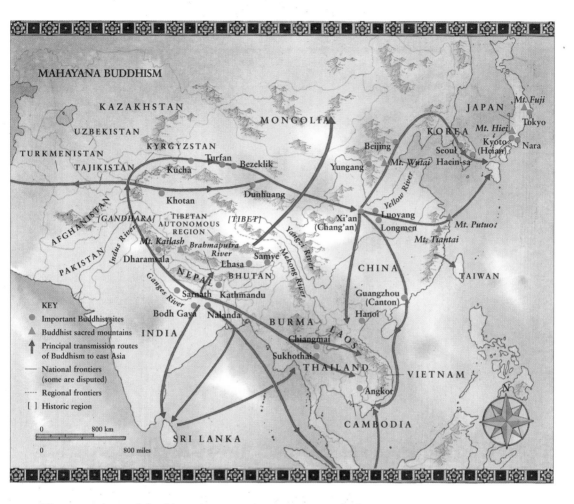

MAHAYANA BUDDHISM

KEY
● Important Buddhist sites
▲ Buddhist sacred mountains
↑ Principal transmission routes of Buddhism to east Asia
— National frontiers (some are disputed)
---- Regional frontiers
[ ] Historic region

0   800 km
0   800 miles

The new path was defined in various ways, but most commonly the adept was encouraged to cultivate the six "perfections" (*paramitas*): generosity, morality, patience, vigor, meditation, and wisdom. At times, this list was expanded to ten, each perfection described as commensurate with one of ten "stages" of spiritual attainment (*bhumi*), such as joy, purity, and so on (see sidebar, p.136).

The Mahayana produced a number of distinctive philosophical doctrines, notably the concept of Emptiness (see pp.140–41). Another striking feature was the new conception of the Buddha as having three forms or "bodies" (*kayas*) (see pp.91–2).

In the Mahayana, faith in the power, omniscience, and eternal spiritual assistance of the Buddha assumed a new sense of importance and Buddhism now took on a decidedly more devotional form. Such Mahayana scriptures as the Lotus Sutra, the Pure Land Sutras, the Garland Sutra, and so on, all describe a *buddha* of cosmic stature. There remained, however, several cosmic *buddhas*: Shakyamuni, Amitabha (see pp.144–7),

The paths of transmission for Mahayana Buddhism. The route into east Asia through central Asia was a particularly important development for the new teachings, making Mahayana the dominant form of Buddhism in a number of countries, including Tibet, Mongolia, China, and Japan.

A woman worshipping at a statue of the Buddha in Hoa Nghiem cave. The Marble Mountains, near Danang, Vietnam, contain a number of such caves which have been used as Buddhist sanctuaries for centuries— since the Chinese form of Buddhism was adopted in Vietnam from the sixth century onward (see box, opposite).

PERIOD OF THE FINAL LAW

History is not a drama in Buddhism in the sense that it has a definite beginning, a purposeful development, and a climactic dénouement. Even in Buddhist cosmology, beginnings and endings are relative as opposed to absolute. It is true, however, that there was a strong Mahayana belief in east Asia that the world was inevitably headed toward a period of dark decline called the Period of the Final Law (known as *mofa* in Chinese and *mappo* in Japanese) because too much time had elapsed since the death of the Buddha and fewer and fewer people understood his teachings. Depending on the *sutra* propounding such views, calculations were made as to when the final period was to begin, usually either in the sixth or eleventh century. This final period could last up to ten thousand years and all sorts of dire consequences were described, such as increases in corruption, conflict, and even a shortening of human life. But the end of this age was unambiguously marked by the advent of a new *buddha*, Maitreya, who will usher in a new era of peace and enlightenment.

Vairochana, Vajradhara, Akshobhya, Bhaishajyaguru, and more, and their accomplishments were beyond imagination. This compared with the early tradition in which the Buddha was a compassionate teacher revered for having destroyed all the anxieties and sufferings within himself, thereby reaching the end of his participation in the cycle of rebirth. But herein lies the basic paradox of Mahayana thought: on the one hand, the concept of *buddha* has been brought closer to the devotee, with the promise that everyone can attain this goal; on the other hand, *buddha*s are described in such expansively cosmic terms—beyond the experience and imagination of most people—that the concept of *buddha* is almost impossible to grasp, thus magnifying the divide between *buddha* and humankind.

The worlds described in the Mahayana *sutra*s are full of wonders that bear little resemblance to this world. Much of this literature presents an idealized cosmos of "*buddha*" realms" or "pure lands" into which the faithful may be born if they pursue certain devotional practices; in these paradisial realms, conditions are perfect, a *buddha* is present to guide the devotee, and progress to complete enlightenment is thereby swift (see pp.144–7).

The Buddha's omniscience permits him not only to know what others are thinking, and why they act in the way they do, but also to see their past lives and their future lives. This enables him to fashion a message or activity tailored to an individual's spiritual condition (see also pp.142–3). But no *buddha* is a creator of the universe or of life within it. The Great Vehicle may have salvific characteristics, but a *buddha* is not accompanied by any sense of the testing, punitive, and forgiving aspects of god, as depicted in the Christian Bible. While there are metaphorical references to the Buddha as "father," this alludes to his commitment to save all sentient life, rather than a sense of responsibility for "his creation." The Buddha bestows the Dharma upon humanity, but it is centered on psychological health and spiritual transformation rather than moral standards. *Buddha*s are also said to be encounterable through practices such as meditative exercise. In the Pure Land tradition, the *buddha* Amitabha invites everyone to seek rebirth in his world so they may practice assiduously under his supervision and thereby reach *buddha*hood themselves without fail. While Amitabha Buddha's land is a paradise, it is not heaven but, like all *buddha*-lands, a unique environment especially conducive to religious realization because it is purified by a *buddha*'s presence. And there are many such lands, indeed all *buddha*s inhabit them (see pp.144–7).

THE GROWTH OF EAST ASIAN BUDDHISM

The spread of Buddhism to east Asia began with the first missionaries to China, who arrived in the first century CE. China had a sophisticated culture with centuries-old traditions of government bureaucracy, literature, philosophy, and so on, and almost immediately translation teams were created to render the *sutra*s into Chinese—a process that continued for eight centuries. By the seventh century, Chinese Buddhism was so fully realized, with its own philosophical schools, traditions of art and architecture, and so on, that it became the form adopted by Vietnam, Korea, and Japan as well.

From at least the third century, the port of Hanoi had served as a stopover point for boats traveling between India and China. In the sixth century, northern Vietnam adopted Chinese Buddhism and this form spread to the south when the country was unified in the fifteenth century.

Although not yet unified politically, all three rival kingdoms in Korea welcomed the arrival of Chinese Buddhism in the second half of the fourth century. From Korea, Buddhism spread to Japan in the sixth century, but in form and language it was thoroughly Chinese.

The pagoda of the Horyuji temple at Nara, Japan, founded by Prince Shotoku shortly after the Japanese imperial family had accepted Buddhism as a state religion in 592CE.

THE *BODHISATTVA* PATH

The concept of *bodhisattva* ("enlightenment being") is at the heart of how the Mahayana defines itself. The word is not uncommon in early Buddhism, where it indicates someone with a relationship to the enlightenment of a *buddha*, either as one destined for enlightenment, or one seeking enlightenment. In the early Pali literature, the only *bodhisattva*s are those who became *buddha*s, namely Shakyamuni in our time. For example, in the Theravada tradition, which counts as many as twenty-four or twenty-seven previous *buddha*s, Siddhartha Gautama is said to be the fourth *buddha* of this epoch, and Maitreya will be the fifth (see p.91). Every epoch, or *kalpa*, lasts for millions of years, and the appearance of a *bodhisattva* or *buddha* is an exceedingly rare occurrence. All *buddha*s have similar careers as *bodhisattva*s who make formal vows to attain *buddha*hood under the *buddha* of their epoch and receive prophecies from that *buddha* as to when and where their goal will be accomplished. Over the course of many lifetimes they then strive to perfect themselves until they succeed. The life of the Buddha is taken as the model of the *bodhisattva*'s career, and there are many *jataka* ("birth") tales of his exemplary behavior in former lifetimes.

With the emergence of the movement within Buddhism that came to be called Mahayana (see pp.132–5), the concept of *bodhisattva* took on a new meaning. It is apparent from the early *sutra*s that the students of the Buddha who became fully enlightened were called *arhat*s ("worthy ones") rather than *buddha*s, but the distinction between the two was not an issue, for they realize the same Dharma. At a council believed to have been held one hundred years after the Buddha's death (see p.47), a disagreement is thought to have occurred over whether the *arhat* ideal was sufficient. From what was to become the Mahayana perspective, the *arhat* path involved different practices and beliefs from the *bodhisattva* path. Becoming an *arhat* was designated as the mundane goal of the mere "listeners" (*shravaka*s) who could do no more than follow what they heard the Buddha preach. This is criticized by Mahayana thinkers as a self-centered path in which individuals are so committed to their own liberation that they lose touch with the world around them and the sufferings of others. By contrast the path of the *bodhisattva* is upheld as ethically and spiritually superior because of its supreme emphasis on the cultivation of compassion toward others who need help. Only the *bodhisattva* path can lead to the transcendental, cosmic status of a *buddha*. Mahayana theorists claimed that the way of the *bodhisattva* was the only complete path that the Buddha had actually taught, labeling the *arhat* path as only a temporary construct meant to prepare his disciples for the final teaching.

In Mahayana culture, all Buddhists who are committed to attaining complete emancipation for themselves and others are deserving of the label *bodhisattva*. Because the concept of personal enlightenment attained without the enlightenment of others would appear, from the Mahayana perspective, not to be a true enlightenment, the *bodhisattva* path is characterized by a rig-

TEN PERFECTIONS

Generosity
Morality
Patience
Vigor
Meditation
Wisdom
Skill in Means
Conviction
Strength
Knowledge

TEN STAGES OF ATTAINMENT

Joy
Purity
Brightness
Radiance
Difficult to Conquer
Facing Nirvana
Far-going
Immovable
Spiritual Intelligence
Dharma Cloud

TARA

One extremely important *bodhisattva* for Tibetans is Tara, who is the feminine aspect of compassion or loving-kindness (*maitri*). The cult of Tara was introduced into Tibet by the Indian master Atisha in the eleventh century CE and has probably gained importance in Tibetan Buddhism due to his own fervor for this deity. Tibetan legends recount how Tara was born from a teardrop of compassion that Avalokiteshvara shed when confronted by the enormity of the task of helping suffering beings. Tara, who has a variety of forms, is said to be the mother of all *buddhas* and her eyes (in the forehead, palms and soles) allow her to see all human pain.

A Tibetan thangka *showing the* bodhisattva Avalokiteshvara (bottom right); Green Tara (center), who represents divine energy; and White Tara (bottom left), who embodies transcendent wisdom. Also depicted is the Gelugpa school's founder Tsongkhapa (top, center), who is flanked by two lamas.

orous standard of compassion, called *karuna*, in which the devotee makes the "*bodhisattva* vow" and promises, according to some Mahayana texts, that his or her final liberation will be postponed until all others can achieve the same. This explains why there are no *buddhas* in our midst, but instead there may be many *bodhisattvas* who are sensitive to an individual's cry for help.

Since a great many beings are far from liberation, there must also be a number of *bodhisattvas* who, like *buddhas*, are active in this world trying to help. *Bodhisattvas* are directed to cultivate a list of six virtues, or "perfections" (*paramitas*), later expanded to ten. The *bodhisattva* path also entails ten stages of spiritual attainment or *bhumi*, which loosely correspond to these virtues (see box, opposite). After progressing to the seventh stage, the *bodhisattva* is capable of becoming a *buddha* if he or she so chooses and has similar supernatural abilities to a *buddha* that allow an appearance anywhere at will. This is the doctrinal basis of faith in the power of what are often called celestial *bodhisattvas*, such as Avalokiteshvara, Manjushri, Kshitigarbha, and Maitreya (see p.91), who have the ability to manifest themselves simultaneously in more than one place.

ART AND ARCHITECTURE *Michael Willis*

THE MAHAYANA PANTHEON

Mahayana Buddhism places special emphasis on *bodhisattva*s or "future *buddha*s" (see pp.132–7). Foremost among the *bodhisattva*s is Avalokiteshvara, whose name means literally the "Lord who looks down in compassion." The earliest sculptures of Avalokiteshvara from India, China, Korea, and Japan portray the *bodhisattva* with his eyes looking serenely downward. Sculptures in India dating to ca. 700CE show him surrounded by panels depicting the Eight Great Perils. Four of these stem from human agency—shipwrecks, wrongful imprisonment, thieves, and conflagrations—and four

HAND GESTURES: *MUDRAS*

Images of the *buddha*s, *bodhisattva*s, and attendant deities are always shown holding symbolic attributes or with their hands held in special positions (*mudra*s). The attributes and positions are numerous and complex, but certain basic gestures are found in all parts of the Buddhist world. Particularly common is the Buddha touching the earth just prior to his enlightenment (see illustration, p.79). When he is shown teaching, both hands are usually raised in front of his chest. Another common gesture, especially in early sculpture, is the right hand raised in salutation, denoting reassurance or freedom from fear (see illustration, p.147).

A figure in a vitarkha mudra *pose—that of "exposition", with the thumb and forefinger forming a circle to symbolize the "wheel of law"—from a fresco in the ca. 6th-century* CE *Buddhist cave monasteries at Bamiyan, western central Asia.*

from dangerous forces in the natural world—lions, poisonous snakes, wild elephants, and disease. Throughout Asia, Avalokiteshvara is invoked by the faithful to protect them from these very real and ever-present threats.

In China, Avalokiteshvara's serenity was accentuated and, because compassion was understood as a feminine quality, the *bodhisattva* was transformed into Guanyin, the goddess of mercy (called Kannon in Japan). In Tibet, Avalokiteshvara (Chenrezi) remained male, but the female aspect of his personality was manifested in the Taras (see p.137), goddesses who were born, according to traditional accounts, from lotuses which grew in the pools formed from Avalokiteshvara's tears of compassion.

Another popular *bodhisattva* is Maitreya, who, many ages in the future, will incarnate himself into the world, meditate at Bodh Gaya, and become a *buddha* to teach the Dharma anew for the good of living beings (see p.91). This great line of *bodhisattva*s and *buddha*s embodies a key Mahayana ideal, namely that while the "*buddha*-nature" or "*buddha*-essence" seems to come and go in the mundane world it is an unbreakable reality that is always present in the heavenly realms, where the *buddha*s, in their celestial bodies (*sambhogakaya*), reside forever. The *buddha*s and *bodhisattva*s are also associated with particular colors and special attributes (see p.78) which allow them to be identified when they are shown in painting. Maitreya, for example, is identifiable from the water-pot and flower which almost always flank his image.

After Avalokiteshvara, who is universally worshipped and has even found his way into Theravada countries, the next most popular *bodhisattva* is Manjushri ("Pleasing Splendor"), considered to be the *bodhisattva* of wisdom. Manjushri is normally shown holding a book and wielding a sword—the book is emblematic of knowledge and the sword represents the power of knowledge to sever the fetters of ignorance. As a result, Manjushri is venerated by scholars in order to improve memory and the ability to master Buddhist texts.

Buddhist manuscripts in the monasteries of Tibet were enclosed between wooden book covers, often painted on either or both sides. This 13th-century example is decorated inside with a triple panel showing Prajnaparamita, goddess of Wisdom, at the center, holding a book and making the mudra of teaching, flanked by attendant boddhisattvas. The nine squares of the adjacent panels each contain either a lama or a bodhisattva.

"EMPTINESS"

ISSUES OF RIGHT AND WRONG
As one might expect, the Emptiness
doctrine resulted in a profound change
in Buddhist values. No longer could
one blithely accept the prevailing
interpretation of the Eightfold Path
(see pp.70–71), that right views or
right speech meant adhering to certain
well-defined standards of what
constituted a right opinion and a
wrong opinion. Insofar as right and
wrong opinions are both empty of any
inherent nature or knowable essence,
they are empty of any inherent reality.
From the perspective of Emptiness, the
only "right view" is no view at all. Yet
to cling to Emptiness as the ideal
doctrine or "answer" is no less a
mistake, for this assumes that
Emptiness itself represents the "right
view" that transcends all others.
Emptiness is not a substance in the
philosophical sense, it is not anything.
In other words, Emptiness is also
empty. Belief in a "non-Emptiness"
also misses the point. But from a
Mahayana perspective this "no-thing"
is the defining element of the world
and everything within it.

No idea better defines the uniqueness of Mahayana thought than that of
shunyata or "emptiness," a notion at once alarming, confusing, and mysteri-
ous. The concept can be found in nascent form in early Buddhism with the
doctrine of non-self, or *anatman*, which holds that each individual is empty
of any permanent, fixed identity. In the Mahayana, the adjective *shunya* or
"empty," is expanded and considered as a religious quality in itself, expressed
by adding the abstract suffix *ta*, resulting in the word *shunyata*, which translates as "emptiness" or "void." The profound conclusion was reached that
all phenomena, even the very concept of such things as "phenomena," are
characterized by this quality of "lacking"—"being empty of" any unambigu-
ous, permanent, identifying mark. And it is this "lack" that is the actual key
to understanding the religious truth about phenomena. Thus did Emptiness
come into being, a new expression of the ultimate truth of existence.

The concept of Emptiness was first developed in the Prajnaparamita
("Perfection of Wisdom" *sutra*s) (see pp.196–7*),* where it was argued that
the truth of the world is beyond dualistic distinctions. These texts refuted
the position taken in the canonical Abhidharma (see pp.192–3), which
explained the lack of an unchanging self in the individual by positing a temporary conglomeration of individual components that are themselves substantial and identifiable. The conceptual mistake of the Abhidharmists was
to replace the essence, or self, of a person with a multitude of minute
essences, which still implied that the world as perceived should be accepted
as real. To Mahayana thinkers, these individual components, called *dharma*s
(not to be confused with the Dharma, the body of the Buddha's teachings),
are as devoid of any unchanging essence as the individual.

It is further argued that the analytical thinking in which we habitually
engage will produce ideas, interpretations, opinions, and so on, that we will
cling to because of their plausibility. From the point of view of Emptiness,
these "realities" are not entirely false, but they are not entirely true either. In
the terminology of Nagarjuna, they are "conventionally true," and clinging
to conventional views of individual identity only prevents one from grasping what is "ultimately true" (see sidebar, p.132). This notion of Emptiness
thus reflects a renewed understanding of the basic Buddhist doctrine of
Dependent Origination, which concludes that all known realities are constructed realities whose identities are merely intellectual conveniences used
to order the world so that it can be understood.

When the truth of the empty nature of all identities or categories of
identity is realized, then ordinary distinctions such as pure/impure, good/ bad,
attractive/unattractive, even me/you become meaningless (see sidebar, left).
The Emptiness doctrine liberates us from the distorting impact of the preju-
dices which accompany opinions. Liberation is found at the point at which
identities disappear, where there are no interpretations or judgments, where
the self and the world are seen for what they are, not for how they relate to
our preconceived categories of how we think things are or should be.

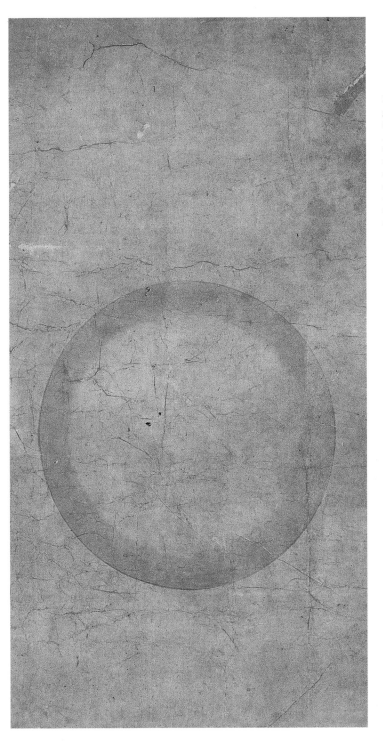

Both Ox and Self Forgotten, *one of the ten paintings from the Zen tradition's Ox-herding sequence, a series of works by the 15th-century Japanese monk Shubun which represents the individual's path from ignorance—the illusion of self—to enlightenment. The circle may be interpreted as representing two seeming opposites: ignorance and full realization or non-attachment, according perfectly with the Mahayana notion of ultimate emptiness.*

"SKILL IN MEANS"

One of the distinguishing characteristics of Buddhism is the principle of *upaya*, or the "skill in means" to teach or lead others to truth. This idea was most clearly developed in the Lotus Sutra, a Mahayana scripture (see pp.198–9), but Buddhism in all its forms assumes that an enlightened teacher will use whatever means are available to communicate truths that are often counter-intuitive. In part this reflects the Buddhist view of language as an imperfect medium of communication; it also indicates a fundamentally flexible approach to doctrine or dogma. In Buddhism, there is no shame in admitting that a lecture which is an inspiration to one person will fall on deaf ears for someone else. There are examples in the early literature of individuals who heard the Buddha preach and simply left when the lecture ended, unmoved; there are even stories of people who sought him out for religious discussion but departed unconvinced by his answers. The Buddha explained that when a crowd gathered to hear him speak, those present all heard different sermons because each listener comprehended only what

A Japanese monk engaged in a tantric ritual in which the flames of the fire, which symbolize wisdom, consume the wooden sticks, which represent the mental afflictions of attachment and ignorance believed to be obstructing an individual's path to truth.

KISA GOTAMI AND THE MUSTARD SEED

The remarkable ability of the Buddha to convey his message to individuals (see main text) is illustrated by the story of a young woman called Kisa Gotami, who, after an arranged marriage, found that her in-laws regarded her as a less than ideal bride. She was desperate to win their approval by producing a male heir, but she and her husband had difficulty conceiving.

As preparations began to find a more "suitable" wife, she became pregnant and bore a son. For a time, her troubles seemed to be over, but then the infant became ill and died. Completely beside herself, she ran into town to seek someone who could bring her baby back to life. Taking pity on her, the townspeople suggested the Buddha, who they described as a "miracle worker" living in a forest outside of town. She found him and begged him to restore her son's life. The Buddha promised to do so if she could bring him one mustard seed from a home where no one had ever died.

Although mustard seeds were common enough, Kisa Gotami found that every household had experienced a death in the family. Slowly, the truth dawned upon her that what had seemed to be a simple request was actually impossible. Returning to the Buddha, she confessed her error and deep appreciation for the "truth of impermanence." Without any explicit statement from the master, she now realized the profound implications of the First Noble Truth of *duhkha*, and joined the community of nuns.

he or she was able to comprehend at that moment. In Mahayana thought, one of the supernatural abilities ascribed to a *buddha* is the ability to preach a different message to everyone in the room at the same time, tailoring each message to fit their individual approaches to life. But even without such displays of the paranormal, the Buddha was always seen as possessing an uncanny ability to discern the best way to instruct an individual, based on an assessment of their mental situation. At times this consisted of communicating a religious truth without any explanation at all (see box, above).

In east Asia, the doctrine of Skill in Means led to a host of new interpretations of the scriptural material. The fountainhead of this movement was the Lotus Sutra, which enjoyed much greater influence there than in the rest of the Buddhist world. This *sutra* categorizes the Dharma into teachings of expediency and teachings of truth. The common division of the community into several "paths" or approaches to faith and practice is explained as a formula constructed merely for convenience. The *sutra* explains that the Buddha at times uses skillful means to help his followers progress step by step, but the truth is that there is only a "single path," the *buddha* path, to *buddha*hood for everyone.

Beginning in late sixth-century China, this model of expedient versus actual was used throughout east Asia to make sense of the many disparate teachings found in the hundreds of scriptures within the region's canons. Scriptures and doctrines were classified on the presumption that the Buddha used his "skill in means" to guide his followers from concrete to abstract truths, from moral to metaphysical understandings. Perhaps the most revolutionary use of this doctrine came with the Pure Land school in China, when Daochuo labeled all teachings and practices devoted to reaching Amitabha's Pure Land as the Buddha's true intent, and all other religious activities as expedients that were to be abandoned (see pp.144–7).

PURE LANDS

By convention, the general term "pure land" denotes the so-called "purified field" that surrounds all *buddha*s, who by virtue of their great compassion and wisdom naturally create a space without defilements. The phrase "pure land" derives from an abbreviation of a line from a Chinese *sutra* translation, wherein Amitabha Buddha ("Infinite Light"; known in China as Amituo Fo and Japan as Amida Butsu) is described as vowing to purify his realm for others who desire to venture there. Although there is no such term in Sanskrit, there were doctrines in India which stated that *bodhisattva*s would transform this world and that such idealized *buddha*-fields (*buddhakshetra*) existed in each of the four directions as goals for the next life.

In his sixth-century CE commentary on the Lotus Sutra, Zhiyi, a prominent member of China's Tiantai school (see also p.200–201), wrote of an "absolute" purification of this world through the salvific light of the Dharmakaya (the Buddha's "Dharma Body,"—see sidebar, p.100). At that time, there were many popular practices devoted to the *buddha* in the east, Akshobhya ("Imperturbable", known in China as Achu), and the *buddha* in the west, Amitabha. Rituals developed that were directed toward rebirth in the purified realms of the transcendental *bodhisattva*s Maitreya (Mile Fo) in the Tushita heaven and Avalokiteshvara (Guanyin), either in his own land or in residence with Maitreya or Amitabha. Maitreya, as the prophesied future *buddha*, and his Pure Land proved especially attractive to a wide range of

RECITING A SACRED NAME

Daochuo's student, Shandao (613–681CE), further clarified two essential points made by his master: the acceptance of one's own spiritual limitations and the role of Amitabha as an agent of salvation. Shandao's unique vision concluded that among the many diverse and difficult practices directed toward the goal of rebirth in the Pure Land, the *buddha* Amitabha had already suggested one practice as superior to all others—the simple recitation of his sacred name in the formula *"Nianfo Amituo Fo"* ("Take refuge in Amitabha Buddha").

Called *nianfo* in Chinese (and *nembutsu* in Japanese, from *"Namu Amida Butsu"*), it was a practice that anyone could perform, requiring only sincerity and a minimal amount of concentration to be effective. Shandao asserted that Amitabha was unique in that he sought to help everyone, not only the most adept,

thereby reversing traditional Buddhist notions which equated difficult practice with higher attainment. The ritual recitation of Amitabha's name, along with the ritual chanting of Pure Land *sutras* (see also pp.84–5), gave rise to a range of elaborate and moving musical ceremonies still practiced today.

In twelfth-century Japan, Honen developed several important effects of Shandao's doctrine, among them the recognition of the equal status of women and lay people, including those of the lowest social classes. Honen's writings (see box, p.147) were taken by some to mean that there was no point in monasticism, that the established monastic orders had been undermined, while Amida Butsu had been raised to the role of savior through whom devotees could attempt to reach the Pure Land. However, Honen continued his monastic status, as did his lineage for a further 700 years.

devotees, ranging from monks to the empress Wu Zetian (reigned 690–705CE), who declared herself to be his incarnation (see also p.91).

Eventually, a belief in the so-called Pure Land, also called Sukhavati ("Abode of Bliss"), created by Amitabha Buddha or Amitayus came to overshadow all others, so that by the medieval period—that is, the seventh century in China and the thirteenth century in Japan—terms like Pure Land Teaching and Pure Land School clearly designate this tradition exclusively. It is likely that the names Amitabha and Amitayus originally denoted two different figures (referring to "light" and "life" respectively), but when the common element *amita* ("infinite" in Sanskrit) was transliterated into Chinese as Amituo, this name came to represent a single conflated *buddha*. Under one of these two names this *buddha* occurs in literally hundreds of Mahayana *sutra*s and other texts. In contrast to the defiled human world, the Pure Land is described as a kind of paradise devoid of diversions, such as women and conflict, and superior to any heaven because Amituo resides there, prepared to preach the Dharma to all those who ask for assistance. There is strong evidence that devotees throughout the Indian Buddhist world strove to attain rebirth in Sukhavati after death, and this conception also took root in the Chinese imagination. The fundamentals of the philosophical system that underpins Pure Land teachings (see also pp.200–203) were laid down in China during the sixth and seventh centuries CE by a series of monks now considered to be the Chinese patriarchs of the Pure Land tradition: Tanluan, Daochuo, Shandao (see box, opposite), Jiazai, and Huaikan.

Tanluan (474–542CE), a student of Nagarjuna's Madhyamika tradition (see p.197) and devotee of the Nirvana Sutra (see pp.206–7), had become despondent after learning of the Buddhist doctrine of historical decline, which described an age of increasing social chaos in which the quality of Dharma teaching would decrease along with the capacity of individuals to understand it and hence to attain enlightenment (see sidebar, p.134). Living at a time of warfare and political disunion in China, Tanluan believed that this degenerate age had arrived. However, he found hope in a *sutra*, the Sukhavativyuha Sutra, on Amitabha Buddha and his Pure Land (see pp.202–3), which described how individuals who aspired to Amitabha's presence could actually attain it. Tanluan made the important contribution of aligning Pure Land ideas with mainstream Mahayana notions of the *bodhisattva* path, arguing that those who were reborn in the Pure Land to attain enlightenment would subsequently return from there in order to assist others, in fulfillment of the *bodhisattva* vow (see p.137).

Daochuo (562–645CE) also began as a devotee of the Nirvana Sutra before his "conversion" to the Pure Land Teaching. In his treatise Anleji ("Collection [of Passages] on [the Land of] Peace and Joy"), Daochuo laid out for the first time a systematic framework of doctrines and practices for the Pure Land. He adroitly explained how the path to the Pure Land was parallel to, and of equal value to, the traditional *bodhisattva* path

Seated gilt-bronze Chinese figure of Amitabha Buddha (Amituo Fo), eyes downcast in contemplation, and with one leg crossed underneath the flowing robes. Early Tang dynasty, ca. 7th–8th century.

(see pp.136–7), but offered a much higher chance of success in this degenerate age because Amitabha Buddha actively aided the devotee. Daochuo asserted that the traditional *bodhisattva* path, which he labeled the path to personal sainthood, though deserving of esteem, was essentially hopeless for most devotees because it was too rigorous.

Not long after the creation of the ideas behind Chinese Pure Land Teaching, Buddhism began to make a serious impact in Japan. During the Nara period (710–794CE), the first Japanese Buddhist essays appeared, including a treatise on Pure Land Buddhism. Although there is evidence in this early period of a belief in the Pure Land of Maitreya, the term Pure Land Buddhism in a Japanese context always refers to the belief system surrounding Amida Butsu. In the Heian era (805–1185), a slow growth in the faith in Amida is evident both among the aristocracy in Kyoto (Heian), and among the populace as a whole, largely owing to itinerant holy men who disseminated the faith in the countryside. In 985CE the scholar Genshin (942–1017) had a great impact with Ojoyoshu ("Birth in the Land of Purity"), a work that illustrated most graphically the glories of Amida's Pure Land. Genshin was a member of the Tendai, the Japanese sect which followed Tiantai concepts introduced from China by Saicho in 805. In the ninth century, under Ennin's leadership, forms of *samadhi* practice from China were introduced, which included chanting the name of Amida as an aid to meditation.

Just as had happened in China, prior to the onset of the Kamakura period (1185–1333) Japan experienced a period of domestic chaos and the Buddhist doctrine of historical decline gained credibility. It led many Buddhists to view the attainment of individual liberation by conventional means

An important part in the development of Buddhism as a popular religion in Japan was played by the introduction of the Tendai sect's slightly esoteric rituals, particularly the chant in praise of Amida Butsu and the promotion of the importance of the Lotus Sutra. A monk at Chion-in temple in Kyoto cleaning the altar decorations.

THE JODO SCHOOL

The Japanese monk Honen (see main text) was probably the first person in Buddhist history to state overtly that since the time of Shakyamuni there have been no *buddhas* and that therefore people should abandon any hope of becoming one, except in the Pure Land (Japanese, Jodo). He set down his doctrine in a treatise called the Senchakushu ("Passages on the Selection of the *Nembutsu* in the Original Vow"), a work kept secret during his lifetime for fear of provoking a reaction from the monastic and intellectual forces of established Buddhism. The work was printed and publicly distributed after his death but was repeatedly suppressed in an attempt to halt the rapid expansion of Pure Land beliefs.

By the Tokugawa period (1605–1868), however, Honen's Jodo school had become the personal faith of Japan's ruling shogunate.

Honen offered a new Buddhist paradigm in which there were no more illusions about personal sainthood in this world. In effect, anyone who sought enlightenment was lowered to the status of an ordinary person, while Amida was raised to the role of transcendent, universal savior through whose assistance devotees could reach the Pure Land, the only place where enlightenment could be achieved.

A late 12th-century cypress wood statue of Amida Butsu, making the abhaya mudra *gesture of reassurance.*

as hopeless. The most persuasive response to this situation came from the most pivotal figure in Japanese Pure Land Buddhism, the Tendai monk Honen (1133–1212), who is considered the founder of Japan's first Jodo (Pure Land) school or sect. Honen's revelation came while reading the work of the Chinese master Shandao (see box, p.144), whose writings had previously received little attention in Japan. Honen was particularly struck by Shandao's assertion that the oral recitation of Amitabha's name was the one true practice precisely because it was easy to do and therefore had the most universal application. Honen developed the doctrine further and his public lectures in Kyoto drew huge numbers of students from all levels of society.

Honen's student Shinran (1173–1263) took things a stage further by declaring himself a failure at monasticism, publicly taking a wife, and giving up all hope of attaining the Pure Land by his own efforts. Shinran developed a radical doctrine that rejected all forms of practice and piety as *jiriki*, or salvation by one's own power, which he claimed indicated a lack of faith in the Buddha's message. In its stead he advocated *tariki* ("other-power"), which credited Amida Butsu as the only true cause of anyone reaching the Pure Land, which he saw as tantamount to realizing *nirvana*. Shinran saw the practice of repeating the *nembutsu* as unnecessary, since for him it was not a means to any end but simply an expression of gratitude to the Buddha. Shinran's followers eventually formed the independent Jodoshin ("True Pure Land") school. The first Buddhist order to permit its clergy to marry, Jodoshin remains the largest religious organization in Japan today.

ART AND ARCHITECTURE *Michael Willis*

DEPICTING THE PURE LAND

One of the most representative features of the Pure Land movement is a practice known as "mindful recollection of the Buddha". At its most basic level, this involves the visualization of the special marks of his glorified body and the repetition of his name. Visualization could be performed in private meditation or during collective worship; recollection and repetition of the name could be done silently or aloud. These practices are found in many strands of the Mahayana tradition. What distinguishes Pure Land devotees is their devotion to the *buddha* Amitabha/Amitayus, in particular, their single interest in gaining rebirth in Sukhavati, his "Abode of Bliss," or Pure Land, as described in the Sukhavativyuha Sutra ("Describing the [World of] Bliss Sutra") texts (see pp.202–3).

This early 10th-century silk scroll from Dunhuang portrays Avalokiteshvara carrying a lotus and a censer, leading a soul, represented by the well-dressed woman, to the halls of paradise (at the top of the painting). The blossoms symbolize blessings. People on their deathbed might hang a scroll painting of Avalokiteshvara or Amitabha before them so as to ease their passage to paradise and salvation.

The employment of specific spiritual techniques to achieve that end are especially clear in the Guan Wuliangshou Fo Jing ("Visualizing the Buddha of Limitless Life Sutra" or "Contemplation Sutra"). This text tells us that the Buddha gave Queen Vaidehi, mother of Ajatashatru, a vision of all the heavenly worlds, which were made visible in a golden ray that shone from the Buddha's forehead. The queen acknowledged that all the celestial worlds were pure and brilliant but that she wished to be reborn in the world of Amitabha. To help her and subsequent devotees achieve this end, the Buddha instructed Vaidehi (and Ananda, his favorite pupil) in a series of increasingly complex visualizations. Each was to be mastered before the next was undertaken. The astonishing richness of these meditative techniques, and their potential for use in the arts, is shown by the eighth visualization, which focuses on Amitayus, the *buddha* of Limitless Life, and includes some powerful descriptions of the "Most Happy World":

"You should think of the *buddha* of Limitless Life [Amitayus]. Why? Because the Body of the *buddha* is the Body of the Universe and it is within the mind of all beings. Therefore when you think of that *buddha* your mind becomes the One who has the thirty-two Magnificent Figures and the eighty Virtues. It is the mind that is to become a *buddha* and it is the mind that is the *buddha*. The Ocean of Omniscient Wisdom of all *buddha*s

grows up from the mind. . .When one has achieved this visualization, one can hear the murmuring sound of the streams and see the rays, jewel-trees, and sheldrakes and mandarin ducks, whose voices praise the Wonderful Law." As the visualizations progress, they become ever more elaborate. Toward the end of the series, the devotee is instructed to see himself or herself sitting in a lotus flower and to imagine the lotus opening before the *buddha* and *bodhisattva*s that have been previously visualized. When this has been achieved, one is guaranteed rebirth in the Pure Land, cutting short hundreds of incarnations in more mundane bodies.

Although the visualizations in the Guan Wuliangshou Fo Jing read almost like descriptions of some of the scenes portrayed in Buddhist paintings, particularly those in some of the more elaborate works of art produced in Tibet (see illustration above), direct parallels between the arts and textual sources are rare. In part this is due to the fragmentary nature of the evidence, much of the ancient painting and sculpture in India and China having been lost and the texts themselves having been subject to a subtle reworking process in the course of transmission. In India, archaeological evidence for devotion to Amitabha appears in the first two centuries CE. His name is mentioned in an inscription and a number of stelae from northwest Pakistan (ancient Gandhara) show Amitabha flanked by devotees on small lotuses.

Visualizations commonly implore the meditator to think of the figure of the buddha Amitabha, who was in Sukhavati when he was struck by a light that shone from the Buddha. Amitabha took this as his signal to manifest Avalokiteshvara, Tibet's most revered bodhisattva. Amitabha radiated his thoughts into a lake, where they produced a lotus that fell apart to reveal Avalokiteshvara. The bodhisattva then changed himself into a monkey and sought union with Tara to produce the ancestors of the Tibetan people. This Tibetan painting, probably dating to the 18th century, shows various paradisial places of purity and power, together with buddhas, bodhisattvas, lamas, and primates.

PART 2 • CHAPTER 9   *Mark L. Blum*

CHAN AND ZEN— THE WAY OF MEDITATION

ZEN IN EAST ASIA

*A gilt bronze statue of the Indian
scholar Bodhidharma, the founder
of Chan/Zen in east Asia,
from the Son (Zen) monastery
of Haein-sa, South Korea
(see illustration, opposite).
Bodhidharma emphasized
the practical over the
intellectual and asserted the
primacy of achievement
through personal effort.*

Zen Buddhism is characterized by devotion to the practice of meditation and a rather irreverent, often unpredictable, teaching style. Although it has its roots in Indian Buddhism, and first reached east Asia via China, Zen is best known in the West as a distinctively Japanese form of Buddhism. The name Zen is the Japanese transliteration of the Chinese word, Chan. This is an abbreviation of *chan-na*, which is in turn a transliteration of the Sanskrit *dhyana*, meaning meditation. Reflecting both the Indian Buddhist emphasis on meditation and Chinese Daoist concepts, such as the importance of intuition and the inability of words to convey profound truths, Zen has been highly influential within all those Buddhist countries directly influenced by Chinese culture, including Taiwan, Korea, Vietnam, and, of course, Japan.

Unlike the older Buddhist schools, which early Zen practitioners regarded as stale and overly scholastic, Zen's authority stems not from scriptures, but from its lineages of "enlightened" masters. Zen traditionally defines itself through four principles: transmission outside the orthodox Buddhist teachings through its lineages; a belief that truth is not dependent upon established doctrine and a belief in the value of experience over the value of scripture; a direct pointing to the mind; and an emphasis on examining one's original nature and the attainment of enlightenment. Proponents of Zen call it the "Buddhism of enlightenment," claiming that it is the one school that can bring an individual to experience the fully awakened mind of a *buddha*.

It is said that Zen originated with the Buddha's disciple Kashyapa, also known as Mahakashyapa ("Great Kashyapa"). During one of his sermons, the Buddha answered a question by merely holding up a flower and smiling. Of all in attendance, only Kashyapa understood—he immediately attained complete enlightenment. This story provides the basis for the Zen belief that profound truth can be transmitted from "mind to mind," without the mediation of language.

Kashyapa is considered the first of twenty-eight Indian patriarchs in the lineage. The last was Bodhidharma, who traveled to southern China ca. 520CE and became the first Chinese patriarch of Chan (Zen). By the late seventh century CE, there were monasteries practicing Zen (Chan) in various parts of China. The most important was the Eastern

Mountain school in Hubei province, founded by the fifth patriarch, Hongren (601–674CE). After his death, Huineng (638–713CE), a peasant who had become enlightened upon hearing a phrase from the Diamond Sutra (see pp.183–4 and 197), was chosen as successor over Shenxiu (605–706CE), a senior monk who stressed purification of the mind through long-continued practice. These differences in approach led to the "sudden enlightenment" stance of the Southern school (Huineng's successors) and the "gradual enlightenment" stance of the Northern school (Shenxiu's successors). Although the Southern school's view prevailed, the tension between the two standpoints has remained. By the ninth century, there were five "houses" of Zen, all belonging to Huineng's lineage, and Zen continued to expand with imperial support during the Song dynasty.

In Vietnam, the Zen (Thien) tradition arrived in 580 with the Indian monk Vinitaruci, and a second transmission was brought from China in the eighth century by Wu Yantong. From the thirteenth century Zen was integrated into Vietnam as a result of its close ties to the royal court. In Korea, where Zen is known as Son, and Japan, the twelfth to thirteenth centuries provided fertile climates for planting Zen roots that were to have a profound impact on both civilizations. The Korean masters Chinul (1158–1210) and T'aego (1301–82) established the Chogye school based on direct links with China's Linji tradition. Similarly, the Japanese monks Eisai (1141–1215) and Dogen (1200–53) both studied under Chinese masters and then founded the Rinzai (Linji) and Soto (Caodong) schools respectively (see pp.154–5).

A monk crosses the courtyard of Haein-sa monastery, South Korea. Located within beautiful woodlands in what is now the country's Kaya-san National Park, Haein-sa houses one of the great collections of Buddhist scriptures (see also illustration opposite and on pp.100 and 187). Although Zen's religious authority is based on the role of individual teachers rather than texts, this does not mean that Zen does not find inspiration in scripture. Historically it has derived much of its philosophical inspiration from the Lankavatara, Diamond, and Avatamsaka sutras (see pp.196–211)

ZEN APPROACHES TO MEDITATION

A Soto Zen monk sitting straight-backed on his cushion, or zafu. He is engaged in a form of zazen known as "just sitting," that aims at a state of awareness of the very ground of one's own being.

Meditation has always been central to Zen practice—the very name Zen derives from a Sanskrit word for meditation (see p.150). Yet there has always been a certain degree of controversy within Zen over the way meditation is defined and the extent to which practice is essential to the attainment of enlightenment. Initially, the emphasis was very much on seated meditation (*zazen*)—one early legend of Bodhidharma (see p.150) recounted that the great patriarch sat for so long that his legs atrophied and fell off. However, the sixth patriarch, Huineng (see p.151), suggested that enlightenment is not dependent upon seated meditation, a view propagated by his

MONKS AND MEDITATION: *ZAZEN* IN RINZAI AND SOTO MONASTERIES

Although the main Japanese Zen schools (see p.154) differ in their approach to meditation (see below), in both Rinzai and Soto monasteries, *zazen* plays a central role in the monks' daily lives. Indeed, its omnipresence is inescapable—the *zendo* (meditation hall), where monks spend up to seven hours a day practicing *zazen*, also serves as refectory and dormitory.

Zen monks meditate in a sitting position, straight-backed and cross-legged, keeping their eyes half open in order to maintain participation in the external world. In Soto monasteries, *zazen* tends to be a rather solitary affair—the monks face the wall, with their backs to each other (see photograph, opposite). In Rinzai monasteries the monks sit facing each other, and in seeing others doing their best, one's own energy is enhanced. This includes observing the monk who parades slowly in front of everyone, ready to strike on the shoulder with a stick anyone who seems to be losing his concentration.

successors, the Southern school of Chan or Zen. In contrast, adherents of the Northern school (see p.151) believed that "gradual enlightenment" was the result of a long period of regular meditation practice.

Mazu (709–788CE) was another master opposed to the notion that one can gradually progress toward enlightenment through meditation. Mazu asserted that it is only because one already has *buddha*-nature that full awakening is possible. He came to criticize any kind of "artificial striving" for enlightenment in stages, teaching that practice becomes meaningful only with a complete breakthrough to understanding. Following Huineng, Mazu stressed the sudden, unexpected nature of the enlightenment experience.

Linji (died 866CE) and Dahui (1089–1163), descendants of Mazu in lineage and ideology, stressed this realization. They championed a confrontational directness in teaching and criticized a form of meditation called "quiet sitting," which was aimed at cultivating mental stillness. Linji taught the value of sudden realization built upon faith in one's own *buddha*-nature. Dahui urged the use of *koan*s (see sidebar, p.155) to aid this manifestation of inherent spirituality. He characterized the form of meditation taught by Hongzhi (1091–1157), a contemporary Zen master, as "silent illumination," calling it a false form of practice that "confuses the sickness with the remedy, denying the experience of enlightenment." In turn Dahui's approach was labeled "*koan*-gazing Zen" by Hongzhi, and both labels stuck, with "silent illumination" describing the *shikan-taza* ("just sitting") of the present-day Soto school and "*koan*-gazing Zen" the methods of the Rinzai school (see p.154).

However, to a large extent, the primary difference between the Rinzai and Soto schools is one of emphasis or approach rather than of substance. Both trace their lineage to Huineng, and both stress that meditation has value not as a method for the attainment of wisdom, but as the embodiment of wisdom itself. Meditation is seen as a dynamic, active state of heightened awareness; *buddha*-consciousness is found in the things of everyday life, with meditation being the best way to reorient the mind so that it is able to appreciate its encounters with this other dimension of reality.

RINZAI AND SOTO

Rinzai and Soto are the two largest Zen sects in Japan today. Both have their beginnings in the transmission of Chinese Chan lineages to Japan by Eisai (1141–1215) and Dogen (1200–53) (see p.151), yet each sect gradually became transformed in the Japanese cultural environment.

Born into a family of Shinto priests, Eisai (or Yosai) became a monk in the Tendai school. He made two trips to China, where he studied under a Linji master (see p.153), returning with a certificate of enlightenment and a commitment to establish Zen in Japan. As founder of Kenninji, a Rinzai monastery in Kyoto still active today, Eisai also taught tantric rituals (see illustration, p.142) and the importance of the monastic precepts.

During the fourteenth and fifteenth centuries, the Rinzai school enjoyed enormous prestige under the Ashikaga shoguns, resulting in an administrative system of public support based on Chinese models called the Five Mountains (*gozan*) and Ten Temples (*jissetsu*). Historically, Rinzai's spread was therefore among the élites of *samurai* culture. Throughout Japan, the majority of its temples were built in urban centers, unlike those of Dogen's Soto school, which spread in rural areas. With the decline of military culture in the nineteenth century, the Rinzai school became smaller. Although today it is by far the smaller of the two sects, many of the original Rinzai temples built in the medieval period in the former centers of political authority in Kyoto and Kamakura remain active monasteries.

Although their goal is the awareness of the Absolute, immanent in all reality, the Rinzai and Soto schools differ in their approach to practice. Dogen considered enlightenment and the practice of *zazen*, or seated meditation (see p.152) to be one and the same. Soto rejects the use of techniques or goals in meditation as misleading, as it believes there is nothing external to search for. Although *zazen*, in its ideal state of pure-awareness, is designated as particularly meaningful, it is thought that all activity should be meditative—that is, accompanied by focused concentration. Typical Soto monastic life pays great attention to detail, with rules in place to guide most activities, including eating and even using the toilet. Although there are exceptions, typical Soto temples do not rely on *koan*s (meditation problems or puzzles—see sidebar, opposite) or regular meetings with the Zen master.

The Rinzai tradition believes that unless one awakens to the Absolute, Rinzai will have no transformative effect. Compared with Soto's values of patience, deportment, and diligence, Rinzai is thus more goal-oriented, and does not hesitate to use psychological tools to trigger such an awakening. Today's method of study through *koan*s in advanced practice derives from the approach of the great Rinzai master Hakuin (1685–1768). Both the use of *koan*s and frequent encounters with the Zen master create a tension in the individual conducive to the sought-after breakthrough—the psychological event called *satori* (see p.78) or *kensho*. Rinzai monasteries tend to be less tightly regulated than those of Soto, because the individual's concentration is directed toward his or her *koan* rather than the details of daily life.

MEDITATION PUZZLES

Difficult questions or stories, often taken from classic accounts of Chan masters in China, are posed to students of Zen to push them toward spiritual breakthroughs. Known as *koans*, their difficulty lies not only in decoding the symbols used—as in "How is it that one hair digs many ditches," wherein one must realize that the hair represents the Absolute and the ditches the myriad phenomena of the material world—but more importantly in the individual's response to the intellectual impasse they produce, from where the leap to deeper understanding is possible. Hakuin's revival of the Rinzai school arose from his conviction of the value of *koan* practice. He created many *koan*s himself, the most famous of them being, "What is the sound of one hand clapping?"

A self-portrait by the great Rinzai Zen master, poet, artist, and calligrapher Hakuin (1685–1768). The forceful lines of his garment seem to contrast with the slightly shy look of this otherwise powerful religious leader. It was not uncommon for Zen masters to be drawn in an exaggerated, serio-comic fashion utilizing a limited number of strokes.

ZEN MONASTIC LIFE

Ladles and running water used for the strictly prescribed act of ritual purification of the hands and mouth to be undertaken by visitors to a Japanese temple.

When the Buddhist tradition of monasticism was transmitted to China, it underwent various changes owing to the differences between Indian and Chinese culture and spirituality. Of all the schools of Buddhism, it was Zen that brought monasticism to its most disciplined state of development. Although the earliest Chan text records are largely anecdotal, with teaching methods including the use of shouting, beating, and slapping, the fourth patriarch Daoxin (580–651) mentions specific rules for his monastery, such as requiring manual labor of all monks in support of the institution. But it was Baizhang Huaihai (720–814CE) who established the monastic code and institutional organization, still followed today, that marked the separation of Zen monasticism from the rest of Chinese Buddhism in a way that serves its religious goals and assures its financial independence.

Zen monasticism exists today in Japan, Korea, Vietnam, and China (although much reduced in the latter since the Cultural Revolution). Monastic customs differ, but Japan may be taken as representative. Zen monastic life is based on humility, self-discipline, and aspiration for insight. The monk's only personal possessions are the basic articles required for monastic life: a razor, a set of bowls, his robes and surplice (a loose, white vestment), cotton leggings, a large bamboo hat, and straw sandals worn without socks even in the winter.

Meditation is just one part of the monk's training, which also includes mendicancy, work, ritual, and study in the form of *sutra* chanting and training in the meditation problems known as *koan*s (see pp.154–5)—although there are exceptions: typical Soto temples do not rely on *koan*s. The day begins at 3.30 or 4.00am and officially ends at 9.00pm (although in Japan this is generally followed by compulsory "night sitting," called *yaza*). Daily meditation (*zazen*) generally runs for two hours in the morning and

SETTING OUT ON THE PATH

Zen monastic life is physically and mentally demanding; it is therefore standard for a monk seeking entrance to be refused initially, as a form of test. He must show his sincerity by waiting in the monastery entrance for two days, then spending three to five days in a small room meditating alone. When he is finally admitted to the meditation hall, or *zendo*, the novice first prostrates himself three times before the image of the *bodhisattva* Manjushri, who symbolizes the wisdom that he is seeking to attain. The novice is then assigned the space of one *tatami* mat—about three feet by six (one by two meters)—on which he will live, sleep, and meditate. After a few days he meets with the Zen master. This private meeting—the first of many during his monastic career—begins the novice's formal study as a Zen monk.

A monk passing through a walkway at Japan's remote, 13th-century Eiheiji training monastery, northeast of Kyoto, holds his food aloft in the Soto Zen ritual manner, deliberately imparting a religious spirit to an otherwise ordinary activity. Novices are required to run when moving about the building—vigorous exercise is part of the Soto creed.

three to five hours in the evening. The monastic schedule includes intensive meditation sessions, called *sesshin* in Japan, which are held from one to twelve times a year. These often attract monks and lay people from outside the monastery and may involve eight to fifteen hours of *zazen* a day for a period of five to seven days.

Mendicancy these days is rarely needed financially but is continued for its physical and spiritual benefits. Work within the monastery includes cleaning, gardening, temple upkeep, and cooking. Monasteries are guided by the principle of Baizhang, "A day without work is a day without food." Physical labor, whether it be in the kitchen or in the fields, not only contributes to self-sufficiency in food but helps focus the mind. Even simple assignments such as washing rice are seen as opportunities to deepen one's concentration. Zen monastic life aims at extending the mental concentration cultivated during *zazen* to all activities. The goal is never one of escape, but of preparing a monk or nun to live a life of spiritual awakening whether in the monastery or in the outside world.

ART AND ARCHITECTURE *Mark L. Blum*

ZEN AND THE ARTS

A number of artistic traditions have emerged as the result of inspiration derived from Zen experience or the outlook on life peculiar to this form of Buddhism. While Zen manifests the same kind of ambivalence toward art as it does toward meditation (see pp.152–3), with respect for its value but non-attachment to any particular example of it, its monasticism is tempered with an appreciation of personal expression, including artistic creation. Not only did the general public soon come to recognize the value in the art produced by Zen monks, professional artists also found inspiration in their work.

Most of the arts associated with the Zen tradition have their origins in China, but it is the Japanese adaptations that have received the most attention in the West. There are various art-forms associated with Zen, including painting, calligraphy, archery, *kendo* swordsmanship, and so on, but all are considered paths to truth in and of themselves. For this reason, there is no conflict, particularly in Japan, when a monk chooses to devote a considerable amount of his time to artistic pursuits.

Zen art is characterized by its concise but also highly suggestive modes of expression, resulting in a paradox of compactness and openness. This is religious art that has no drama, no passion, and usually no narrative—it is aimed at producing insight rather than devotion. Often implicit to the point of obscurity, like a *koan* (see pp.154–5), much Zen art challenges the viewer to "get" the painting, the poem, or the tea bowl.

It was during the Song dynasty (960–1279) in China that both Chinese painting and Chan as a monastic institution reached their apogee, leading to a fruitful interaction between the two. Monks and professional painters began to produce Chan-inspired ink paintings. The techniques of Chinese painting derive from calligraphy; as monks began to exploit the potential offered by calligraphic brush techniques for quick, dramatic, and flexible expression in painting, professional painters drew from the Chan/Zen heritage of religious anecdotes and its favorable regard for spontaneity.

Thematically, Zen culture is expressed in painting in three basic ways: portraiture, landscapes, and descriptive scenes illustrating famous Zen stories, such as encounters between master and disciple, and depictions of *koan* themes. "Ox-herding" pictures, which use the motif of a young man chasing a large ox to depict ten stages in the path of spiritual progress, are also intended for teaching use (see p.79 and illustration on p.141).

Portraits were created to record a famous master's countenance and were hung on the walls of a temple to document its lineage history. One of the earliest extant Zen-inspired portraits is *The Second Patriarch Setting His Mind in Order*, created by the ninth-century CE Chinese recluse Shike. It is an expressly informal work, depicting the Chan patriarch Huike (487–593) slumped in contemplation, his eyes downcast. Shike's impressionistic treatment of the monk's robes was imitated and expanded by later painters, and is vivid in the work of the thirteenth-century artists Liangkai (early thirteenth century) and Muqi (ca. 1210–ca. 1288). Liangkai's *Dancing Budai* shows the sparsely drawn figure of a monk walking barefoot with the mere outline of the bag and stick he is carrying, yet the monk's wild smile and splayed fingers mark him as eccentric and not wholly of this world, a popular theme in Chan/Zen paintings.

Chan/Zen landscape paintings often express the enormity of the universe. In his *Fisherman*, Mayuan (1190–1230) paints only in one corner of his silk canvas, suggesting the immensity of cosmic space. *Sunset in a Fishing Village* by the monk Muqi depicts little more than mountain peaks jutting through a mist with a few scattered roofs and one tiny fisherman throwing his net into the river from a boat, similarly emphasizing the smallness of man against nature. The monk Yujian had great influence in Japan. His *Landscape at Lu-shan* is a marvel of abstraction and spontaneity.

In Japan, the Chinese ink painting tradition was popularized from the fourteenth century by artists also working in the Zen tradition. The fourteenth-century professional painter-turned-monk Kao (died 1345) created powerful images of monks to illustrate Zen themes. His spontaneously lifelike drawings of the Tang-dynasty poets Hanshan (Japanese, Kanzan) and Shide (Japanese, Jittoku) were often copied by later artists. The early fifteenth-century monk-painter Josetsu's *Catching a Catfish with a Gourd*—in which the fish looks larger than the gourd—is a parable on the irrationality of seeking enlightenment. His incisive line style was expanded by Shubun and Sesshu, two monk-painters based at the Shokokuji Zen monastery in Kyoto. In their works, the level of abstraction increases until natural shapes appear boldly realistic and yet impossibly arresting in their depiction. Sesshu's *Winter Landscape* skillfully mixes thick strokes and dramatic contrasts to express an aesthetic of composition that is purely Japanese.

In the Tokugawa period (1603–1868), Zen painting became more personalized. The Rinzai Zen master, or *roshi*, Hakuin (1685–1768) (see pp.154–5) often gave paintings to lay visitors who came seeking religious advice. Although he had no artistic training, Hakuin's unique creations are remarkably compelling and at times humorous; in them we are given the rare opportunity to see how an enlightened mind expresses itself. His *Blind Men Crossing a Bridge* is not only visually stunning—a closer look at what appear at first to be ants crawling across bamboo reveals them to be blind

OPPOSITE   *This simple ink painting is entitled* Morning Glory *and dates from 1830–40. The hanging scroll would have hung on its own in a room used for tea rituals (see p.161), its subtle monochrome shades helping to create the harmonious meditative atmosphere required. The brocade edgings are decorated with dewy grass and the silk surround is a blue damask with a wave-on-water motif. All this has been carefully selected and executed to enhance the restraint of the painting.*

This 17th-century Japanese calligraphy was written by a Chinese monk called Nangen, who at the age of fifteen entered the Zen temple at Manpukuji, near Kyoto, Japan. The large character reads "kokoro," meaning heart—a reference to the place of prominence accorded in Zen Buddhism to the Heart Sutra.

ZEN POETRY

Throughout the history of Zen, countless monks have used poetry to express their spiritual experiences. The following *haiku* (a seventeen-syllable poem intended to produce sudden insight in the reader) by the Japanese poet Basho (1644–94) expresses much of the same concise Zen spirituality that can be seen in painting, garden design, and other Zen art forms:

The old pond, ah!
A frog jumps in:
The sound of the water.

men—but a didactic reminder of the critical importance of keeping one's attention focused. The quickly executed works of monks such as Torei, Jiun, and Sengai move toward greater and greater abstraction—at times these pieces are only shapes, as in the evocative circles drawn by Torei and others.

The practice of drinking tea is extremely old in China, but it was in Kyoto in Japan where, as a by-product of the conversations between Zen monks and the nobility in the fifteenth century, the preparation, serving, and drinking of powdered tea was formalized in a way that combined aesthetics with meditative calm. Special rooms, such as the one constructed at Ginkakuji by Shogun Ashikaga Yoshimasa (1438–91), were built by the nobility for the purpose of enjoying tea. It was the monk Shuko who—having learned the value of combining meditation with artistic pursuits from his teacher, the poet Ikkyu—formulated the four principles that still govern the way tea is used today: harmony, reverence, purity, and tranquillity.

In the sixteenth century, tea ceremony (*chanoyu*) aesthetics took a leap forward under the influence of Sen no Rikyu (1522–91). A master of taste, Rikyu eschewed the opulence of palaces and mansions. He redesigned the tea room (*chashitsu*), transforming it into a small, rustic place, where the elegance and simplicity of the tea ceremony could be savored. The entrance to this new tea room was so low that visitors had to bow to enter, and *samurai* were forced to leave their swords outside. Inside was an almost blank space—only one piece of art was allowed to adorn the room (see illustration, p.158)—where an imperfect yet extraordinary aesthetic experience could unfold. Rikyu termed this an expression of *wabi*. Words such as *wabi* and *sabi* were borrowed from descriptions of solitary monastic hermits to describe an aesthetic of understatement and natural decay.

In this narrow, unfurnished room, the guest enters a world of quiet elegance. His or her thoughts naturally focus on the highly refined performance of the tea master and the beauty of the carefully selected utensils, such as the iron kettle, the ceramic tea bowl, the lacquered container for the bright green powdered tea, and the silk tea cloth. These are enhanced by the gestures of politeness when the hot tea is given and received, and by the exquisite calligraphy in the hanging scroll or carefully arranged flowers which may be the room's only form of decoration. Today, the tea ceremony remains a unique fusion of contemplative calm and aesthetic brilliance.

The creation of a tranquil, external place is exemplified by an aspect of Zen culture well known in the West, that of garden design. An ancient Chinese craft in origin, beautiful gardens adorn the grounds of Buddhist temples throughout east Asia, but it was in Japan that the combination of Zen spirituality and garden aesthetics developed to a point at which garden design and care came to be seen as a religious activity. Gardens in Zen monasteries are objects of meditation, visual tableaux that are thought-provoking and suggestive of religious or cosmic themes. In that they are also intended to leave the viewer with a deep impression of natural beauty, Zen gardens embody a paradox, for their conception is artificial. Yet, as in all Zen art, the garden designer's intention is to create forms that are suggestive of something beyond the forms themselves.

The best known designer of Zen gardens is Muso (1275–1351), a charismatic monk who was repeatedly appointed to the abbotship of large Zen monasteries only to escape, seeking seclusion. At Saihoji and Tenryuji, both in the environs of Kyoto, Muso redesigned existing gardens into breathtaking encapsulations of the emotional power that nature can evoke. An exquisite composition of seasonal plants, Tenryuji contains a pond dug in the shape of the character for "mind" (*kokoro*) and kept clear by natural springs, suggestive of the unfettered mental state that is enlightenment. Viewed from the temple veranda, a small series of rocks behind the pond suggests a distant waterfall, but in fact no water passes through it. At Saihoji, Muso also included a "mind" pond, and planted more than twenty varieties of moss on earth, trees, and rocks, earning it the name Moss Garden. Unlike most Zen gardens, which are designed to be looked at from the outside, that at Saihoji is a "walking garden," intended for strolling. The combination of the hard, jutting rocks and the soft moss blanketing the ground suggests the complementary opposites of *yin* and *yang* (*in* and *yo* in Japanese), or the contrast between aesthetically comforting surroundings and the austerity of monastic life.

Zen's dry landscape genre also creates powerful images. The most famous example is the so-called Rock Garden at Ryoanji temple in Kyoto, where carefully raked pebbles and different sized rocks give the impression of islands in a river, or random thoughts in the viewer's mind.

Japan's ruling aristocratic warrior class were the chief patrons of Zen, which, in turn, embraced certain martial disciplines as aids to enlightenment. This samurai sword guard, or tsuba, *is decorated with an intricately crafted religious motif, which appears to be a hermit or monk meditating under a tree in blossom. Zen's acceptance of martial arts meant that a spiritual basis was provided for the samurai's single-minded pursuit of skills in swordplay and archery.*

PART 2 ● CHAPTER 10 *Todd T. Lewis*

TANTRA

THE DIAMOND VEHICLE

The esoteric spiritual school that developed within Mahayana Buddhism is most commonly known as tantric Buddhism, or Tantra, after the texts known as *tantras* (see pp.208–11). This school is also called Tantrayana ("Tantra Vehicle"), and Mantrayana ("Mantra Vehicle"), but the most usual term is Vajrayana ("Diamond-Thunderbolt Vehicle"). This refers to the indestructibility of a diamond (*vajra*) and its ability to cut through all other materials, and to the belief that the tantric path has the power to cause the rapid destruction (hence "thunderbolt," another meaning of *vajra*) of the fetters of ignorance (*avidya*) that bind all living beings to *samsara*. Tantric Buddhists aim to attain enlightenment rapidly in a single lifetime through powerful techniques learned under the guidance of an accomplished adept, or saint (*siddha*).

This esoteric and mystical form of Buddhism is highly characteristic of Tibet, where it is believed to have spread from India in the eighth or ninth century CE. It is impossible to discern the earliest history of tantric Buddhism because its transmission was oral, although many of its fundamental concepts draw upon *yoga* traditions dating back to the time of the Buddha.

Tantric Buddhism first arose in northern India around 600CE as a spiritual "counterculture" among *siddhas* who rejected the monastic establishment of the Sangha as having become scholastic and hierarchical. Accounts suggest that these monasteries had developed in such a way that many of the monks appeared more concerned with their status as professors of philosophy than in being exemplary spiritual figures. In response, there arose a series of spiritual innovators, or *mahasiddhas* ("great saints," or "great adepts;" see pp.164–5), who experimented with distinctive meditative practices (*sadhanas*) that focused on deities from the Mahayana pantheon. However, these *siddhas* also found the Mahayana culture spiritually complacent, especially its teaching that the qualities necessary for enlightenment could "ripen" only over several lifetimes.

Other trends within Mahayana philosophy also contributed to the rise of the Vajrayana. The philosopher Nagarjuna equated *samsara* with *nirvana* (see p.69) and asserted the immanence of enlightenment within all spheres of human experience justified the search for insight. The Tathagatagarbha doctrine (see p.205), which argued that all beings possess an innate "*buddha*-embryo" (*tathagatagarbha*), supported the same view. The Chittamatra school, which focused on consciousness as the locus of spiritual transformation, advocated the visualization of divinities, a common tantric

In this photograph by the author, a tantric master or vajracharya *from Nepal's Newar community chants during a ritual for generating blessings. He holds a* vajrakila *("vajra-dagger"), one of the three ritual implements of the* vajracharya, *along with a bell and* vajra *("diamond thunderbolt"; see pp.164–5). The* vajrakila *is believed to fend off or destroy demons (see p.166) that are attracted to impure offerings. During the early Buddhist missions in the Tibetan world and Japan, tantric rituals were important in establishing the new faith. Most popular were those rituals promising to transfer merit to the dead and lead their spirits to a good rebirth.*

practice. The Buddha's prediction that Buddhism and human spiritual capacity would inevitably decline, suggested to Vajrayana's exponents that more radical practices were necessary for the attainment of enlightenment.

Ironically, the beliefs and practices of the *mahasiddha*s were eventually absorbed by mainstream scholars and monastics. The distinctive teachings, meditative practices, and related rituals of the *mahasiddha*s came to be written down in coded and esoteric language in the texts called *tantra*s, which were guarded from any inquisitive non-initiates.

In the last centuries of Indian Buddhism, Tantra moved from the periphery to become part of the dominant Buddhist culture—today it is practiced in Tibet and other culturally Tibetan regions, such as Ladakh, Bhutan, and among Nepal's Newar ethnic community. Tantric traditions were also transmitted to east Asia, where they developed in China and Korea as the Zhenyan and Milgyo schools respectively, although both later declined. It manifested as the Shingon in Japan, attracting a vigorous following and inspiring rich artistic and ritual traditions, where it survives until the present.

WOMEN AND TANTRA

Although the social context of early tantric Buddhism remains obscure, there is no doubt that an important part of the tantric subculture celebrated the spirituality of women. In so doing, the earliest tradition opposed the patriarchy of Indian caste society and the Vinaya rules of the monastic establishment. Many of the *tantra*s state that respect for women is one of the essentials for enlightenment.

In Mahayana philosophy, all dualism must be rejected to reach *nirvana* realization—Tantra put their sexual equality idea into practice by encouraging seekers to transcend their attachment to gender ideology. The enlightened goddess Prajnaparamita is visualized as the embodiment of *prajna* ("wisdom") (see illustration, p.87); even more revered in Vajrayana practices is the *yogini*, a goddess capable of cutting through attachments and leading the practitioner to fully experience *prajna*. Tantric advocates note that without the gift of food from the woman Sujata, the Buddha would not have survived his austerities or achieved his enlightenment; seekers on the Vajrayana path likewise assert that they must merge the dynamic energies of male and female to achieve *nirvana*.

THE BELL AND THE THUNDERBOLT

Tibetan monks performing a prayer ceremony in a courtyard of the Jokhang monastery in Lhasa, Tibet's most sacred temple, founded in 647CE. Before each monk are the two most common implements used in tantric rituals—a vajra *("diamond thunderbolt") and a bell, each symbolizing the two main principles of a* vajracharya's bodhisattva *service: the* vajra *conveys the ideal of skillful compassionate practice and the bell, empty yet beautifully resonant, symbolizes wisdom (prajna). By selfless service, a* vajracharya *can utilize his own body as a vessel for divine presence and his mind can generate powers which he can share with others. A third implement is the* vajrakila *("vajra-dagger," Tibetan* phurbu: see illustration on p.163).

The sages who discovered specific means to rapid *nirvana* realization are called *mahasiddha*s ("great saints," or "great adepts"). One text, preserved in Tibetan, records brief biographies of eighty-four *mahasiddha*s who lived between 700CE and 1100CE and the meditation practices they favored for reaching enlightenment. The *mahasiddha*s came from every walk of life and included kings and priests, farmers and beggars, housewives and prostitutes. Most were wandering mendicants and eccentrics or, as one scholar has characterized them, spiritual anarchists. Luipa ate fish entrails, Virupa frequented taverns, Shanaripa was a hunter, Aryadeva gave as an offering one of his eyes, Vinapa played the lute. Each saint encountered a teacher who set him or her on the path to realization: some teachers were male ascetics, others were women in unexpected guises. The most renowned Tibetan *mahasiddha*s include Naropa (eleventh century CE), his disciple Marpa (a farmer by birth), and, most popular of all, Marpa's disciple Milarepa (see sidebar, opposite).

Each *mahasiddha* is associated with a particular tantric practice (*sadhana*) which the saint passes down to his disciples. A *siddha* reaches enlightenment and comes to possess characteristic supernormal power, or *siddhi* (hence their title of *siddha*). These abilities included telepathy, clairvoyance, extraordinary strength, and flight. Most *siddha*s regarded themselves as *bodhisattva*s who applied their expertise to the development of ritual techniques aimed at multiplying the blessings that arose from their tantric powers and and sharing them with society at large.

Those who came to practice meditation and ritual in the Vajrayana tradition are called *vajracharya*s, or "*vajra* masters." This role arose and developed during the last centuries of Indian Buddhism (in the period up to about 1200CE; see box, p.54), as ritual became an integral part of the tradition in the process of its spread to Nepal, Tibet, and Japan. In the Newar community of Nepal, *vajracharya*s are a caste of Buddhist priests that specialize in Vajrayana meditation and ritualism (see p.163). A *vajracharya* must be initiated and undergo training to wield the ritual bell and thunderbolt (*vajra*), implements needed to perform tantric rituals. One or more initiations into a tantric *sadhana* practice must be undergone, since meditation, visualization practice, and *mantra* recitations are essential to the success of a *vajracharya*'s ritual service. In the main rituals, the *vajracharya* calls upon celestial *buddha*s and *bodhisattva*s (see p.138) to abide in the ritual space (most often a special flask), transform a variety of ritual offerings into blessed substances, and thereby generate spiritual "medicine" for those connected with the ritual. They are also called upon to control the deities, spirits, and ghosts that affect human life.

In an interesting if still not completely understood historical connection, the earliest *vajracharya*s also adopted one of the most important Vedic Hindu rituals, the fire sacrifice or *homa* (see p.16). But while they adopted roughly the same ritual procedure—offering many kinds of grains and clarified butter into a fire—they used different *mantra* chants and transformed the symbolic meaning of the ritual entirely. For example, the various offering substances do not feed the gods but now symbolize the individual's attachments and ignorance, and the flame is visualized as consuming the individual's or society's obstacles to enlightenment. *Vajracharya*s in Nepal, the Tibetan cultural region, and Japan (see illustration, p.142) still perform this ritual which began more than 3,500 years ago.

MILAREPA

Milarepa (1052–1135) is the most renowned *siddha* in Tibet, beloved for his very human biography and for the thousands of songs that are attributed to him. He was born into a rich family, but when his father died his paternal aunt and uncle reduced him and his mother to beggary. When he grew up, it is said that Milarepa studied black magic in order to impose disaster on his relatives and so recover his property.

Initially elated at exacting revenge, Milarepa later felt remorse and sought out the *mahasiddha* Marpa, who agreed to be his teacher. Discerning that Milarepa first had to erase his bad *karma*, Marpa subjected him to great trials, including building, demolishing, then rebuilding towers. After spending a long period of meditation in remote Himalayan caves, Milarepa realized *nirvana*. His name comes from the fact that he specialized in heat-generating meditation (*tummo*) while wearing only a cotton robe (*mila-repa*).

TANTRIC DEITIES

In the tantric tradition, the three elements of the Triple Refuge (Buddha, Dharma, Sangha; see sidebar, p.107), like other central aspects of Buddhist practice, have been overlaid with additional esoteric meanings. "The Buddha" becomes represented by the tantric *guru* who bestows initiation; "the Dharma" becomes the male tantric deities whose forms, in visualization meditation, are the bodily expressions of the highest truth; and "the Sangha" consists of the female deities called *yoginis* (see p.163), since in their company a practitioner experiences *prajna* and thus enlightenment. (Some Vajrayana traditions even have disciples "take refuge" in four rather than three "jewels": Buddha, Dharma, Sangha, and the Guru.) These deities came to dominate tantric Buddhist art, and largely replaced the historical Buddha, the celestial *buddhas*, and compassionate *bodhisattvas* as objects of meditative practice.

The Vajrayana builds upon existing Mahayana ideas about celestial *buddhas* and *bodhisattvas* and asserts that, at times, demons confront humanity; accordingly, compassion demands that these Buddhist divinities assume wrathful forms that can respond with force either to disperse or destroy the demons, which may be understood literally or, from the more profound esoteric perspective, as the psychological hindrances to spiritual progress, such as greed, lust, anger, and delusion. The wrathful forms of the enlightened deities fuse an outer appearance of malevolence with an inner one of compassion.

Every fierce form of a *buddha* or *bodhisattva* has a "seed *mantra*," which the practitioner chants to begin the process of visualization, and a "heart *mantra*," which elicits the deity's compassion. According to tantric interpreters, these *mantras* work by affecting the practitioner without engag-

THE *PANCARAKSHA*

Mahapratisara is one of five tantric deities featured in the *Pancharaksha* ("Five Protectors"), dating from around 800CE and one of the most popular Buddhist texts in Tibet, Nepal, China, and Japan. Chanting this text is thought to bring blessings to oneself, one's home, family, and entire community. Each of the five deities has a *mantra* and an icon that one should visualize while chanting; there are also stories appended to each that attest to the success of the practice. In the case of Mahapratisara, one should chant her *mantra*—"Om manidhari vajrini mahapratisare raksha raksha mam sarvasattvanama hum hum phat phat phat svaha"—

after visualizing her emanating from her "seed syllable" *pra*, seated in the lotus position, with a *stupa* on her crown, four faces (black, yellow, green, white), and eight arms holding certain objects.

The stories in the text associated with the *sadhana* practice of this tantric goddess are recounted by the Buddha, who gives the *mantra*, reveals the *sadhana*, and promises a host of blessings. These include freedom from harm by spirits and ghosts, contagious diseases, poison, fire, weapons, and snakes; one earns merit, wealth, and healthy children. The text also recommends the creation of amulets and prayer flags inscribed with her *mantra*.

ing his or her intellect. On the esoteric level, every wrathful deity—many of which, in Tibetan Buddhism, serve as Dharmapalas ("Protectors of the Dharma")—has an appearance which contains complex symbolism.

An example of this is the deity Mahakala ("Great Black" or "Great Time") (see illustration, right), who the initiate will learn—through instruction, chant, and meditation—has two *sadhana*s devoted to him. The first of these emphasizes his function as the protector of Buddhist institutions, a role that led to statues of him being placed at the entranceways to monasteries in northern India, Nepal, and Tibet. He can also manifest as a wolf or tiger, as shown on either side in the illustration, in order to guard these sacred precincts.

The second *sadhana* utilizes Mahakala as a meditation deity (*yidam*). In this aspect, Mahakala has been described as the wrathful manifestation of the *bodhisattva* Avalokiteshvara, who is especially dedicated to the prompt defeat of any obstacles to happiness. A crown is worn that bears the image of the Buddha touching the earth to bear witness to his defeat of Mara. Mahakala may also bestride a demon, recognized as an obstacle to enlightenment and an indicator of Mahakala's ability to facilitate meditative success.

As "Great Time," Mahakala holds a blade, which symbolizes the means to sever all discursive conceptions, and a skull-cup to symbolize wisdom or insight. Both implements are also utilized by initiates in their *sadhana*. Finally, Mahakala may wear a garland of fifty skulls to illustrate his dual worldly and transcendental roles as a tantric deity—they serve to scare off evil beings, but they also represent the fifty vowels and consonants of the Sanskrit alphabet, thereby encompassing the whole of pure *mantra* sound which, when bound with Mahakala meditation, enables the practitioner to overcome time and obtain enlightenment.

Wrathful deities are embodiments of enlightened beings who have assumed wrathful forms in order to produce transformative effects on the minds of disciples. Yamantaka is a manifestation of Manjushri (see pp.78–9), who originated when Manjushri visited hell to subjugate Yama, the Lord of Death, because he was interfering with the law of *karma* by claiming victims "before their time." Manjushri assumed the form of a demon whose appearance frightened Yama literally to death. This form of Manjushri became known as Yamantaka, "Subduer of Yama." In Tantra, the individual who opens his or her body, speech, and mind to transformation by the visualization of these deities and through other tantric practices, can effectively overcome the "inner demons" that obstruct the path to liberation.

Tibetan tradition recounts how the great siddha Padmasambhava, who founded Tibet's first monastery in the 8th century CE, forced Tibet's pre-Buddhist gods to serve as Dharmapalas. One of the most popular of these is Mahakala ("Great Black" or "Great Time"), shown here on a stone stele.

OVERLEAF *Monks carry food offerings into the main hall during a ceremony at the Tibetan monastery of Nechung near Dharamsala, India. Nechung is the abode of a protector deity called Pehar, whose five forms are said to have been converted to Buddhism by Padmasambhava.*

LAMAS AND TULKUS

After a period of support from the Tibetan monarchy, Buddhism was suppressed in Tibet around 840CE when the state became engulfed by civil strife and chaos. Two centuries later, the faith had to be reintroduced from India by *siddha*s and scholars, and the political forces that dominated subsequent Tibetan history were the four main monastic orders (the Sakyapa, Nyingmapa, Kagyupa, and Gelugpa) formed by the disciples of these Indian teachers. First the Sakyapa school and finally the Gelugpa ("Yellow Hat"), headed by the Dalai Lamas (see box, opposite), came to rule the country—the only time in the Buddhist world when the Sangha assumed secular power.

Another unique feature of Tibetan Buddhism was the high percentage of men who became monks (*gelong*), perhaps a quarter of the male population by the early twentieth century. Tibetan Buddhism was formerly often called "lamaism" in the West, from the term *lama*. This is the Tibetan translation of the Sanskrit *guru*, and is used of someone who has mastered tantric *sadhana* meditation practices and related ritualism. Only a small number of monks reach this exalted position. Given Tibet's large Sangha, it is not surprising that while some monks practiced meditation in pursuit of the highest spiritual goal, many others worked as ritualists, scholars, printers, and doctors. Many simply kept the large monasteries functioning.

A distinctive type of leadership in the various Tibetan orders is that provided by the *tulku*, or reincarnate teacher. The *tulku* builds on the Mahayana theory of the Three Bodies of the Buddha (see pp.91–2) and the expectation that enlightened *bodhisattva*s (or, in some instances, *buddha*s) take repeated birth in a human body (*nirmanakaya*) in order to help humankind by teaching, healing, and by their example. At death they are reborn to resume these activities as leader of the same monastic order or monastery headed by their predecessor. Several thousand *tulku*s have been recognized in Tibet, almost all men. Some families, particularly aristocratic ones, are famed for having produced many *tulku*s, and it is not unusual for disputes to arise over the recognition of a new incarnation (see sidebar, left).

One reason for such disputes is that major *tulku*s traditionally possess large *labrang*s ("households"), which own land and other resources to support the incarnate teacher, providing for his material needs and those of a regent and teachers before he comes of age. Prior to the Chinese occupation of Tibet in the 1950s, *labrang*s of the greatest lineages once included extensive landholdings, bonded laborers, and multiple buildings.

This reincarnation system often produces remarkable individuals who inspire disciples with their learning, teachings, and spiritual charisma. Stories in Tibet recount how *tulku*s remember the names of former disciples and very specific details of their previous life. The *tulku* system makes believable the immanent reality of the cosmic *bodhisattva* who can control his destiny in the intermediate state (*bardo*) between births, and who with inexpressible compassion returns to assume another mortal body and resume his holy work. These great *lama*s are given the title *Rinpoche* ("Precious One").

IDENTIFYING A TULKU

The means of finding a *tulku*'s infant successor are fairly consistent across the Tibetan schools. Usually, late in life the *tulku* will give clues about the direction in which his next rebirth will occur, in some cases writing down details about the circumstances. After his death, his leading disciples will follow these signs and perhaps consult with another *tulku* or an oracle for more specific guidance. A party from the monastery, often disguised as laity, will seek out families with children of suitable age. When a candidate is found, the delegation examines the child's physical features for auspicious marks and asks questions to discern the child's moral character. Next they present the child with a series of items, such as rosaries, ritual implements, or tea cups, from which the child must correctly and repeatedly choose those used by the last *tulku*. If the child does so, he is acknowledged as the new *tulku* and is taken to the monastery with great fanfare to begin his studies, in some cases accompanied by his parents.

THE DALAI LAMAS

Historically, the most influential *tulku* is the Dalai Lama, head of the Gelugpa order, who is regarded as an incarnation of the *bodhisattva* Avalokiteshvara. Since the mid-seventeenth century, the Dalai Lamas have been Tibet's political and spiritual leaders, based in Lhasa. The term "Dalai," means "Ocean [of Wisdom]," a Mongol title that was conferred by Altan Khan on the monastic reformer and meditation master Sonam Gyatso (1543–88). Later, the title of Dalai Lamas was applied retrospectively to two earlier *lamas*, making him the third. After his death, the fourth Dalai Lama was found in Mongolia. When Ngawang Losang Gyatso, the "Great Fifth" Dalai Lama (1617-82), deposed the king of Lhasa, the Gelugpa school assumed political control of the capital, and soon extended its authority to central Tibet's other major cities by annexing monasteries in Shigatse and then beyond, unifying state rule from Mount Kailash to Kham province in the east.

The "Great Fifth" built the Potala palace, made an alliance with China's new Manchu emperors, and recognized the Panchen Lama, the abbot of the Gelugpa school's Tashilhunpo monastery in Shigatse, as a *tulku* of Amitabha. The current (fourteenth) Dalai Lama, Tenzin Gyatso (1935–), fled Tibet in 1959 and has since been the focus of efforts to preserve Tibet's Buddhist culture in the face of the policies of the Communist Chinese state, which occupied Tibet in 1950.

The Dalai Lama addressing monks in Dharamsala, Himachal Pradesh province, India, seat of the Tibetan government-in-exile.

HARNESSING DESIRE

The Vajrayana school argued that the self-restraint of early Buddhist monasticism did not succeed in giving individuals mastery over their desires, but only suppressed them. For the Vajrayanists, the best way to conquer desire is to experience it fully and thereby drain it of every mystery—only then can one truly reach *nirvana*. Tantric traditions thus seek to harness desire in order to defeat it: to use metaphors from the *tantra*s themselves, they aim "to use a thorn to remove a thorn," or "to pour water in the ear to remove all water from the ear."

Vajrayanists acknowledge that their path is a dangerous one for the uninitiated. They also warn those undergoing the initiation into a *sadhana* practice that breaking the rules (for example, by using tantric practices for profane ends, or sharing the secrets with non-initiates) may result in insanity or many births in hell. But for those who are ready, and can keep to their vows, the tantric path promises *nirvana* in a single lifetime. Hence, the tradition is controlled by revered *guru*s who must judge the readiness of their disciples and choose the *sadhana* suitable for them. The initiation procedure (see box, opposite) can be a lengthy process, perhaps taking several days to complete.

A belief in bodily and cosmic energy is a central part of the beliefs and practices of Tantra. It is these energies which are harnessed in the initiate's search for enlightenment. The colors of these Tibetan prayer flags symbolize the five elements— space, water, fire, air, and earth—that constitute the essential ingredients of life.

Tantra views the body and its energies as realms of experience capable of leading persons to enlightenment, building on an assumption, first made in Hindu *yoga* tradition, that humans are microcosms of the universe. Although the *sadhana*s differ in their details, there are said to be subtle channels of energy running up the body in the spine, along which there is said to be a series of specific centers called *chakra*s ("wheels"). The goal of *sadhana*s is to move the energy released, called *bodhichitta* ("awakening mind"), upward until it reaches the "crown *chakra*" at the top of the head, the seat of spiritual evolution, and produces the experience of incomparable bliss, transformed consciousness, and *nirvana*.

Male and female bodies are said to possess distinctive and complementary energies, which Buddhists identify as *upaya* ("means") and *prajna* ("wisdom" or "insight") respectively. With female energy identified as *prajna*, it is not surprising that women and female tantric deities (*yogini*s and *dakini*s) are particularly celebrated in many *tantra*s. When these male and female forces are conjoined and cultivated, the energy unleashed can be harnessed and moved through subtle channels of the body.

Some *sadhana*s call for male and female partners to practice sexual *yoga*. In this act, the couple join as divine consorts to magnify and move the innate energy upward in both. Profane pleasure-seeking and orgasm represent failure, since union should deflect the sexual energy into the mystical channel of enlightenment. Such practices may have won the Vajrayana a receptive audience within lay communities of married householders.

THE DIVINE PATH

The tantric path requires close and highly individual guidance in order to master its rigorous disciplines. After initiation (see box, below), most tantric traditions specify a host of further preliminary practices before the full *sadhana* can be attempted. Breath control, prostrations before images, and the memorization of *mantra*s can be demanding. Most *sadhana*s require individuals to master extensive visualizations of themselves as enlightened beings—often occupying sacred spaces called *mandala*s (see pp.88–9)—as well as using ritual hand gestures (*mudra*s), dance, *mantra*s, and special ritual clothing, all to create a rich identification with the divine. To transcend any attachment to one's ordinary profane identity, initiates may indulge in normally proscribed acts in order to experience identification with the body, speech, and mind of the deity. When the identification is complete, the *tantra*s assume that the seeker will also attain the enlightenment of the focal divinity.

TANTRIC INITIATION

When a tantric master accepts a disciple to study a meditation discipline (*sadhana*), an initiation (*abhisheka*) must be undertaken to inform the disciple about the details of practice, transfer to him or her the blessings of the relevant deity on whom the practice is focused, and protect the pupil from the powerful spiritual and emotional forces to which he or she will be exposed. The teacher begins with his own visualizations: of himself as the focal deity; of ritual objects (*vajra*, bell, water vases) as pure manifestations of the elements of enlightenment; and of an image (or *mandala*) of the deity infused with the divine presence. The teacher gives the disciple blessed water for ritual purification, and has the disciple repeat the *bodhisattva* vow (to save others as oneself), sealing the vow by ringing the bell and displaying the *vajra*. He then touches a sculpture of the deity to the head of the disciple, visualizing an image of the deity issuing from it and merging with the initiate's body.

Symbols of the deity are touched to the body of the disciple at the *chakra* points (see main text). The disciple holds a rosary with the teacher, and the master utters the deity's "heart *mantra*" (see p.166) while simultaneously visualizing the *mantra* going out from his heart to that of each disciple. Other offerings and ritual gestures seal the *sadhana* transmission and connection through the teacher. Some initiations include the vow to practice the *sadhana* every day for the rest of one's life.

PART 3

HOLY WRITINGS

In the early 20th century, the Anglo-Hungarian explorer Sir Aurel Stein discovered a rich trove of Buddhist scriptures and 9th–10th century wall paintings in central Asia. This image from Ming-oi, near the Dunhuang caves on the edge of the Gobi desert, emphasizes the importance of writing in monastic life by portraying a senior monk holding a pen and a pothi *leaf as he instructs an audience of younger monks.*

PART 3 • CHAPTER 1 *Mark L. Blum*

ASSEMBLING THE DHARMA

THE BUDDHA'S "DHARMA BODY"

THE WORDS OF THE BUDDHA
The purpose of Buddhist texts was not
to provide a convenient reference work
but rather to reproduce the Buddha's
words and in doing so to acquire
spiritual merit. For example, even the
earliest of the Mahayana *sutras*, which
were conceptualized as written texts,
promise their audiences blessings for
preserving, reading, reciting, and
copying the *sutra* for others. Scholars
speak of the "cult of the book" in
Mahayana, because the physical form
of *sutras* is revered as an embodiment
of truth. The Lotus Sutra even
instructs its audience to erect shrines to
house copies of itself, before which
believers should make offerings.

When the Buddha was facing death, he addressed the belief held by some of
his followers that their religious community would be dispersed once he was
gone. To dispel this sense of depair, he made it explicit that in his absence
what he had preached to them was to become their new authority: "that
which I have proclaimed and made known as the Doctrines and the Discipline, that shall be your Master when I am gone."

Herein lies the inspiration for the Buddhist community's collective
memory of the Buddha's words, the Dharma, to become a timeless expression
of the Buddha himself. In collecting these words of truth after the Buddha's
death, in essence his followers assembled the Buddha's "Dharma Body."

According to tradition, that process began with the convening of an
assembly in a large cave at Rajagriha, during which each monk recited what
he had remembered of the Buddha's sermons, and rulings were made on
matters of monastic discipline (see also pp.186–7). The elders reviewed and
corrected this material, and from this collective effort the Buddhist canon
was born. Subsequent generations of monks were then required to learn a
portion of this material, a process which continues to the present day. Once
the scholastic writings that explained the content and intent of this material
had also become accepted as canonical, the threefold division of authoritative scripture known as the "Three Baskets" (Tipitaka in Pali, Tripitaka in
Sanskrit) was in place.

In keeping with the general transition in India from an oral to a written culture, Buddhists began to write down their canon in the first century
BCE (see pp.180–81). The texts of the Mahayana tradition began purely as
written documents and are often much longer as a result. This physical
embodiment of the truth in written form also led to new forms of religious
expression. Like relics, Buddhist scriptures became physical objects to be
revered on an altar, buried in the ground to sanctify a site, or placed inside
statues of *buddha*s and *bodhisattva*s to transform them from objects of
beauty to symbolic representations of the Buddha himself. Mahayana Buddhism is known for the adoption of Sanskrit as its normative language, and
for its "cult of the book," in which *sutra*s are revered. The Lotus Sutra, one
of the oldest Mahayana scriptures (see pp.198–201), explicitly states that
whosoever makes a copy of this *sutra* gains incomparable amounts of merit.

A 19th-century tablet of part of the Pali canon, the Tipitaka. It is one of 729 marble stelae that stand within the precincts of the Kuthodaw pagoda in Mandalay, Burma (Myanmar), and together contain the entire text of the canon. Each tablet is housed in its own miniature pagoda. (See also illustration on p.190).

Mahayana Buddhism expanded the *sutra* "basket" to include hundreds of new texts, which can often be identified by their grand opening scenes in which the Buddha emerges from a deep meditation and miracles subsequently occur. It is presumed that the content of the Buddha's sermon bestows upon his audience the transcendent insight he has just experienced in his trance state.

As Buddhism expanded outside the Indian subcontinent, conceptions of the Dharma changed in response to the historical circumstances of translation. Although only fragments exist of the canons translated into central Asian languages—and these have survived only because they are preserved within the massive canons existing in Chinese and Tibetan translation—there is so much material lost in India that a study of the Indian Mahayana tradition is impossible without them. Chinese translations begin with the arrival of the Parthian An Shihgao in 148CE; Tibetan translations probably began some time in the seventh century. In both cases, translation activity continued for centuries, with each canon growing as new material was added.

LANGUAGE AND TRANSLATION

One of China's oldest and best known Buddhist buildings, begun in 589CE, is the Big Wild Goose pagoda in the Da Cien temple, Xi'an. The current seven-story structure dates from the Tang dynasty (618–907CE), constructed to house the many scriptures brought back from India by the pilgrim and translator Xuanzang (602–664CE), and to serve as a center for their translation.

One of the most troublesome aspects of the study of Buddhism is its lack of a single authoritative language. For Sri Lanka, Burma, Thailand, Cambodia, and Laos the canonical language is Pali; for Tibet and Mongolia it is Tibetan; for China, Vietnam, Korea, and Japan it is Chinese. This linguistic diversity caused a host of questions about language to arise in the Buddhist tradition. Should there be one language designated as embodying the linguistic forms held most sacred to Buddhism? What value should be afforded to translations of scripture, and who authorizes a translation as correct or proper?

Because such fundamental terms as *karma* or *nirvana* appear in Sanskrit, today Sanskrit is often regarded as the authoritative language of Buddhism. It is likely that the Buddha spoke a related dialect called Magadhi,

THE LIMITATIONS OF LANGUAGE

Whether any language is a suitable medium for communicating the Buddha's message has long been a subject of debate among Buddhists. Some believe that truth cannot be communicated by resorting to the use of words, others that truth is something that is necessarily embedded within language.

Mahayana culture is particularly critical of language, because words inevitably mean different things to different people. To put it another way, no word can hold a perfect correspondence to what it represents—all language is therefore suspect. Composed in language, scripture is viewed by some Buddhists as thereby having lost its absolute authority—they view it as representing "conventional truth" (see sidebar, p.132). Moreover, the highest levels of truth embody concepts such as Emptiness (see p.140), which proposes impermanence. For some, then, language is simply too unstable to be a reliable vehicle for truth. This idea is expressed most explicitly in the Zen school (see pp.150–61), which believes in a transmission of truth that is non-verbal.

now a dead language, although he undoubtedly also learned Sanskrit (see p.17), because its use was common among India's élite. He is said to have advised his disciples to preach in the local language when in remote areas— a suggestion said to have given rise to the principle, later enshrined in Buddhist doctrine, that no one language has any more authority than any other. However, after the Buddha's death, Sanskrit began to dominate the religion.

The tradition of linguistic adaptation made it easy for the translation of scripture to occur, a process that began in earnest during the centuries around the turn of the Common Era, when the first Mahayana *sutras* were conceived and written in Sanskrit (see pp.196–211). Due to the enormous distances these *sutras* had to travel, and because the canon is defined differently by each Buddhist school, translations proceeded piecemeal and a comparison of canons reveals many differences between traditions.

The canon in Pali was first transmitted to Sri Lanka, from where it spread, unchanged, to southeast Asia. By contrast, the northern Indian Buddhist scriptures that spread into central Asia around the same time (the third century BCE), began in Sanskrit but underwent extensive translation as they were transmitted into a multiplicity of linguistic regions along the major trade routes, from Bactria in the west to Turfan in the east (see map on p.133). In the second century CE, the first translations into Chinese appear, and this activity continued over a thousand years. In the late eighth century CE, Tibetan translation efforts similarly began under royal sponsorship.

The peoples of southeast Asia did not translate the Pali canon when they received it, on the grounds that it was believed to be the word of the Buddha and to do so would be irreligious. The Mongolians accepted it in Tibetan form, and the Koreans and Japanese in Chinese. In China and Tibet, the texts translated were overwhelmingly Mahayana. Unlike the Pali *sutras*, which are essentially written records of an oral tradition, the lengthy Mahayana *sutras* were conceived in written form, but often took years to translate. In the modern period, there has been an effort to bring these scriptures into the living languages of Buddhist countries, and of course into European languages as well.

FORMS AND MEDIA

The transmission and preservation of Buddhist scriptures have played a major role in the development of media for the recording of language, principally in the historical form of books. More modern technological advances have allowed greater numbers of people easier access to Buddhist scripture.

Writing was not unknown in India at the time of the Buddha, but religious texts were preserved orally, and the "books" of early Buddhism in the canon, or Tipitaka, initially followed tradition. This is the reason for Buddhist *sutra*s to begin, "Thus have I heard … ," and why they contain so many mnemonic devices.

According to tradition, the first Buddhist text in material rather than oral form was the Pali canon produced in Sri Lanka in the first century BCE (see p.187). This was written on leaves of the talipot (or fan) palm tree, which was the general medium for writing throughout the Indian subcontinent and Tibet. After the young leaves were cut from the tops of the palms, they were blanched, dried, and then burnished. The text was inscribed with a metal stylus on the smooth surface, which was then covered entirely in ink. Finally, the ink was wiped away, but remained in the etched marks. Talipot is remarkably durable if protected from insects and damp. The oldest extant Buddhist palm-leaf manuscripts are Perfection of Wisdom texts dating to the eleventh century CE or shortly before.

However, as palms only grew in tropical areas, other media including birch bark, cloth (including silk), and even copper plates were also used. Birch bark was obtained from the common birch tree that grows widely in the Himalayas. The bark was cut into long, thin strips with the text written across the narrow measure. The strips were then rolled to make scrolls. The world's earliest surviving example of a written Buddhist text, dating to the first century CE, is a fragmentary birch bark scroll found in the Gandhara region (northern Afghanistan and Pakistan).

The scroll format traveled with Buddhism from northern India to central Asia and thence into China. Yet scrolls such as the Diamond Sutra (see pp.183–4) were found to be impractical for everyday reading and recitation. This problem led to them being folded like a concertina so that the desired section could be found quickly and easily. Stitching one side of such books led to the printed booklets that were widely used in east Asia from the sixteenth to the early twentieth centuries.

Buddhist sacred texts can be found in a wide variety of media. For example, in addition to scrolls, birch bark was also used to make looseleaf manuscripts. Pieces of bark were cut into sheets or leaves which were kept flat and stored between wooden boards. Old examples of this type, Vinaya texts dating from between the fourth and eighth centuries CE, have been recovered from Gilgit in the Himalayas. The leaves are quite narrow—about 5 inches (12cm) high—with the writing horizontal across the front face of each sheet. The folios are numbered, and the presence of small holes in the center of the pages indicates they were held together with a string.

The translation of Buddhist *sutra*s into Chinese began around the same time as the invention of paper there, in the second century CE. Some surviving examples of Chinese *sutra*s written in ink on paper were produced as early as the third century CE (see p.198). The next significant technological leap, in around the seventh century CE, was the invention of printing (see pp.182–3), born from the zeal in China to distribute Buddhist scripture. Woodblock printing sparked a revolution in the dissemination of books, particularly Buddhist, throughout east Asia and Tibet. From the Tang period onward, each succeeding Chinese dynasty sponsored the editing, carving, and printing of the Buddhist canon, a precedent that was duplicated in Korea, Tibet, and Japan. The standard twentieth-century Chinese-language canon, the Taisho Tripitaka, was produced in moveable type in Japan between 1924 and 1932, and totals 2,184 works in fifty-five volumes, each of a thousand pages.

Modern distribution methods mean that *sutra*s printed in one country are easily obtainable in another for the first time. The digital age is also having a major impact, and today there are a number of projects to enter Buddhist scriptures in Pali, Tibetan, and Chinese into computer databases—with revolutionary results. In the past, scholars spent months poring over hundreds of pages of scripture to find a word or phrase. Using digitized texts on CDs and the internet, words or phrases among the 55,000 pages of the Taisho canon, for example, can be found in seconds (see also pp.232–3).

A talismanic inscription—part of the mantra *of Avalokiteshvara (*Om mani padme hum*)— carved into a rock-face on a Buddhist pilgrimage route near sacred Mount Kailash in western Tibet, the snow-capped peak of which can be seen in the background.*

ART AND ARCHITECTURE *Michael Willis*

THE BUDDHIST ART OF THE BOOK

The Prajnaparamita texts ("Perfection of Wisdom" *sutra*s) from eastern India (see pp.180–81), produced in the great Buddhist monasteries that flourished under the Pala kings (who reigned from the eighth to twelfth centuries CE), were sometimes decorated with miniature paintings showing *buddha*s, *bodhisattva*s, and tutelary deities. The paintings cover just part of the folio, with most of the surface being given over to the text itself. The inside faces of the accompanying book covers provided a larger surface for painting. The covers were made of thin pieces of wood, and since text was seldom written on the face of the board, the smooth inner surface could be completely covered with miniatures. A number of examples from the twelfth century CE and later have survived and these generally show *jataka* scenes (illustrating the Buddha's former lives) or seated Buddhist divinities. They are extremely important for the history of Indian painting because they give an idea of the kind of frescoes that once decorated the monasteries of eastern India and which are now only known from fragments. Most covers on old books are later replacements, testimony to the fact that libraries and manuscripts were maintained with great care.

Birch bark and palm leaf manuscripts (see pp.180–81) had been prevalent in India for more than a thousand years before the introduction of paper in the thirteenth century CE. As a consequence, the horizontal format and other characteristics of Indian books were perpetuated even after paper came into general use. This was due to deference to established practice and

A cover for a 19th-century Burmese palm leaf manuscript of the Buddha's first sermon, "Turning of the Wheel of Law." The circles represent the wheel of the Dharma.

A Yogachara text printed in the 20th century from the 13th-century woodblocks kept at South Korea's Haein-sa monastery.

the sanctity of the book in Mahayana Buddhist practice. Tibetan manuscripts on paper thus replicate the general shape of much older palm leaf and birch bark books. The larger scale that paper allowed meant that title pages could be more elaborate and carry larger miniatures. The frontispiece often includes sheets of silk to protect the writing and images from wear. Tibetan book covers, again due to their larger size, are often elaborately carved on the outside with Buddhist divinities and symbols (see illustration on pp.184–5). Following older practices, the inner faces of these covers are painted with images, with the larger format giving rise to much greater elaboration. In this well-developed tradition of book production, there was little place for books bound in cured leather, as such materials were considered inappropriate for the texts of a religion that advocated compassion and non-violence.

In addition to being written by hand, Tibetan books and prayers are also printed from woodblocks. This technique, along with paper, was invented in China. The custom of preparing rubbings of ancient inscriptions, prevalent from Han times onward, may have been instrumental in the invention of the technique itself, but the real impetus for Chinese woodblock printing was the dissemination of Buddhist texts during the period of the Tang dynasty (618–906CE). The method consists of tracing characters in reverse on a flat block of hard wood and carving around them so that only text remains. Ink is applied to this flat surface, and a page of paper laid on top and pressed down.

Textual references indicate that Buddhist *sutra*s and images were being printed on silk and paper as early as the seventh century CE. Aside from the early *dharani* texts, the oldest surviving printed work is a Chinese

translation of the Vajrachedika Prajnaparamita Sutra. Recovered from Cave
17 at Dunhuang in central Asia and now preserved in the British Library,
this is generally referred to as the "Diamond Sutra." The text is printed on
a scroll nearly 20 feet (6m) in length with a frontispiece showing the Buddha surrounded by monks, nobles, and protective deities. The colophon at
the end reads: "Reverently commissioned for universal free distribution by
Wang Jie on behalf of his parents on the 15th day of the 4th moon of the
9th year of Xiantong [11 May 868]." The sentiments are entirely within the
devotional ambit of Mahayana and its "cult of the book" (see pages 55 and
sidebar, p.176).

The translation of Buddhist works into Chinese was a great intellectual project that involved several generations of scholars from India, central
Asia, and China. To complete their work, a number of monks—most
famously the seventh-century scholar Xuanzang—made the long journey to
India from China in order to collect texts (see illustration on p.178). Once
the translations had been completed to an acceptable standard, woodblock
editions facilitated the further spread of Buddhism and assured the integrity
of its doctrines. To produce the entire Tipitaka in China, 130,000 blocks
were carved and printed in 983CE in Chengdu, Sichuan, a site selected for its
mulberry trees, the pulp of which is ideal for paper-making.

The most celebrated and best-preserved example of the canon in Chinese was cut in Korea in the mid-thirteenth century. This is now preserved

This large (730mm by 273mm) book cover is painted with five buddha images, each displaying a different hand gesture or mudra (see p.138). They are either the five transcendent or celestial buddhas or their manifestations, the five human buddhas who are each saviours of the world in their respective epochs (see p.78). The five buddhas are a key doctrine of Mahayana doctrine, but followers of Theravada also believe in them. This is the inner face of the book cover, which would normally be kept face down against the leaves of the manuscript. It was painted in Tibet, possibly as early as the 14th century.

in the monastery at Haein-sa (see illustrations on p.183 and p.187). Of the more than twenty versions of the Buddhist canon in Chinese, this is regarded as the most meticulously prepared and complete.

That printing and the propagation of Buddhism went hand in hand is indicated by the fact that the oldest surviving specimen of printing is also from Korea. This is a *dharani*, or prayer, which dates from the eighth century CE and was found in a *stupa* in the Buddhist temple of Pulguk-sa. From Korea, printing traveled to Japan, where it was used, most notably, between 764CE and 770CE to produce the *dharani* prayers which were placed inside the one million miniature wooden *stupas*—known as the Hyakuman To—commissioned by Empress Shotoku to commemorate her defeat of a rebellion.

The reproduction of certain texts and prayers in great numbers is closely related to the practice of producing numerous small tablets from molds. These votive tablets typically carry Buddha images and texts (see illustration on p.79). The practice was widespread in India, Burma, Thailand, and central Asia and it is still common in Tibet. The printing of *dharani*s and the making of tablets, like the spinning of Tibetan prayer wheels, can be regarded as a physical parallel to the spiritual exercise of constantly repeating prayers and invocations. The underlying assumption of all these activities is that constant repetition of special religious formulas is a powerful tool for moving the devotee along the path.

PART 3 • CHAPTER 2 *Kevin Trainor*

THE THREE BASKETS

THE TIPITAKA

In the closing moments of the Buddha's life, tradition records that he reassured his personal attendant Ananda by reminding him that his final passing away did not mean the end of his teaching. After his death, the Buddha said, he could turn for instruction to the Dharma ("doctrine") and Vinaya ("discipline") that he had taught and explained. This twofold organization of the Buddha's teaching represents the whole of the Buddha's oral instruction to his community of followers over the course of forty-five years. According to Theravada tradition, this enormous body of oral teachings was given a fixed and authoritative form in a communal recitation held in the city of Rajagriha (present-day Rajgir) during the first rainy-season retreat after the Buddha's death (see pp.176–9).

Nowhere in the collection itself is there an explicit reference to the Tipitaka (in Sanskrit, Tripitaka), the "Three Baskets" of the Buddha's teaching, though there are passages referring to a specialization of labor and expertise among those in the Sangha responsible for memorizing and expounding the Buddha's teaching. Some were learned in the discourses (in Pali, *sutta*s, in Sanskrit, *sutra*s), others in the discipline (*vinaya*), and still others in the summaries (*matika*s)—lists of doctrinal topics used to systematize the Buddha's teaching for the purposes of analysis and instruction. This last category of teaching probably represents the foundation of the "third basket," later known as the Abhidhamma Pitaka (Abhidharma in Sanskrit, the "Basket of Scholastic Doctrine").

The earliest direct references to the Tipitaka occur in inscriptions from the second century BCE, and these refer to groups of people within the Sangha responsible for memorizing and reciting three distinctive genres of oral tradition. It is likely that these three general categories of Buddhist teaching were collections that expanded in the centuries following the Buddha's death, and as the Buddhist community fractured into a diversity of distinct schools, several different versions of the Tipitaka were compiled, portions of which still survive. The only complete Tipitaka collection extant today is that of the Theravada tradition, which is preserved in the Pali language, and it is this version that is described here. While the Pali canon is widely accepted among followers of the Theravada to be the literal "word of the Buddha," it is unlikely that the dialect or dialects spoken by the Buddha were equivalent to the Pali language preserved in the Tipitaka.

Several factors contributed to the formation of a closed canon of texts within Theravada. It is widely accepted that the Pali Tipitaka was first committed to writing in Sri Lanka in the first century BCE (see sidebar, opposite),

A librarian at Haein-sa monastery in South Korea, famed for its possession of 81,000 original engraved wooden printing blocks dating from the 13th century, when an officially sponsored complete edition of the Tripitaka (in Pali, Tipitaka) in Chinese was printed.

THE WRITING DOWN OF THE PALI CANON

Accustomed as we are to the reading of written texts, it is difficult to appreciate the value attributed to oral transmission within early Buddhism. For the first several centuries after the Buddha's death, his authoritative teachings were passed down within the Sangha from teacher to student, and to know a teaching meant not simply to have read it but to have committed it to memory. It was only under circumstances of extreme social disintegration caused by invasion, warfare, and famine that members of the Sri Lankan monastic community turned to writing to preserve the Buddha's teachings. Tradition records that in the first century BCE five hundred *arhat*s gathered together at a cave temple at Aluvihara in central Sri Lanka and wrote down the entire Tipitaka along with the Pali commentaries. Subsequently, the copying and dissemination of Buddhist texts became important practices, and it is these written texts that have served as the basis for much Western scholarship on Buddhism since the nineteenth century. However, memorization and oral recitation of the Buddha's teachings continued to be highly prized practices in Theravada Buddhist cultures. As one Pali aphorism has it, "Knowledge in books [is like] money in someone else's hands: when you need it, it's not there."

and this no doubt facilitated the process of codification. In addition, splits within the Sri Lankan Sangha at this time probably also contributed to the fixing of the canon. The Mahavihara community claimed to be the exclusive bearer of orthodox tradition, buttressed by its closed collection of scriptures, its extensive corpus of written commentarial tradition, and by a series of monastic chronicles that narrated the lineage of the fraternity and its royal supporters. In the twelfth century CE it became exclusively identified with Sri Lankan Theravada tradition when the Sangha was reunited under Mahavihara leadership (see pp.124–5).

The collection of written Pali canonical texts preserved in Sri Lankan and southeast Asian Theravada tradition is voluminous. It includes more than ten thousand of the Buddha's discourses and runs to more than fifty volumes in its printed Western edition. While most of the manuscripts upon which modern editions are based date back only to the eighteenth and nineteenth centuries, the Pali Tipitaka is widely acknowledged to preserve some of the earliest historical sources for reconstructing early Buddhist tradition. It should not, however, be equated with "original" Buddhism.

THE VINAYA PITAKA

THE ORDINATION OF WOMEN
The Vinaya account of the
establishment of the women's monastic
lineage reveals that the Buddha was
concerned about the effect this might
have on lay opinion. After first
resisting the request of his aunt
Mahaprajapati for ordination, the
Buddha finally agreed to ordain
women with the understanding that
they observe a series of additional
rules that symbolically and
institutionally subordinated the
women's community to that of the
men. While the account depicts the
Buddha explicitly affirming that
women are capable of attaining
nirvana, he also appears concerned to
avoid criticisms that might have arisen
had the women's community been
given more independence from male
supervision. However much the
Sangha represents an ideal of social
disengagement, the Vinaya also reflects
an awareness that the continued
survival of the Sangha depends upon
lay approval and material support.
The women's ordination lineage died
out in Sri Lanka in the eleventh
century, but there have been recent
controversial attempts to reestablish it
(see pp.222–5).

The first of the three collections of texts that comprise the Tipitaka is
the Vinaya Pitaka ("Basket of Monastic Discipline"), commonly called the
Vinaya, and its priority in the scriptural canon suggests its importance for
the Sangha and for Theravada tradition. The collection falls into three
general divisions. The first, the Suttavibhanga ("Explanation of the
[Patimokkha]"), includes a comprehensive set of rules for monks and nuns
called the Patimokkha, consisting of 227 rules for men and 311 rules for
women. The Suttavibhanga also narrates the specific circumstances in the
life of the Sangha that led to the establishment of each rule. The significance
of these rules for the life of the monastic community is ritually embodied
through the Patimokkha (Sanskrit, Pratimoksha) ceremony, which members
of the Sangha perform twice monthly during the Uposatha observance days
(see box, opposite, and p.108).

The second division of the Vinaya is called the Khandhaka ("The
Multitude") and it has two sections. The first provides a lengthy narrative
of the Buddha's life from his enlightenment up to the ordination of his two
chief disciples, Sariputta (in Sanskrit, Shariputra) and Moggallana

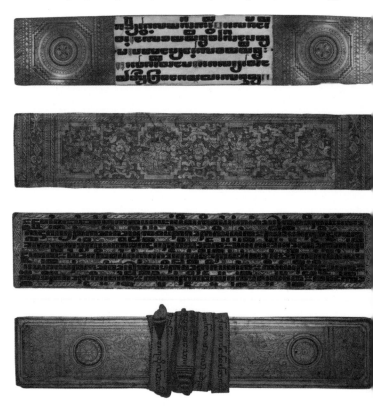

Three examples of covers from copies of the
Kammavaca ("Official Act of the Sangha"),
a collection of extracts from the Vinaya
Pitaka. These texts were often copied in
Theravada countries, but Burmese families
might commission an often ornate copy of
the Kammavaca to commemorate the entry
of a son into monkhood. From left to right:
an 18th-century gilded and lacquered
wooden cover with Pali text in Burmese
script on ivory; a 19th-century gold and red
lacquer-decorated cover alongside an
example of the Pali text in black lacquer;
and a 19th-century red and gold cover with
a woven manuscript ribbon.

THE UPOSATHA HALL AND THE PRATIMOKSHA

One of the primary sources of unity within local Theravada monastic communities has been the regular observance of the Pratimoksha (Pali, Patimokkha) ceremony. All higher-ordained members of the community gather together in the Uposatha hall twice each month and ritually affirm their collective purity with respect to each of the regulations. Even though this public recitation no longer provides the context for publicly confessing disciplinary infractions, it continues to define collective identity within local monastic communities and within their broader fraternal affiliations. The ritual boundaries (*sima*s) which circumscribe specific local monastic residences determine where monks participate in the twice-monthly ceremony, and a special, ritually bounded structure is traditionally set apart within the monastery grounds for this ritual, as well as for formal acts of the Sangha such as ordination. The ceremony also serves as a symbolic assurance to the laity that the

A portion of a 3rd- or 4th-century CE Sasanian-style fresco from Miran, central Asia, showing Siddhartha (left) expounding the Vinaya law, accompanied by six early disciples and members of the Sangha.

local Sangha continues to abide by the Vinaya and thus remains a highly productive "field of merit" for those who support its upkeep with material donations.

(Maudgalyana), as well as rules for important rituals such as ordination and Patimokkha recitation. The second section provides a more detailed elaboration of monastic deportment and responsibilities, outlining a set of standards that governs interactions both within the community and between monastics and laity. It also includes a narrative of the establishment of the women's monastic order and the first and second councils.

The third section of the Vinaya, the Parivara ("Appendix"), gives detailed summaries of the extensive material found in the previous two sections. These summaries organize the contents of the Vinaya into a variety of forms that facilitate the instruction of new members of the community.

The detailed and complex code of monastic discipline outlined in the Vinaya may strike many contemporary Westerners as legalistic and unnecessarily concerned with matters of external behavior. But such a perspective fails to recognize the extent to which Theravada Buddhist tradition has linked mental cultivation and the realization of the Dharma with the total pattern of life defined by the code of monastic discipline. The Vinaya has served Theravada Buddhist communities for more than two and a half millennia as the foundation for practicing the Buddha's path to *nirvana* and for ensuring the continued survival of the Buddha's Dharma.

THE SUTTA PITAKA

The Kuthodaw pagoda in Mandalay, Myanmar (Burma), the capital of King Mindon (reigned 1853–78) in upper Burma, was where the monarch convened a Buddhist council in 1871 for the purpose of establishing a definitive text of the scriptures. The texts verified at the council were engraved on stelae, each of them housed in one of the individual pagodas visible here (see also p.177).

The Sutta Pitaka ("Basket of Discourses") is the most famous section of the Theravada canon. By far the largest of the three collections of texts that comprise the Tipitaka, it consists of more than thirty volumes of *sutta*s (Sanskrit, *sutra*s) or discourses attributed to the Buddha and his early followers, and is traditionally grouped together under five sections: the Digha Nikaya ("Group of Long Discourses"); the Majjhima Nikaya ("Group of Medium-Length Discourses"); the Samyutta Nikaya ("Group of Connected Discourses"); the Anguttara Nikaya ("Group of Discourses Arranged Numerically in Ascending Order"); and the Khuddaka Nikaya ("Group of Small Texts"), a miscellaneous collection of texts not clearly fitting into any of the other collections.

The discourses typically open with the formula, "Thus have I heard...," a statement traditionally linked with the disciple Ananda's recitation of each discourse when the collection of the Buddha's teachings was communally established after his death (see pp.176–9 and 186). This concern to trace the *sutta*s back to eyewitness, or more accurately "earwitness," testimony suggests the importance that Theravada tradition has accorded the historical link between its teachings and the life of Gautama Buddha. The *sutta*s also generally specify where the Buddha was residing when he gave each teaching and who his audience was, again suggesting that however universal the truth of the Buddha's teachings, each discourse is expressed in a manner appropriate to the specific concerns and abilities of those to whom it is directed.

Despite the wide range of questions addressed by the Buddha in the Sutta Pitaka, the discourses also suggest that the Buddha did not consider all questions worthy of investigation. For example, he refused to answer speculative questions about the age and extent of the universe, the relationship between the life-force and the body, and the continued existence of the Buddha after death. One famous discourse in the Majjhima Nikaya relates that when a monk threatened to leave the Sangha unless the Buddha answered these questions, the Buddha responded with the simile comparing the monk to a man shot with a poisoned arrow (see p.70). The man foolishly refused treatment until he knew several particulars about the archer who had shot the arrow, the bow that was used, and the arrow itself. The Buddha urged his followers to avoid wasting time and energy with such speculative debates and to focus instead on what really matters: the cause of suffering and its cessation.

Although it is held that some monks and nuns memorized the whole of the Sutta Pitaka, it is clear that parts of the collection were particularly influential because of their relevance to the regular activities of the monastic community and the needs of the laity. For example, because Sangha members regularly recite texts from the Mahaparitta ("Book of Protection"), a special set of protective verses collected from various parts of the Sutta Pitaka, these discourses are widely known and venerated even though they are not a separate collection within the "Basket of Discourses" (see sidebar, p.85). Some of these verses come from the Khuddakapatha ("Short Passages"), a brief collection of passages in the Khuddaka Nikaya that probably originated as a kind of primer for novice monks and nuns. Two other texts from the Khuddaka Nikaya, the Jataka ("Birth Stories") and the Dhammapada ("Verses of the Dharma") have also been very influential. Both of these texts are frequently quoted when monks instruct the laity and scenes from the Jataka, which recounts the previous lives of the Buddha, feature prominently in Buddhist temple paintings (see sidebar, right). Novice monks commonly memorize all 423 verses of the Dhammapada, a collection of excerpts in verse form from the Buddha's teachings. One of the first complete Buddhist texts widely translated into Western languages, the Dhammapada has been well known in Europe and North America since the middle of the nineteenth century. Verse 183 of this text has come to be regarded by many as a summary of the Buddha's entire teaching: "Avoiding every bad deed; cultivating what is beneficial; purifying one's own mind; this is the instruction of the *buddha*s."

JATAKA STORIES

Stories about the previous lives of the Buddha circulated widely in the Buddhist world and appear in a number of early texts. The most well known is the Jataka ("Birth Stories"), a collection of more than five hundred stories that forms part of the Sutta Pitaka. The date of this compilation is uncertain, but already in the second century BCE recognizable *jataka*s were being shown in relief sculpture in north India. The stories demonstrate how the Bodhisattva took the opportunity of each rebirth to cultivate generosity, compassion, and other noble qualities. While the *jataka*s reinforced the unique character of the Buddha-to-be, they also made him more accessible and the path to enlightenment more tangible. He had many different lives and passed through a broad cross-section of possible rebirth statuses, being born as king, prince, nobleman, minister, Brahman, merchant, deer, bird, antelope, dog, horse, monkey, bull, ox, ascetic, tree-spirit, and even celestial being. The stories thus represent in dramatic terms the working out of the principle of *karma* and provide a living tableau of the varieties of sentient experience. The Jataka is also among the canonical texts that monks most commonly draw upon in teaching the laity.

THE ABHIDHAMMA PITAKA

The third collection of writings within the Tipitaka is the Abhidhamma Pitaka (Abhidharma Pitaka in Sanskrit, the "Basket of Scholastic Doctrine"), and its form and content differ greatly from the other two collections. While the latter are for the most part set in a narrative form in which the Buddha responds to particular questions or incidents in the life of his community, the contents of the Abhidhamma Pitaka are highly abstract and systematic. One might describe them as an attempt to express what the world looks like from the perspective of one who has gained perfect enlightenment. Despite the difficulties of comprehension that these texts pose, Theravada tradition has celebrated their great value, particularly as a support for those engaged in advanced forms of meditation. The texts are held to be so profound that even lay people can benefit greatly from hearing them recited, even if they cannot consciously grasp their meaning, and excerpts are commonly chanted at funerals and during festivals.

The Abhidhamma has seven books. The first, the Dhammasangani ("Enumeration of Phenomena"), details the eighty-two *dharma*s or phenomena that constitute all reality according to Theravada tradition. (Other Buddhist schools identified different numbers of *dharma*s; the Sarvastivadins, for example, recognized seventy-five.) Eighty-one of these are "conditioned" or come into existence interdependently; one is unconditioned: *nirvana*. Viewed from the perspective of perfect enlightenment, these *dharma*s are the basic factors that account for all experience, and the Buddha's path of deliverance can be understood as the means for coming to see things "as they really are"; that is to say, as constituted by the conditioned arising of these *dharma*s. One who directly perceives these phenomena realizes the non-existence of any permanent self and therefore puts a final end to any sort of desire or attachment. Such a person has realized *nirvana*, the one unconditioned *dharma*. Abhidhamma thus deals with both the process of realization and the truth to which that process leads; it has been described as an exploration of reality that encompasses philosophy, psychology, and morality.

These *dharma*s are explored using a variety of approaches by the other six books: the Vibhanga ("Book of Treatises"), the Dhatukatha ("Discussion Concerning the Elements"), the Puggalapannati ("Description of Individuals"), the Kathavatthu ("Points of Controversy"), the Yamaka ("Books of Pairs"), and the Patthana ("Book of Relations"). The latter is the longest in the entire Tipitaka, exceeding six thousand pages in the Siamese (Thai) edition. It examines the twenty-four laws of conditionality that define all the possible relationships among the *dharma*s, and it is considered the most profound expression of the Buddha's perfect enlightenment (see box, opposite).

This monument at Bodh Gaya marks the spot traditionally associated with the Buddha's meditation on the Abhidhamma during the fourth week following his enlightenment.

SARIPUTTA

On entering the image hall of a Sri Lankan Buddhist temple, one typically sees an image of a monk at the Buddha's right side; this is his great disciple Sariputta (Shariputra in Sanskrit), esteemed by Theravadins as second only to the Buddha in his grasp of the Dharma. Tradition has it that when the Buddha was teaching the Abhidhamma to his mother (see box, opposite), he also descended each day from heaven to instruct Sariputta.

THE BUDDHA PREACHES THE ABHIDHAMMA TO HIS MOTHER

Despite evidence that at least parts of the Abhidhamma Pitaka were composed after the Buddha's death, Theravada tradition maintains that the whole of the teaching goes back to the Buddha himself. According to this school, he meditated upon the contents of the Abhidhamma during the fourth week after his enlightenment (see illustration, opposite), and as he reflected on the seventh book (the Patthana), his body gave off brilliant multicolored rays, a sign of the text's profound truth.

Theravada tradition further maintains that Gautama Buddha, like his predecessors, rose up into the "Heaven of the Thirty-three" in order to teach this truth to his mother who descended there to hear it, having been reborn as a male *deva* in the Tushita heaven. It is said that he taught this text for three months. One of the most celebrated incidents in the Buddha's biography follows this heavenly sojourn when he descends to the city of Samkashya along a jeweled ladder, flanked by the gods Brahma and Shakra (Indra) on ladders of silver and gold. The Buddha's ascent to the Heaven of the Thirty-three was immediately preceded by his performance of the "Miracle of the Double" at Shravasti, in which he rose into the sky and flames and water emerged simultaneously from his body (see p.122).

This 18th-century painting in Bangkok's Buddhaisawan chapel shows the Buddha descending to Samkashya along a jeweled ladder.

COMMENTARIES AND CHRONICLES

The mountain in Sri Lanka known as Sripada or Adam's Peak, seen here silhouetted on the cloud cover, has been a place of Buddhist pilgrimage for centuries (see p.112). The English name derives from a Muslim tradition that the strange indentation on top of the mountain (believed by Buddhists to be the Buddha's footprint) was caused by Adam having stood there on one leg for a thousand years in penance.

Theravada Buddhist tradition is defined not only by the Tipitaka; it also possesses an extensive commentarial literature of great antiquity and authority. Like the Tipitaka itself, these are traditionally traced back to the first council immediately following the Buddha's death. These orally transmitted traditions of interpretation, it is said, were brought to Sri Lanka in the third century BCE by Mahinda (Mahendra), the monk credited with introducing the Buddha's teaching to the island (see pp.124–5). It is not known in what language the early oral commentaries were composed, but by the time the scholar Buddhaghosa, the most revered author of Pali commentaries (see sidebar, opposite), encountered them in written form at the Mahavihara monastery in Sri Lanka in the fifth century CE, they were preserved in the Sinhala language. Buddhaghosa organized and translated this vernacular tradition into a comprehensive collection of Pali commentaries that established a framework for the interpretation of the Tipitaka for Theravadins down to the present day. So authoritative were his translations, one account has it, that the earlier Sinhala commentaries were burned after he completed his work.

PALI CHRONICLES

The fifth century CE marked the period during which Mahavihara monks began to compose the highly influential Pali *vamsa* or "chronicle" texts. Like the Pali commentaries (see main text), the earliest examples of this literature are based upon earlier Sinhala traditions no longer extant, and they provide valuable sources for the history of Theravada tradition in India and Sri Lanka.

An extensive chronicle literature developed in south and southeast Asia, including compositions in vernacular languages. A central preoccupation of this literature is the continuity of Theravada tradition as defined through unbroken monastic lineages and the preservation and veneration of the Buddha's relics. The chronicle literature thus established the importance of particular Buddhist religious sites and of ritual practices such as *stupa* construction and pilgrimage (see pp.108–9 and pp.112–13). In the past century these chronicles have played a prominent role in forging Sinhala Buddhist nationalist sentiments (see p.229). The powerful influence of these traditions is suggested by the periodic expansion of the Pali Mahavamsa ("Great Chronicle"), which was most recently updated in the late 1980s under the auspices of the Sri Lankan government.

The Pali chronicles record that the Buddha visited Sri Lanka; on one visit, illustrated in this painting at Kelaniya temple, Sri Lanka, he is said to have driven the yakkhas *(demons) off the island by expanding his meditation mat, which is ringed with fire.*

Buddhaghosa is traditionally credited with composing commentaries on all the Tipitaka books, with the exception of several writings in the Sutta Pitaka known as the "Group of Small Texts." These were supplied by other commentators, most notably Dhammapala in the fifth and sixth centuries CE. The Pali commentaries, in turn, gave rise to an extensive Pali subcommentarial literature. At the same time, some Pali commentaries were translated back into vernacular languages, making them accessible to a broader lay audience.

As well as clarifying the meaning of individual words and grammatical ambiguities in the canonical texts, the commentaries also guided the interpretation of individual passages in a manner consistent with the larger body of the Buddha's teaching, all of which, it is said, serves the purpose of helping beings realize *nirvana*. In addition, the literature is a rich repository of stories that help scholars to reconstruct the history of Buddhism and ancient Indian and Sri Lankan society. The extensive body of Pali commentaries and also the Pali chronicle literature (see box, above) bears witness to two fundamental dynamics running throughout Theravada history: it simultaneously provides evidence for the historical and geographical diversity of Theravada traditions, and highlights an ongoing Theravada preoccupation with the continuity, through both texts and relics, of the Buddha's presence.

BUDDHAGHOSA

According to tradition, Buddhaghosa, whose name means "Speech of the Buddha," was born near Bodh Gaya and had a brahmanical training, but later converted to Buddhism and went to the ancient Sri Lankan capital, Anuradhapura, to translate the Sinhala commentaries preserved by the Mahaviharins into Pali. As a test, the Mahavihara monks instructed him to write a commentary on two lines of the Samyutta Nikaya. The result was Buddhaghosa's famous Visuddhimagga ("Path of Purity"), a huge encyclopedia of the Buddha's path to *nirvana*. It is said that the *deva*s twice hid his text, but each time Buddhaghosa rewrote it without changing a single syllable. He went on to compose commentaries on most of the Tipitaka (see main text).

PART 3 • CHAPTER 3 *Mark L. Blum*

MAHAYANA SCRIPTURES

PERFECTION OF WISDOM *SUTRAS*

Although accurate dating of the first appearance of any scripture in Buddhism is difficult, many scholars believe that the production of Mahayana *sutra*s (see p.132) began in the first century before, or perhaps shortly after, the beginning of the Common Era.

Early Mahayana thought is revealed in the Lotus Sutra (see pp.198–201), the Pure Land *sutra*s (see pp.202–3), and the corpus of scriptures known as the Prajnaparamita ("Perfection of Wisdom" sutras), each presenting somewhat different conceptions of the cosmos and humanity's relation to it. The Perfection of Wisdom *sutra*s derive their name from their singling out of wisdom from the list of virtues ("perfections") that all *bodhisattva*s cultivate. The Prajnaparamita is thus an extensive treatise on the nature of religious wisdom; it focuses on the absolute as *shunyata*, or Emptiness (see pp.140–41)—a notion not entirely absent in early discourses, but not of central concern.

Pre-Mahayana traditions often spoke of the importance of grasping the significance of non-self (*anatman*), impermanence (*anitya*), and suffering (*duhkha*). Many Buddhists, though, found *anatman* counter-intuitive and one new explanation asserted that while there is no permanent substance underlying an individual sentient being, the component parts (*dharma*s) of

The Turfan basin in eastern Turkestan in central Asia (present-day Xinjiang Autonomous Region, China), stands astride the ancient Silk Road, part of the network of trade routes along which the Mahayana Buddhist sutras were transmitted into China and beyond. The basin is the location of many early Buddhist sites and caves, including those at Bezeklik, seen here, where there is also a monastery cut into the side of a gorge in the Flaming Mountains. The frescoes in the monastic cells at Bezeklik date to the 8th–10th centuries CE.

all beings have an unchanging "own-nature" (*svabhava*) (see p.192). The Perfection of Wisdom *sutras* view this analysis as insufficient—instead, they assert that individual *dharma*s are also without a fixed self-nature. This position was to some extent an attack on the assumption that *nirvana* was a "thing" that one could gain or attain. The Prajnaparamita's core criticism was that in striving to develop more refined statements on truth, many people became attached to their "correct" opinions. In the Perfection of Wisdom tradition, all opinions must be abandoned because they inevitably prejudice perceptions: Emptiness means to be emptied of all speculative thinking (see pp.140–41).

The dating of the Perfection of Wisdom *sutras* is unclear, but the oldest one, the "Perfection of Wisdom in 8,000 Lines," appears to have emerged, at least in an early form, in the first century BCE. Based on this, the second-century CE Buddhist philosopher Nagarjuna, who also expounded the doctrine of Two Truths (see p.132), founded an interpretive tradition known as Madhyamika ("School of the Middle Way") or Shunyatavada ("School of Emptiness"). Nagarjuna had an enormous impact on the evolving Mahayana tradition. According to him, the Buddha's teaching of Dependent Origination means that nothing can be known except in terms of something else. *Nirvana* itself only has meaning because it is set apart as the opposite of the messy, karmic world of *samsara*. Thus *nirvana* for Nagarjuna is just another dimension of the world before us: we simply cannot perceive it because we are unable to abandon our dualistic mode of comprehension. Although he does not quote the Perfection of Wisdom *sutras* directly, what Nagarjuna brought out from their doctrines is not simply that all the phenomena of the universe are dependent upon each other, but the more difficult concept that this interdependence *is* the universe itself. This tradition thus deconstructs individual identity of any kind, concluding that what we perceive is only the illusion of separate entities.

A Tibetan translation, ca. 1500, of the "Perfection of Wisdom in 8,000 Lines," probably the oldest of the Mahayana sutras, *dating to the 1st century* BCE. *The cover, shown here, is decorated with paintings of the Buddha (left) and the Perfection of Wisdom (right), personified as the four-armed goddess Prajnaparamita.*

LITERARY FORMS
The Perfection of Wisdom *sutras* take a variety of forms, from the extreme brevity of the Heart Sutra, which consists of a single, direct statement on the unity of opposites ("Form is none other than emptiness; emptiness is none other than form"), to the lengthy "Perfection of Wisdom in 100,000 Lines." They also include practical homilies, such as those in the Diamond Sutra ("True charity occurs only when there are no notions of giving, giver, or gift").

THE LOTUS SUTRA

As with many Buddhist scriptures of Indian origin, it is uncertain when the Saddharma Pundarika ("White Lotus of the True Law," better known as the "Lotus Sutra"), was created, but it is generally dated to the early phase of Mahayana, either the first century BCE or the first century CE. It became one of the most influential of all Buddhist scriptures, particularly in east and central Asia, where its cultural impact is profound. The Lotus Sutra's popularity is attested by the early Chinese catalogs, which record no fewer than seventeen Chinese translations (of which only three remain). The earliest surviving text of the *sutra* is a Chinese translation made in 286CE by the central Asian missionary and scholar Dharmaraksha. Since the end of the nineteenth century, a number of Sanskrit texts have been discovered in Nepal, Tibet, Kashmir, and central Asia, each somewhat different in content.

The Lotus Sutra is a long scripture, with twenty-seven or twenty-eight chapters, and tradition has found it convenient to divide these into two sections. The first fourteen chapters are called the section on "expedient teachings," the means of communicating the Dharma through parable and example. The remaining chapters expound the doctrine of the eternal nature of the Buddha. Zhiyi (538–597CE), the great Chinese scholar of the Lotus Sutra, labeled the first half the "traces" of truth and the second half the "actual" truth. Today, three doctrinal themes are generally identified in this work: a universal path to liberation; the eternal nature of the Buddha; and a pragmatic course for human endeavor represented by the *bodhisattva*. But whatever theme it is presenting, the Lotus Sutra is characterized by a polemical attitude toward the non-Mahayana goal of *arhat*ship and a narrative style that is grandiose.

One of the problems addressed in the Lotus Sutra, and indeed in all Mahayana *sutra*s, is the absence of the Buddha from the world and the corresponding loss of his salvific teaching. In the chapter entitled "The Life Span of the Tathagata [the Buddha]," the Buddha reveals that hundreds of thousands of billions of eons (*kalpa*s) have passed since he became a *buddha*, and that he only gave the appearance of departing from the world in order to prevent people from taking his presence for granted. In fact, he says, "I have always been here. I shall never pass away." This process of redefining the Buddha transforms him into a symbol of omniscience and transcendence, a cosmic entity capable of summoning *buddha*s residing on other planets to come and bear witness to this wonderful *sutra* called the Lotus. Far from being lost, the Buddha's salvific powers are much in evidence, because since he appeared on earth, hundreds of billions of sentient beings have attained the point where they will pass out of the cycle of rebirth. While he preaches, according to the text, celestial drums resound in heaven, celestial jewels rain down from the heavens, and so forth.

The *sutra* is also known for its skillful use of parables and metaphors, many of which are alluded to so frequently in the literature of China, Korea, and Japan that early Western scholars of those cultures saw the influence of the Lotus as akin to that of the Bible in the Christian world. The *sutra* includes numerous popular and frequently quoted parables. In one well-known example, a young son runs away from home and is gone for fifty years. In the interim, the father becomes rich and powerful, while the son lives from hand to mouth without job or home. One day, the aged father accidentally spots his son and has him forcibly brought to his residence. Without meeting him directly, the father offers his son a menial job for relatively high wages. The son accepts, not knowing who his employer is. Rewarded for his honesty and hard work, he is quickly promoted. When the father is near death, he calls a meeting of prominent members of the community and his staff, including the

The frontispiece from a 17th-century manuscript of the Lotus Sutra, painted in gold, silver, and blue on indigo paper for a prominent family. Two bodhisattvas (bosatsu in Japanese) are seated on lotus petals in a pagoda, which has guardian figures nearby.

An extract from a Japanese edition of the Lotus Sutra, which is one of the oldest of all Mahayana sutras. It is said that to make a copy of the Lotus Sutra is a way to earn much merit.

son. He then announces that he is the man's father and is passing on his fortune to him. Aspiring only to a decent living for an honest day's work, the son is astonished. The *sutra* then explains that the son represents a Hinayana follower (that is, a non-Mahayana Buddhist) who works hard but only aspires to the modest goal of *arhat*ship. The Buddha is the father who holds a far greater treasure—*buddha*hood—than the son can imagine.

Another much quoted parable is "The Burning House," and here once again a wealthy father represents the Buddha. Some children are happily playing inside their house when it suddenly catches fire, but they are so focused on their games that they fail to notice. The father implores them to leave the house, but they do not heed him. He considers carrying them out, but there are too many of them and the doorway is narrow. Instead he tells them that outside he has prepared an unusual array of carts pulled by oxen, antelope, and goats. Excited by this news, they all run for the door, pushing and shoving in great haste. Once they are outside, the father gives each of them a large cart adorned with jewels and bells, accompanied by attendants. Although these are not what he described while the children were in the burning house, they are more than pleased with what they find. From the perspective of the Buddha, most people are unaware that the greed and attachment which accompany their struggles for wealth and power (represented by the children's games) create an anxiety that is dangerous to their spiritual well-being (this danger is represented by the fire). But when this point is expressed directly it is too often unappreciated, so the good teacher is not above exploiting his listeners' tendency for attachment by using enticements (the animals) to lead them to a more profound understanding (the jewels and bells, representing the Dharma).

The ultimate objective of the *sutra* is traditionally seen to be, in essence, that doctrines of the Buddha have the nature of cosmic truth; that faith is important for participating in that truth; and above all, that there is "one vehicle" (*ekayana*) for expressing the truth. ("One vehicle" is a synonym for Mahayana, and "one" should be read as "universal.") The story of Devadatta in chapter twelve of the Lotus Sutra illustrates this. A cousin of the Buddha, Devadatta initially joined the community of monks under the Buddha's leadership, but then grew jealous of him. He did his best to divide the Sangha and even made several attempts on the Buddha's life. But then we learn that in a previous life he did many good deeds and as a result it is predicted that he, too, will eventually reach *buddha*hood. The moral is that even the most evil person can be liberated and reach self-perfection.

The Lotus Sutra became the doctrinal basis for China's Tiantai sect, founded in the late sixth century CE (see also pp.144–5). Zhiyi, considered its second patriarch, used earlier Chinese philosophical categories of *li* (underlying or inherent principle) and *shi* (the expression of this principle in phenomena) to construct a systematic understanding of Buddhist philosophy in which the Lotus Sutra is regarded as the most complete expression of Buddhist truth. One of Zhiyi's most influential achievements was to organize the vast array of Buddhist teachings and scripture into a five-tiered chronological scheme, reasoning that the Buddha's doctrine of Skill in Means (see pp.142–3) meant that he had ordered the presentation of his Dharma in a way that enabled his listeners to proceed from the relatively simple to the complex, from concrete to abstract truths. Zhiyi combined the doctrine of a universal *buddha*-nature in the Nirvana Sutra (see pp.206–7) with the Lotus Sutra's creative approach to teaching and practice in a way that proved extremely influential throughout east Asia.

NICHIREN'S VISION OF UTOPIA

One of the strongest expressions of faith in the Lotus Sutra is found in the work of the Japanese monk Nichiren (1222–1282). Although Nichiren had quit the Tendai sect, his belief in the Lotus Sutra as the pinnacle of all Buddhist expressions of truth was unshaken. He reasoned that as the *sutra* was the embodiment of infinite power, if all other religious institutions would recognize its authority and abandon their beliefs its enormous salvific power would protect Japan from the threat of Mongol invasion. Nichiren was totally committed and prepared to die for his cause. He regarded Buddhism not so much as a means to individual emancipation as the basis for realizing a utopia.

Drawing on Tantra symbolism, Nichiren fashioned a ritual system that used a *mandala* with the Lotus Sutra in its center. The ritual object of reverence in Nichiren temples has always been a scroll with the name of the *sutra* in the center and pithy phrases and names of celestial *bodhisattva*s around it. The core religious practice for Nichiren is to face this scroll and repeatedly recite the phrase *namu myoho renge kyo*, or "Homage to the Wondrous Sutra of the Lotus."

Triptych of Nichiren calming the sea on his way into exile. He saw it as his destiny to lead the world into a new era governed by a purer form of Buddhism.

PURE LAND *SUTRAS*

An 18th-century printed Chinese text with an illustration of the Pure Land, from a monastery in Rehe, Mongolia. It conveys the "cloud-nature" of the paradisial realm of Amitabha, who is seated at the center, flanked by Avalokiteshvara and Mahasthamaprapta. Pure Land followers believe they can attain this realm, where the conditions are ideal to attain nirvana, *if they show the necessary devotion.*

All *buddha*s are believed to purify, by their very presence, the realms where they dwell, and therefore in one sense every *buddha* resides in a "pure land." However, what is termed Pure Land Buddhism (see pp.144–7) specifically refers to the doctrines, practices, and beliefs that focus on Amitabha Buddha, the *buddha* of Infinite Light, alternatively called Amitayus, the *buddha* of Infinite Life (and known as Amituo Fo in China and Amida Butsu in Japan). Both because he presided over the western paradise called Sukhavati—one of the paradises that are said to exist in each of the four cardinal direction— and because of his enormous appeal as a result of the qualities associated with him, Amitabha Buddha features in literally hundreds of Mahayana *sutra*s.

The development of the Pure Land school in east Asia was influenced by one group of writings in particular, consisting of three *sutra*s and a treatise (see box, opposite), which form the principal authoritative basis for the Pure Land sects established in Japan in the thirteenth century.

The first two of the three *sutra*s share the same Sanskrit title—Sukhavativyuha Sutra ("Describing the [World of] Bliss Sutra")—although their titles in Chinese translation differ. The Western world follows east Asian tradition and they are conveniently labeled as the Shorter Sukhavativyuha Sutra and the Longer Sukhavativyuha Sutra. The Shorter Sukhavativyuha Sutra is chiefly concerned with describing the wonders of Amitabha Buddha's Pure Land, although it also discusses in some detail the characteristics of Amitabha himself. In other words, it establishes this particular *buddha*-realm as a genuine paradise. It also promises that Amitabha will protect all who cultivate the mindfulness practice that takes this *buddha* as its object. The word used in the *sutra* to describe such practices is *nianfo* (Chinese) or *nembutsu* (Japanese), a word that originally referred to a wide array of *buddha* contemplation practices. After the establishment of the Pure Land school in China in the seventh century CE, in which the practice of invoking Amitabha's name became authoritative, this *sutra* was interpreted as implying that the invocation *nembutsu* practice (see box, p.144) was singled out by Amitabha as deserving of special attention.

The Longer Sukhavativyuha Sutra is known for its lengthy description of the career of the *bodhisattva* Dharmakara, his compassionate vows to assist the world should he attain *buddha*hood, and the confirmation that he has indeed reached his goal and should be

THE JINGTU LUN

The title of the fourth central Pure Land text refers to it as a commentary on the Longer Sukhavativyuha Sutra, but generally it is simply known as the Jingtu Lun ("Pure Land treatise"). The treatise was accepted as equally authoritative as the three Pure Land *sutras* but it exists only in Chinese translation. Originally written by Vasubandhu, who may or may not be the same Vasubandhu known for his Abhidharma and Yogachara scholarship, this work contributed significantly to the development of Pure Land practices. The Jingtu Lun offers five forms of devotion: expressing reverence for Amitabha Buddha; praising his virtues by reciting his name; vocal statements of aspiration to be born in the Pure Land; contemplation of the physical form of Amitabha Buddha, the *bodhisattvas* who also reside in his Pure Land, and the Pure Land itself; and transferring one's own merit to other sentient beings to assist them in also reaching the Pure Land.

known by the name Amitabha Buddha. From the earliest strata of Mahayana *sutras*, the Longer Sukhavativyuha Sutra is structured to impress upon the believer the fact the forty-eight separate vows enumerated therein (the earliest version has only twenty-four) are actually there because they were promises made if Dharmakara became a *buddha*, and, as Amitabha, he is now a *buddha*. The eighteenth vow is widely viewed as the most important statement of the *buddha*'s covenant with sentient beings, promising to bring them to his Pure Land if they have the right attitude: "May I not attain complete enlightenment if, once I have attained *buddha*hood, there are any sentient beings in any of the ten regions of the universe who are unable to attain birth in my realm despite embracing a single-minded desire to be reborn in my land with sincerity, faith, and joy, even down to those [who embrace this attitude] for as few as ten moments of thought. This excludes those who have committed the five grave offenses [see p.207] and those who have slandered the Dharma."

The third *sutra* is the somewhat enigmatic Guan Wuliangshou Fo Jing ("Contemplation on the Buddha of Infinite Life Sutra" or "Visualizing the Buddha of Limitless Life Sutra," or simply "Contemplation Sutra"). Of later date than the other two *sutras* or the Pure Land treatise, it differs from the Longer Sukhavativyuha Sutra, which excludes from the Pure Land those who have committed one of the five offenses or *icchantika* (see p.207), in explicitly permitting offenders to be reborn in the Pure Land, following the trend expressed in the Nirvana Sutra. Addressed to a woman, the *sutra* extols thirteen different forms of visualization meditation connected with Amitabha and the glories of his realm. It then describes nine different grades of people according to their spiritual capacities, as well as how their experiences of rebirth in the Pure Land will differ as a result of these differences. Finally, it recommends the recitation of the name of Amitabha for those in the ninth and lowest category of believer who are unable to do the difficult visualization and contemplation exercises extolled in the *sutra*. But for Shandao and Honen (see pp.144–7) it is in this section that Amitabha's true intention is revealed, for they argue that the purpose of the Pure Land *sutras* is to provide universally accessible avenues to spiritual emancipation for ordinary people.

YOGACHARA *SUTRAS*

Some two centuries after the lifetime of the philosopher Nagarjuna (second century CE), there arose a new Mahayana school usually known as Yogachara ("Practice of Yoga"). The name is testimony to the prevalence of yogic traditions of meditation and controlled exercise in all Indian religions of this time, including Buddhism. The Yogachara school reflects a feeling that the doctrine of Emptiness—expounded in the Perfection of Wisdom *sutras* and clarified in the logic of Nagarjuna—went too far in negating the reality of phenomena as asserted by the Abhidharma philosophers. Yogachara instead presents a study of the phenomena of consciousness, combined with specific meditative disciplines to effect a fundamental transformation of that consciousness.

The *sutras* that have been most influential for the development of this school are the Sandhinirmochana ("Revealing the Esoteric [Meaning]") Sutra and the Lankavatara ("Entering into Lanka") Sutra. The Abhidharma Sutra is frequently cited, although the complete text is now lost. Another work, the Avatamsaka ("Flower Garland") Sutra, also exhibits some Yogachara themes. The Sandhinirmochana Sutra expresses most of the fundamental Yogachara doctrines: the three natures of phenomena—imaginary, dependent, and perfected; the meditative practices of calmness and insight; and the radical doctrine of an unconscious, or "storehouse" consciousness. Written somewhat later, the Lankavatara goes further and asserts that phenomena have no existence independent of the mind that perceives them. It describes conscious experience as operating like waves on the surface of an ocean—a metaphor that was to have great resonance in the later tradition. It is also the scriptural source of vegetarianism as a Mahayana ideal.

The Yogachara school is also called the "Mind Only" or "Consciousness" school (Vijnanavada), and its thinkers assert that our primary religious concern should be about the relationship to what we perceive. The focus is not on what we perceive but how the perceiving organ, the mind, is functioning—for it is the mind that determines the meaning of perception, not its object. They argue that our mental functions can never be considered objective because everyone's mind is shaped by its unique experiences, both external and internal. Not only is the mind that processes the data different from every other mind, but the sensory apparatuses used to take in that data are also in some sense "programmed" by the mind. In this view, our eyes are not neutral sensors sending unaltered light information to the brain. Each pair of eyes can only function insofar as they are part

Frontispiece from a late 16th-century folding format edition of the Dafungguang Fo Huayan Jing or Flower Garland Sutra (in Sanskrit, Avatamsaka Sutra), depicting the Buddha surrounded by arhats and bodhisattvas. The core text of China's Huayan school, a rival to the Tiantai, the approach of the Flower Garland Sutra was highly intellectual. It taught the emptiness and interpenetration of all phenomena, but acknowledged that few could ever follow its teachings. Like the Lotus Sutra for the Tiantai, the Flower Garland Sutra was said by the followers of Huayan to be the highest form of truth in existence.

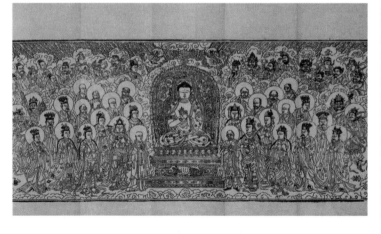

A South Korean monk meditating on a rock. One of the important scholars in the Yogachara school's development was Vasubandhu, who stated unambiguously that everything we know and perceive is an internal mental function. The tradition states that proper meditation is the key to liberation specifically because it enables the practitioner to overcome such dualistic perceptions of subject and object, which reaffirm the presumption of the self as a subject separate from what is perceived. This conclusion provoked much debate but it clarified the core message of the school's founder, Maitreya (ca. 270–350CE), that what Buddhism is really concerned about is the nature of subjectivity.

f something called "visual consciousness," and the precise manner in which nat operates can never be the same for any two people, because everyone has unique set of visual experiences upon which to draw.

If there is no perception without interpretation, it is ultimately the mind nat determines what we see, hear, taste, and so on. The Yogachara under-:anding of how the mind dominates or "constructs" our experience infers the xistence of two mental functions that are uncannily close to Freud's theory of go (*manas* or *adana*) and unconscious (*alaya*), though these two "levels" or activities" of consciousness operate somewhat differently. In its analysis of he three natures of phenomenal knowledge—imaginary, dependent, and per-:cted—the Yogachara tradition states that every thought, utterance, and ction produces a seed of karmic information that is deposited in the uncon-:ious, or "storehouse" consciousness (see sidebar, right). These seeds natu-ally associate with the individual's presumptions about the world, which perfume" them until they ripen to the point of manifesting as a new event.

"THE EMBRYO OF A BUDDHA"
According to the Yogachara idea of "storehouse consciousness" (see main text), the unconscious mind also contains karmic seeds from previous lives that have yet to mature. This creates the potential for endless rebirths with no chance of liberation, were it not for the fact that we are also born with pure seeds of the knowledge of truth that is the source of liberation. In the Yogachara *sutra*s these seeds are metaphorically called the "embryo of a *tathagata* [*buddha*]" (*tathagatagharba*) (see p.162). Through meditation, we can weaken our preconceptions and psychological constructs and in doing so nurture the "embryo" to the point where we experience what is called "signless cognition"—perception without identification of either subject (that which knows) or object (that which is known).

NIRVANA SUTRA

The Nirvana Sutra has been one of the most influential *sutra*s in east Asia. The title is in fact derived from two distinctly different *sutra*s, both called *Mahaparinirvana* ("Great Final Nirvana Sutra"), in which the word *nirvana* or *parinirvana* refers to the death of the Buddha, his "final emancipation" (see pp.40–41)

Robed monks paying homage to a statue of the reclining Buddha at Wat Xieng Khuan, near Vientiane, Laos.

The original text, the Mahaparinibbana-sutta in the Pali Tipitaka—which also survives in a Sanskrit and in four Chinese versions—is a short narrative that traces the Buddha's final days on the road at the age of eighty, relating the gastrointestinal infection that caused him such pain and ultimately debilitated him to the point that he knew he would not recover (see p.41). The Buddha utters a final short sermon in which he encourages his followers to ask whatever they are unsure about as he will not survive the next day. Everyone is silent, so he admonishes his disciples with a famous passage in which he points out that just as in life he has never asked them to look to him as the source of their liberation, neither should they do so after his death: "Cleave to the Dharma [teachings], and be an island unto yourselves," he declares. The Mahaparinibbana-sutta ends with a description of the Buddha's funerary procession and cremation, and the distribution of his ashes.

Sometime in the fourth century CE, a quite different Nirvana Sutra emerged that was translated into Chinese between 410CE and 420CE by a monk from central Asia. While the setting and basic storyline are identical to those of the earlier version—the final days of the Buddha, his illness, final sermon, and death—the presentation is entirely different. It is a fully realized Mahayana *sutra*, being very long and grandiose in its narrative style. The text makes liberal use of analogy and folk narratives to illustrate philosophical points, some of which are quite entertaining but whose doctrinal import is less than clear. But the greatest impact of this later Nirvana Sutra lay in its radically new doctrine of religious truth.

The philosophy of the Nirvana Sutra presupposes both the Lotus Sutra and the Perfection of Wisdom *sutra*s, but it goes

eyond them in its assertion of the *buddha*-nature. Sentient beings are said
o possess a sacred nature that is the basis for them becoming *buddha*s.
lthough obscured from view by normal consciousness, and inevitably cor-
upted or defiled by desire, greed, delusion, vanity, fear, anxiety, and so on,
nis *buddha*-nature is in fact our true nature. And, as distinct from the posi-
on taken by the Yogachara school and its *sutra*s, this nature is universal
nd completely unsullied by whatever psychological and karmic state an
ndividual may be in.

One of the most interesting aspects of the Nirvana Sutra is that its
rst half repeats a phrase that is common to many of the Mahayana scrip-
ures in the context of religious aspirations: "this is available to all except
ne *icchantika*." The *icchantika* refers to the five grave offenses or crimes
vhich are considered to be so heinous that those people who have commit-
ed any of them are to be presumed incapable of attaining enlightenment in
nis lifetime. The five include parricide, matricide, physically harming a
uddha, and so forth. But then the *sutra* stunningly reverses its position in
ne second half and makes the bold statement that even *icchantika* have the
uddha-nature. This marked a radical shift in the Buddhist view of the
armic bonds that restrict us.

Traditionally, every individual has been said to possess the power to
hange his future through the proper cultivation of wisdom and compas-
ion, but differences in actual accomplishment are genuine because of dif-
erences in individual spiritual capacity, which is unavoidably the result of
revious *karma*. One Buddhist theory suggested that people should be
ivided into five different classes or "families" of spiritual potential, with
ne class that had none at all, the *icchantika*. The Nirvana Sutra in effect
eclared such speculation to be incorrect, and its new doctrine of truly uni-
ersal spiritual potentiality meant that previous *karma* was no longer an
nsurmountable hindrance for anyone. The *sutra* even went so far as to state
hat the nature of the Absolute is personal, blissful, eternal, and pure—a list
f qualities that stands in contrast to the usual Buddhist view of the known
elf as impersonal, characterized by pain or discomfort, impermanent, and
mpure. The effect of this uncharacteristically positive statement on indi-
idual potential and the joys of *nirvana* was profound in China and
hroughout east Asia as a whole. It affected all the schools of Chinese Bud-
hism, but became most pronounced in the Chan or Zen tradition (see
p.150–161).

Chan also drew heavily on a creative treatise called the "Awakening
f Faith in Mahayana," which sought to clarify further the Nirvana Sutra
eaching of *buddha*-nature. Here, two kinds of enlightenment were
ffirmed: original and experiential. Original enlightenment is the name
iven to our intrinsic but unrealized enlightened nature that makes possible
he enlightenment experience. The treatise uses a metaphor of waves upon
he ocean, saying that what we see are the waves (experiential enlighten-
nent) but these are only surface activity of the mind caused by the winds of
xperience; without the huge body of water underneath that is original
nlightenment, no such waves would be possible. But this does not mean
hat what we experience is any less fundamental, any less real, because both
nderlying water and wave are alike in their wetness.

An 18th-century Japanese ink painting on a leaf of the Ficus religiosa, *better known as the pipal, bo, or Bodhi tree, the species under which the Buddha attained* nirvana *(see pp.34–5). Buddhist paintings on leaves of this sacred tree are a popular genre. This example is one of a traditional series featuring 18 arhats.*

TANTRIC WRITINGS

by John Peacock

The tantric Buddhism, or Tantra, found in Tibet and Tibetan-influenced regions (see pp.162–3) is based on a body of writings known as *tantra*s. In the Tibetan tradition these are considered to be the secret teachings of the Buddha, although modern scholarship reveals that many of these documents were composed more than a thousand years after his death. The word *tantra* itself is Sanskrit for "fabric" or "woven" and is applied to both Hindu and Buddhist forms of practice. In its Buddhist context, the term points to a "woven" interconnectedness of experience whereby the body, speech, and mind of the tantric practitioner are brought into a unique harmony that is directed toward the achievement of *buddha*hood. In general, the tantric path is to be distinguished from the more "gradual" path toward awakening, as tantric practice aims at attaining *buddha*hood in a short a time as possible.

Tantra does not really represent a further development in Buddhist thought since its philosophical basis is to be found in the Madhyamika and Yogachara schools of Mahayana Buddhism (see pp.196–7 and pp.204–5). What characterizes tantric Buddhism is a specific approach to the Buddhist path in terms of meditational practice. Thus tantric literature, rather than being concerned with philosophical debates on subtle points of Buddhist doctrine, is for the most part entirely centered on practice, and much tantric writing is devoted to painstaking descriptions of meditational procedures. Tantric literature is hierarchically divided into four distinct categories: *kriya tantra* ("action *tantra*"), *charyatantra* ("performance *tantra*"), *yogatantra* and *anuttara-yogatantra* ("highest *yoga tantra*").

The vast majority of extant tantric documents are preserved in the Tibetan language. Buddhist tantric literature is written in a highly oblique and obscure literary form known as "twilight language" (*sandhya bhasha*), designed to conceal its contents from non-practitioners (but not, as some early Western commentators assumed, to conceal "degenerate" tantric sexual practices). A brief example of a tantric text (the Vajrayogini) concerned with generating wisdom in the practitioner illustrates "twilight language": "Before me are the forms of wind and fire, surmounted by three human heads and upon the heads is the syllable *A* which is transformed into a skull bowl; inside the skull-bowl are the syllables *go ku na ha da*, which transform into the five fleshes, and the syllables *pi mu shu ma ra*, which transform into the five nectars." Such symbology is incomprehensible without the key provided by the oral commentary of a tantric master.

Using complex symbolism, tantric literature links together visualization practices associated with particular deities (see p.163), and elements of liturgy and ritual, all aimed at the harmonization of body, speech, and mind toward the goal of *buddha*hood. Before aspirants can begin any given tantric practice, they must undergo initiation (*abhisheka*) into it, a procedure that may involve the recitation of an entire *tantra* (see also pp.172–3). The "lower" *tantra*s (*kriyatantra* and *charyatantra*) mainly detail devotional

Two Tibetan monks chanting prayers from sacred texts to exorcise demonic forces from the dancing arena prior to a performance of the Shanak, or "Black Hat Dance," in Himachal Pradesh, northern India. Adorned with silk brocade costumes, the monks wear elaborate wide-brimmed black hats. The Black Hat Dance celebrates the legend that King Langdarma of Tibet, who is said to have been a persecutor of Buddhism, was assassinated in 842CE by a Buddhist monk wearing a black hat and robe, in the sleeves of which he concealed a bow and arrows. This un-Buddhist act is justified on the grounds that it prevented Langdarma acquiring any more bad karma through further evil deeds.

and ritualistic practices centered on particular deities. *Tantra*s of the *yoga* and *charya* class also give extensive descriptions of various complex visual- ization and meditational practices.

The practices detailed in these classes of *tantra* are directed toward a "given" or "chosen" deity (*ishta-devata*), with the aim of progressively incorporating the wisdom or compassion associated with the deity into the psyche of the practitioner. Initially this process starts with the deity being visualized as external to the practitioner (the "generation stage," *kye rim*). When the image can be formed perfectly in the mind, the tantric practitioner progresses to visualizing himself or herself as the deity (the "completion stage," *dzog rim*). Visualizing oneself as the deity during the meditation ses- sion allows one to manifest the qualities of that deity (for example, wisdom or compassion).

While these techniques are also utilized in the *tantra*s of the higher classes (*yogatantra* and *anuttara-yogatantra*), this form of literature becomes increasingly concerned with complex theories of *yoga*. The highest *yogatantra*s outline practices in which the devotee visualizes "winds," "channels," and "centers" of the body. In such visualizations the practitioner learns to manipulate bodily "energies" with the aim of transforming the body into that of a *buddha*. In addition, the highest *yogatantra*s identify the bliss encountered in sexual union with the primordial bliss of the mind. The initiation and practice of the *anuttara-yogatantra*s may therefore involve sexual union with a consort (see p.173). However, in some Tibetan Buddhist schools (the Gelugpa in particular), where the monks are celibate, this process is visualized. In either instance, the union of the female and male is said to represent the union of wisdom (female) and compassion (male) and the iconography of Tibetan Buddhism often depicts deities associated with highest *yogatantra* in sexual union. This process, as it is outlined in the *tantra*s, is not associated with the gratification of desire but, as with all forms of Buddhist practice, with its transmutation. Desire, in this instance, is actively employed as a means to reach the goal of extinguishing desire, a technique that is termed "turning the hindrance into the path."

A manuscript of the Bardö Thol Dro, better known as the Tibetan Book of the Dead. The illustrations depict some of the fierce deities that are believed to appear to the deceased in the days after death, at the end of which the dead person will either be liberated from samsara or be reborn.

THE TIBETAN BOOK OF THE DEAD

The work whose title is regularly translated as the Tibetan Book of the Dead is known in Tibetan as the Bardö Thol Dro, rendered more accurately as "Liberation through Hearing in the *Bardö*." It is drawn from the Nyingmapa school of Tibetan Buddhism and reflects aspects of Nyingmapa doctrine. The recitation of the work by the bedside of a dead or dying person is intended to awake in that person the consciousness that is directed toward liberation (*nirvana*). However, as the eminent Tibetan *lama* Sogyal Rinpoche (1944–) has observed, the Bardö Thol Dro is as much a book aimed at the living as at the dead, because it provides solace for the bereaved and a clear guide to their own death.

The intermediate state (*bardö*) between death and rebirth is said to last for forty-nine days and during this period the consciousness of the deceased will encounter both peaceful and terrifying images. These are considered to be manifestations of the deceased's own mind and are known as the "*mandala*s of the peaceful and wrathful deities." The recitation of the Bardö Thol Dro into the ear of the dead or dying person is meant to act as a step-by-step guide to the arduous journey through the *bardö* state. The recital continues for the forty-nine day period, being addressed to an image of the deceased after the corpse itself has been disposed of. Throughout the recitation, the dead person is constantly reminded that any images with which they are confronted are simply manifestations of their own mind: "Do not be afraid, do not be terrified, do not be bewildered, recognize this as the form of your own mind."

It is believed that if the consciousness of the deceased recognizes the visions correctly as aspects of itself, there is a very real possibility that it will attain liberation from the cycle of rebirth. Failing this the deceased may find a more fortunate rebirth. However, a failure to recognize the symbols encountered in the *bardö* will propel the consciousness into another birth simply by the force of its *karma*.

Different *tantra*s and the techniques contained within them have assumed greater or lesser importance within the various schools of Tibetan Buddhism, depending on the lineage of teachers by whom the teachings were transmitted. For example, Tsongkhapa (1357–1419), the founder of the Gelugpa school (which is headed by the Dalai Lama), instituted a thorough reform of tantric literature and its associated practices and greatly reduced the number of *tantra*s that were regarded as authentic and acceptable by the Gelugpa. In contrast, the oldest school of Tibetan Buddhism, the Nyingmapa, recognizes a prodigious quantity of tantric works, all of which it considers to be authentic.

One specialist area within the corpus of tantric literature is those works which deal with death, rebirth, and the *bardö*, the name given to the "intermediate state" between death and rebirth. These texts are of enormous importance because they clearly reflect the Tibetan position on the process of liberation—they are not derived from Indian Buddhist works but appear to be entirely Tibetan in origin. The most famous of these works, certainly in the West, is the Bardö Thol Dro, which has come to be known as the "Tibetan Book of the Dead" (see box, above). However, this work is just one example of an extensive genre of literature that is to be found in all the schools of Tibetan Buddhism, with each work reflecting the various doctrinal positions of its school. Much of the material in this form of tantric literature clearly reflects the influence of pre-Buddhist (Bön) traditions on the development of Tibetan Buddhist doctrine.

PART 4

BUDDHISM TODAY

A nun silhouetted in a window of Thien Vien Truc Lam, a Zen monastery at Da Lat in the central highlands of Vietnam. Housing large numbers of both monks and nuns, the monastery is one of the largest Zen meditation study centers in Vietnam. The presence of a renowned teacher, Thich Thanh Tu, insures that the center remains popular both locally and with Vietnamese from abroad who return for meditation studies.

PART 4 • CHAPTER 1 *David Chappell*

THE EXPANDING COMMUNITY

NEW BUDDHIST MOVEMENTS

The most dramatic recent developments in Buddhism have been the new popular movements that have arisen since the Second World War. In the past, Buddhist monastics gave educational and moral guidance to society and the state, but today secular institutions have taken over these traditional teaching and welfare roles. In a global culture with modern media, increased social mobility, fewer state controls on religion, and international networking, traditional monastic roles are being questioned, while large new movements focused on the laity are developing different ways to practice Buddhism.

New Japanese Buddhist movements such as Soka Gakkai (see box, p.217) are well known, and several important groups have arisen in other Buddhist cultures, such as Fo Kuang Shan (Fo Guangshan) (FKS) in Taiwan. Founded in 1967 by a monk, Shih Hsing-yun (Shi Xingyun) (1927–), FKS teaches "humanistic Buddhism," which aims to improve life in this world, rather than emphasizing rebirth in the Pure Land after death. From its headquarters near Kaohsiung (Gaoxiong) in southern Taiwan, FKS coordinates a cadre of young, educated monastic leaders, most of whom are nuns, and provides a school system from kindergarten to university level. The influence of FKS extends to overseas Chinese communities through its financial sponsorship of the World Fellowship of Buddhists, founded in Bangkok in 1950, and the World Buddhist Sangha Council, founded in 1966. Two years after the lifting of martial law in Taiwan in 1989, FKS organized its lay supporters into a worldwide organization called the Buddha Light International Association (BLIA), and it now has temples in Australia, South Africa, and thirty other countries. Another socially active movement of Taiwanese origin is the Buddhist Compassion Relief Tzu-chi Association (see p.217),

A very different kind of movement began in Sri Lanka in 1958 when A.T. Ariyaratne (1931–), invited his urban, middle-class students at the Buddhist Nalanda College in Colombo to serve poor villagers by digging wells and teaching healthcare. Further work camps were soon organized on the basis of a process called *shramadana* ("donating labor"). Believing that development must follow a dual track, both personal and social, the group adopted the name Sarvodaya, meaning the "awakening, or uplifting, of all." In 1967 Sarvodaya began the Hundred Villages Development Scheme to teach not only the value of working together, but how to include everyone in discussions and decision-making. By the 1990s half of Sri Lanka's 24,000 villages had enlisted in *shramadana* practice. After civil war broke out in Sri Lanka in 1983, Sarvodaya organized peace negotiations and provided relief for both sides in the conflict. Influenced by Gandhian ideals, Sarvodaya builds inclusive communities in which everyone is valued and minorities are especially recognized. Urban-dwellers find spiritual fulfillment, while villagers feel valued by learning new skills and gain strength through serving others in a constant process of *shramadana*.

New lay-centered organizations have also arisen in South Korea. Although founded in 1916, Won Buddhism became a popular movement only in the 1960s and 1970s, when it grew to more than a million members. The leaders of Won do not follow monastic rules, although female leaders are usually celibate. Established in the 1960s, the Chontae (Tiantai) Order has a core of more than 400 monastics, and has also attracted more than a million lay members. Both movements teach the idea of social service, "meditation in action" (mindfulness during daily activities), and global responsibility.

In Thailand, Buddhism is the official state religion, but various reform movements have arisen as a result of a belief that its rituals have become

Novice monks at the Nan Hua temple of the Buddha Light International Association (BLIA), Bronkhorstspruit, near Pretoria, South Africa. The migration of Asians to other parts of the world and the growth of new Buddhist movements has contributed to the expansion of Buddhism beyond its traditional home in Asia. The BLIA is an international organization of Taiwan's Fo Kuang Shan (see main text).

Buddhist organizations played an important role in the international relief effort that followed the devastating Taiwanese earthquake in 1999. Most prominent was Taiwan's own Tzu-chi association (see sidebar, opposite), which was the first volunteer organization on the scene, even ahead of the national emergency services. Other organizations also made a valuable contribution: here, members of Soka Gakkai International (see box, opposite) assist with the transport of relief goods.

divorced from the spiritual needs of the people. The Santi Asok movement began in 1973 as an internal reform of monastic discipline and quickly attracted 100,000 lay supporters. However, the Supreme Buddhist Council requested the state to arrest and defrock Santi Asok's leader, Phra Bodhiraksa (1934–), for creating a separate Buddhist group. Although the movement has not been disbanded, Santi Asok monks are denied state privileges and are forbidden to wear traditional saffron robes. In contrast, the Venerable Buddhadasa (1906–93) applied Buddhist thought outwardly to economic and political issues in what he called "dhammic socialism." Avoiding the state Buddhist hierarchy, he built a forest retreat, Suan Mokkh, in 1932. Although Buddhadasa's teachings gained him international recognition as Thailand's leading Buddhist intellectual, his ideas lack strong institutional power.

Today, the most successful Thai Buddhist movement is Dhammakaya, founded by a lay woman, Khun Yay Ubasika Chandra Khonnokyoong (1908–2000), whose meditation methods for the laity were inspired by the monk Luang Por Wat Paknam (1884–1959). The movement's beautifully landscaped center at Wat Dhammakaya (founded by Khun in 1970) has become a unifying pilgrimage site for lay practitioners; more than 100,000 white-clad followers have attended some of the ceremonies held there. By organizing meditation programs through universities across Thailand, rather than setting up branch temples, Dhammakaya has avoided the charge of being a sect. In 1995 Dhammakaya produced a CD-ROM of the Pali Buddhist scriptures, and in 1999 its monastic students were the most successful Pali students in Thailand. By 2000, Dhammakaya had fourteen international centers in Europe, America, and Asia. Dhammakaya attracts members of the Thai élite as well as educated and upwardly mobile urban lay people, who are required to give substantial financial support.

At the other end of the economic scale is the Trailokya Bauddha Maha-sangha (TBM, "The Universal Sangha of the Buddha of the Three Realms"), a movement largely comprised of former Untouchables (see p.14) in western India. After the public conversion to Buddhism in 1956 of Dr Bhimrao Ramji Ambedkar, a prominent Untouchable and chief author of the Indian consitution, millions of Untouchables embraced the religion as their best hope for emancipation (see pp.234–7). Encouraged by the Buddha's rejection of the caste system, millions of members are implementing his vision through new institutional structures to provide legal protection, education, social development, and international backing. In a challenge to traditional monasticism, TBM leaders do not have to become celibate monks.

An alliance has developed between TBM and another reform group, the Friends of the Western Buddhist Order (FWBO), founded in England by the Venerable Sangharakshita (born 1925 as Dennis Lingwood). When Ambedkar died suddenly in 1956, Sangharakshita participated at his funeral and gave many talks to Ambedkar's new followers. After Sangharakshita returned to England, he founded FWBO in 1967. The order has grown to include more than eighty centers in Europe and America. In 1978 several of Sangharakshita's students returned to India to assist TBM, notably Dharmachari Lokamitra (born Jeremy Goody in 1947), who is continuing Ambedkar's social revolution.

NEW MOVEMENTS IN JAPAN

Perhaps the best known new lay movements are those that arose in Japan to provide egalitarian support groups for displaced individuals after the Second World War. Many of these movements were centered on the Lotus Sutra (see pp.198–201), especially Reiyukai, Rissho Koseikai (RKK), and Soka Gakkai International (SGI). Based on the teachings of Nichiren (1222–82), these groups focus on chanting the phrase *namu myoho renge kyo* ("Homage to the Wondrous Sutra of the Lotus"; see p.201) as a way to transform one's personal life condition and act as *bodhisattva*s by working toward world peace through the development of culture and education. RKK has sponsored worldwide inter-faith cooperation with the World Conference on Religion and Peace, while SGI has worked more through its school system, at all age levels, and through the United Nations. The third SGI president, Daisaku Ikeda (1928–) began a global mission in October 1960 and there are now members in most countries.

Although a lay organization, SGI was affiliated to a priestly sect called Nichiren Shoshu and courted controversy because of its aggressive evangelism against other religious groups. However, in 1991 SGI rejected the priesthood and is now promoting dialogue as a way to transcend divisions. It has become the most ethnically diverse form of Buddhism today.

TZU-CHI (ZOJI)

Founded in 1966 by a Buddhist nun, Shih Cheng-yen (Shi Zhengyan) (1937–), the Buddhist Compassion Relief Tzu-chi Association (Tzu-chi/Zoji) is the largest non-governmental organization in Taiwan, with annual donations exceeding US$300 million, largely administered by its five million lay volunteers. The livelihood of Tzu-chi's 100 monastics is entirely separate from its relief work, and its financial records are open to public scrutiny.

Tzu-chi is renowned as a source of medical and social welfare aid, and for building hospitals, a medical school, a nursing school, and a university. Their bone marrow register is the third largest in the world, and they run medical missions around the world, including a hospital in Shanghai, China, where financial support from Taiwan for social relief is welcomed. They were prominent in organizing rapid relief following the terrible earthquake that struck Taiwan in 1999: their work included rebuilding 75 of the more than 200 schools destroyed in the disaster.

Shih Cheng-yen interprets relief work not as simply giving to the poor and sick, but as an opportunity to learn from them in order to improve the spiritual condition of practitioners, who are believed to gain important self-knowledge and lasting happiness through such service.

SCHOLARS AND PRACTITIONERS

A quiet revolution is currently taking place in Buddhist education, challenging Buddhist views of history that were once considered sacred. By critically analyzing scriptures and the Buddhist texts discovered at Dunhuang in China (see below), scholars of Buddhism are reassessing sectarian claims, especially about the origins of Mahayana scriptures and of Zen. At the same time, Buddhists east and west are seeking to transform cultural values through non-sectarian, but value-centered, humanistic education.

By the early nineteenth century, one consequence of Western colonialism in the Indian subcontinent was the collection and study of ancient Pali, Sanskrit, and Tibetan texts. Eugène Burnouf (1801–52) compiled a Pali grammar, read Tibetan Buddhist texts, and translated into French a Sanskrit Lotus Sutra which the British scholar Brian Houghton Hodgson (1800–94) had sent to Paris from Kathmandu in 1837. At the same time, Pali texts were also being studied in Sri Lanka, and in 1881 the Pali Text Society was founded in England. In the late nineteenth century, Buddhist texts were being critically studied in London, Oxford, and Paris, much to the surprise of Japanese scholars who visited Europe soon after 1868, when Japan embarked on a period of rapid modernization and opening up to the West.

As Buddhist universities—such as Ryukoku, Komazawa, Otani, Taisho, Hanazono, Rissho, Bukkyo, and Soka—flourished in Japan in the twentieth century, so textual analysis developed also, but only recently have Japanese studies attained a global influence. For example, the Buddha's death was dated at 544BCE by Buddhists in Sri Lanka, India, Burma, Thailand, Laos, and Cambodia, who celebrated its 2,500th anniversary in 1956. At the same time, many Western scholars dated the Buddha's death at 483BCE. But only in recent years have international scholars considered Japanese research in support of a death date in the fourth century BCE (see also p.23).

A more serious issue arose for east Asian Buddhists when textual analysis suggested that Mahayana texts had not been the direct teachings of the historical Buddha, but developed later. The question of origins was compounded for the Zen tradition when a huge library of Buddhist texts (more numerous than the Dead Sea Scrolls) a thousand years old were discovered in 1907 by Sir Aurel Stein at Dunhuang in western China. In studies led by Yanagida Seizan after the Second World War, it was suggested that Zen had not been brought from India to China by Bodhidharma (died ca. 533CE), but had only arisen after his death (see also p.150).

Although most Japanese Buddhist scholars are also priests, sectarian teachings are often isolated from research that contradicts sectarian claims, such as the belief that the Lotus Sutra was taught by the historical Buddha, or that Zen priests receive an unbroken transmission from the Buddha. This separation of scholarship from religious practice was challenged recently by a Japanese movement called "critical Buddhism." The movement is led by two members of Soto Zen and Komazawa University, Hakayama Noriaki and

Matsumoto Shiro, who criticize the Japanese idea of *buddha*-nature as deviating from true, original Buddhism. Many Western scholars applaud this critical spirit, but deny that an "original" Buddhism can be found apart from the diversity of historical interpretations. In Western colleges, Buddhism is generally taught in a secular or inter-religious context, where it is represented as one among many forms of religious expression grounded in a shared humanity.

Buddhism in turn has traditionally challenged academic studies. Zen is famous for its slogan "non-reliance on words and letters" and tells stories of Zen monks who burned Buddhist books and ridiculed scholar monks. Paradoxically, the Zen/Chan lineage in China has the most writings of any Buddhist tradition. Other movements use education to downplay sectarian labels and to promote humanistic and spiritual values. In Taiwan, the FKS and Tzu-chi (see pp. 214–17) emphasize education, social service, and "humanistic Buddhism" (see sidebar, opposite) as ways to build a Pure Land here on earth, and to this end in the 1990s they established six new Buddhist universities in Taiwan and the United States.

A young Theravada monk studying at the 18th-century Wat Saket in Bangkok, one of Thailand's oldest temples. Many present-day Buddhist educational movements seek to underplay the distinctions between the major Buddhist traditions in favor of an emphasis on values shared by followers of all ethical and religious traditions.

THE DIASPORA AND CONVERTS

The first Buddhist temples in the West were built not to convert Westerners but for Buddhist priests to provide services for their compatriots overseas. However, this situation began to change when Anagarika Dharmapala (1864–1933) of Ceylon (Sri Lanka) and Shaku Soyen (1859–1919) of Japan attended the World's Parliament of Religions in Chicago in 1893 as representatives of Buddhism, and began to attract the interest of Westerners. Shaku Soyen's translator was Daisetz Taitaro Suzuki (1870–1966), who was later to become the most influential Buddhist missionary to the West.

A monk in meditation at Samye Ling monastery in southern Scotland, the first Tibetan Buddhist monastery in the West. Established in 1967 by two exiled Tibetan tulkus of the Kagyu Karmapa school, Chögyam Trungpa Rinpoche and Chuje Akong Rinpoche, it was named for Samye, Tibet's first monastery, which was founded in the 8th century CE.

A Japanese Pure Land denomination popularly known as Shin Buddhism was the first Buddhist tradition to establish itself outside Asia. Japanese Shin immigrants founded temples in Hawaii in 1889 and in California in 1899, and by 1930 Shin was the largest Buddhist organization in the West, subsequently becoming known as the Buddhist Churches of America (BCA). By 1997 the number of BCA priests had declined to 61 and only about 17,000 families belonged to the organization. Other Japanese Buddhist denominations based mainly in immigrant communities in the United States—Zen,

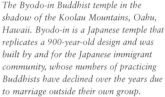

The Byodo-in Buddhist temple in the shadow of the Koolau Mountains, Oahu, Hawaii. Byodo-in is a Japanese temple that replicates a 900-year-old design and was built by and for the Japanese immigrant community, whose numbers of practicing Buddhists have declined over the years due to marriage outside their own group.

Nichiren, Shingon, and Jodo—have experienced a similar decline among the third and fourth generations as increased out-marriage takes place. However, another Japanese group, Soka Gakkai International, was established in the United States in 1960 (SGI-USA) and has become the largest and most ethnically diverse Buddhist organization, with around 45,000 active members. By 1997 its district leaders in nine major cities were 39 percent Euro-American, 27 percent African American, and fewer than 20 percent of Japanese ancestry.

A strong ethnic base is also found among Chinese, Vietnamese, Korean, Thai, and Sri Lankan Buddhist groups in the West. Chinese Buddhists have a substantial presence worldwide, reflecting the large Chinese diaspora. The biggest Chinese temple organization is Fo Kuang Shan (FKS), with offices in more than 30 countries. FKS has twelve temples in Europe, while in 1998 there were eighteen FKS-affiliated temples among the 125 Chinese Buddhist groups in the United States. However, the FKS membership remains more than 95 percent Chinese (see p.214). The second largest international Chinese Buddhist group is Tzu-chi, with more than five million members worldwide, almost all of Chinese origin (see p.217).

The Buddhist Society in London lists more than 350 Buddhist groups of all traditions in the United Kingdom, while there are more than 400 groups in Germany, and 140 Tibetan centers alone in France. Such groups are typically small, but millions of Westerners are sympathetic to Buddhist values and ideas, as is evident from the huge audiences that attend talks by the 14th Dalai Lama (see p.227) and the Zen monk Thich Nhat Hanh (see pp.234–5). Zen is one of the most successful traditions to gain a following in the West, where there are more than 500 Zen meditation centers, largely run by non-Asians with only informal connections to Zen centers in Asia.

WOMEN IN MODERN BUDDHISM

In recent years, the work of remarkable figures such as Voramai Kabilsingh Shatsena, Karma Lekshe Tsomo, and Ayya Khema, three pioneers of female ordination, has begun to bring about historic changes to the status of Buddhist women. In some parts of the traditional Buddhist world, where lineages of nuns either died out centuries ago or were never established in the first place, female practitioners have long had a marginal status, without access to full monastic training. Lineages of nuns enjoying full ordination on equal terms with the male Sangha have existed only in China (including Taiwan) and Korea, whereas in most other countries it has not been possible for women to obtain ordination beyond novitiate status. In Tibet, for example, women are traditionally only ordained as "Eight-Precept" or "Ten-Precept" nuns, whereas full ordination involves accepting about three hundred precepts.

In modern southeast Asia lineages of nuns have been restarted or begun for the first time. This Burmese nun is in a devotional posture at Sagaing, southwest of Mandalay, Burma (Myanmar). Once the capital of the Shan kingdom, Sagaing is now mainly a Buddhist meditation center and near Sagaing Hill there are hundreds of monasteries for both monks and nuns.

BUDDHISM AND FEMINISM IN THE WEST

In the 1970s in the West, the movements of Buddhism and feminism began to interact creatively. As early as 1930, the female writer I.B. Horner had studied Buddhist women and there had been pioneering women who had ventured to Asia as practitioners, including Jiyu Kennett, who returned to the United States in 1969 as a Soto Zen master to establish a center. In 1974 Diana Paul wrote her Ph.D. on the "Buddhist Feminine Ideal," and in 1979 women in Hawaii's Diamond Sangha founded the quarterly *Kahawai: A Journal of Women and Zen*, the first journal in Buddhist history written both for and by women.

In 1980 Rita Gross, an American feminist and Tibetan Buddhist practitioner, discovered that in meditation her rage gave way to calmness, insight, and compassion, while her feminism challenged male-dominated Buddhist hierarchies. In 1981 at Boulder, Colorado, Judith Simmer-Brown organized the first of several Women in Buddhism conferences focusing on the lack of women Buddhist leaders today. In 1993, as a constructive response to the lack of female Buddhist leaders, Gross wrote *Buddhism After Patriarchy: A Feminist History, Analysis, and Reconstruction of Buddhism.*

Nuns at Shasta abbey, established at Mount Shasta, California, in 1969 by Jiyu Kennett for her Order of Buddhist Contemplatives of the Soto Zen Church, a Westernized form of Soto.

A movement for change was initiated in Thailand in 1971 when Vora-ai Kabilsingh Shatsena (1908–) traveled to Taiwan for ordination as the venerable Ta Tao because no fully ordained nuns' lineage existed in Thailand. A Thai wife and mother, she began to wear a yellow monastic robe and to observe the Eight Precepts (see pp.104–5 and p.108) of a novice nun in 1955. Her daughter, Dr Chatsumarn Kabilsingh, who was educated in Canada and India, is today working to establish a Thai nun's lineage and publishes Yasodhara, a newsletter for Buddhist women named for the wife of the Buddha.

A Westerner, the German-born Ayya Khema (1923–97), was active in efforts to restore the full ordination of Theravada nuns in Sri Lanka. She was ordained as a novice nun (*dasasil mata*) in Sri Lanka 1983, and in 1984 she founded Parappuduwa Nuns' Island there as an international Buddhist women's training center. Ayya was also ordained in the Chinese tradition in Los Angeles in 1988 before returning the following year to Europe, where by 1996 she had established 37 new meditation groups in Germany. Thirty Sri Lankan nuns were ordained at Bodh Gaya in India in 1998, and since then the number of full ordinations of women in Sri Lanka has steadily increased.

Moves to establish full female monasticism in the Tibetan tradition began in 1982, when Karma Lekshe Tsomo, an American nun trained by

Tibetan teachers in India, received full ordination in South Korea and Taiwan. In 1985 she acquired land to build a nunnery and set up the Jamyang Choling project, which provides education for women in Dharamsala, Ladakh, and other parts of India's Himachal Pradesh province. Recently, the Tibetan government-in-exile at Dharamsala established the Tibetan Nuns' Project (TNP), which also aims to educate future nuns (see sidebar, right). In 1987 Lekshe organized the first International Buddhist Women's Conference (IBWC) at Bodh Gaya in India, the place of the Buddha's enlightenment. As a result, the International Association of Buddhist Women (Sakyadhita) was formed. The sixth IBWC, held in 2000 in the Buddha's birthplace of Lumbini, Nepal, attracted three hundred women from 24 different countries.

In Taiwan, unlike other Asian Buddhist countries, women are highly active in the leadership of the Buddhist community. More than 80 percent of the monastic Sangha are nuns, who run more than twenty-five of the thirty Buddhist research institutes. These include the Center for Buddhist Studies at Taiwan National University, founded in the 1990s by a nun, Professor Shih Heng-ching (Shi Hengjing). In addition to Taiwan's many young, educated nuns, lay women also have prominent roles. Eighty percent of the five million members of the Buddhist Compassion Relief Tzu-chi Association—founded by the nun Shih Cheng-yen—are lay women, known as "blue angels" from their distinctive blue clothing and social welfare work (see pp.216–7). Another leading Taiwanese Buddhist organization, the Fo Kuang Shan (FKS; see pp.214–7), has been active in supporting the full ordination of Buddhist nuns worldwide, beginning with a ceremony at its Los Angeles temple in 1988 at which Ayya Khema, among others, was ordained. In response to growing support for the full ordination of nuns in Sri Lanka, Tibet, and southeast Asia, FKS sponsored another major ordination ceremony at Bodh Gaya in February 1998 to restart the female monastic lineages in these regions.

In Japan, contrary to Buddhist practice elsewhere, most Japanese Buddhist priests are married and their positions as heads of temples are hereditary (see p.229). Korean Buddhism experimented with non-celibate clergy in the twentieth century, especially under Japanese rule, but has largely abandoned this idea. However, male leaders of the new Won movement (see p.215) usually marry, although its female leaders remain celibate.

Western Buddhism lacks the cultural restraints on female advancement found in Asian traditions and is also concerned with equitable and power-sharing structures that differ from Asian hierarchical social models. Euro-American Buddhist groups often follow the Japanese model and allow married clergy, but there are interesting variations. For example, Zen Mountain Monastery in New York State supports monastic celibacy, but also allows married couples if both are practitioners.

Some of the recently founded Buddhist groups are promoting more egalitarian roles for women and men that avoid the lay and monastic structure entirely. The Friends of the Western Buddhist Order (FWBO) makes no distinction between married or single practitioners, with the same ten precepts for men and women. The Indian Buddhist movement Trailokya Buddha Mahasangha (TBM) and Japan's Soka Gakkai International (SGI) (see p.217) are also beginning to include women in leadership roles.

DOLMA LING

In 1991, with the support of the 14th Dalai Lama, the Dolma Ling Training Institute for Tibetan nuns was founded by the Tibetan Nuns' Project (see main text) at Dharamsala, India, the headquarters of the Tibetan exile community. The institute is open to nuns from all schools of Tibetan Buddhism. It offers a model for nunneries throughout Tibet by providing a detailed educational program for its 40 nuns, consisting of a 13-year curriculum of traditional Buddhist philosophy and debate (see illustration, opposite), along with modern courses in science, mathematics, Tibetan history, computer skills, basic medical training, and English. When their studies are complete, the nuns will fill an important role as teachers, both in the nunneries and throughout the Tibetan exile community.

OPPOSITE *Tibetan Buddhist nuns participate in a debating session in the courtyard of Dolma Ling nunnery, Dharamsala, India.*

PART 4 • CHAPTER 2 *David Chappell*

SOCIETY AND THE SANGHA

GOVERNMENT AND POLITICS

Burma's (Myanmar) best known opponent of military rule is the devout Buddhist Aung San Suu Kyi (center; 1945–), who was awarded the Nobel peace prize in 1991 for her policy of peaceful political activism in the face of violent state repression.

Since the time of the Buddha, the fortunes of the Sangha have depended, to a greater or lesser extent, on its relationship with local secular authorities (see pp.118–19). The emperor Ashoka of the third century BCE (see pp.50–53) enthusiastically supported the Sangha, but also decreed that any monks who encouraged schism and deviation were to be expelled from the monastic community. Similar policies of state "sponsorship," which often effectively means state control, are found today in varying degrees in Thailand, Burma (Myanmar), Vietnam, North Korea, Laos, Cambodia, and China.

Buddhism in Laos, North Korea, and Vietnam lacks educational facilities, financial support, and an effective national organization, and Buddhist temples function for the most part only locally and at subsistence level. The tightest political structures exsist in China. During the Cultural Revolution (1966–76), all religious practice was banned and two-thirds of the approximately 100,000 Buddhist temples existing in 1949 were destroyed. However, persecution is not a new phenomenon in China. From the fifth century CE, the Chinese government appointed "Sangha supervisors" to insure that monks posed no political threat. Buddhism sometimes creates cultural tensions—for example, monasticism conflicted with family duties—but politically the clergy's immunity from military service, the exemption of temple lands from taxation, and the siphoning of wealth into the monasteries were seen as even greater liabilities. During state persecutions of Buddhism in 446CE, 576CE, and 845CE, monks were laicized, scriptures and temples were looted and destroyed, and temple lands were confiscated on a vast scale.

In China today, the Religious Affairs Bureau supervises all religions. Under this bureau, the Chinese Buddhist Association represents Buddhists, and similar organizations exist for other religions. Fayuan monastery in Beijing and the Shanghai Buddhist Institute are

His Holiness the 14th Dalai Lama, Tenzin Gyatso (1935–), the spiritual and political leader of the Tibetan exile community, is probably the best known Buddhist figure in the world, particularly in the West, where his tireless efforts to promote inter-religious harmony and to preserve Tibet's traditional Buddhist culture have won countless admirers. He was awarded the Nobel Peace Prize in 1989.

state-sponsored seminaries, but education in these institutes is limited and most graduates are unable to offer intellectual or social leadership. The state has preserved some famous monasteries and built a pagoda near Beijing to house a tooth relic of the Buddha, but such moves are primarily aimed at encouraging tourism and fostering good relations with China's Buddhist neighbors. Freedom of belief is allowed as a private matter, but no public propagation of religion is permitted and no religious organizations may exist except state-approved ones—hence the persecution of Falun Gong, a Buddhist-based popular movement that emerged in the 1990s (see box, p.228).

Before 1950, Tibet was the only Buddhist country with a government led by monks. Its entire complex religio-political structure was attacked and dismantled in the wake of the occupation of the country by Communist China in 1950, especially following the failed Tibetan uprising and the departure of the Dalai Lama in 1959. Almost all of the 6,500 temples that existed in 1950 were destroyed, mostly during the Cultural Revolution. After 1978, an effort was made to redress some of the excesses of the

BUDDHIST LEADERS
The most famous Buddhist leaders today are those who advocate peaceful activism in response to violence: the Dalai Lama (see above), and Aung San Suu Kyi of Burma (see opposite). Other Buddhist advocates of non-violent political and social reform have included Dr Bhimrao Ramji Ambedkar (1891–1956) in India, Daisaku Ikeda (1928–) in Japan, Sulak Sivaraksa (1933–) in Thailand, and the Vietnamese Thich Nhat Hanh (1926–), a peace activist during the Vietnam War who now lives in exile in France (see pp.218–19).

FALUN GONG

Falun Gong (FG) is an interesting example of the typically Chinese cross-fertilization of religious and ethical traditions. Founded in 1992 in China, it draws on Daoist and Buddhist physical and mental techniques to produce what the founder, Li Hongzhi, calls the "wheel of the law" (Chinese *falun*), a protective and liberating "revolving cosmic energy" in the lower abdomen which in turn promotes Buddhist enlightenment. FG members believe that their practices not only improve their individual lives, but promote honesty, harmony, and health in society. The movement advocates truthfulness (*zhen*), goodness (*shan*), and patient endurance (*ren*), which cultivate the inner self (*xinxing*), transform negative into positive, and transcend the world of rebirth.

In spite of Daoist influences, such as abdominal energy, the movement's primary identity is Buddhist. Li legally changed his birthday to April 8, the traditional date of the Buddha's birth, and he is sometimes depicted by followers sitting, Buddha-like, on a lotus seat.

In 1999, FG's website claimed a membership of one hundred million followers, although fifteen million is a more realistic figure. News of the group's strength came as a surprise to most of the world, including the Chinese government officials who awoke on April 25, 1999, to find ten thousand FG members standing quietly outside their living compound. The aim of this silent protest was to win a retraction of attacks on FG in the Chinese state press. Instead, the government banned FG as an anti-government movement, confiscated and destroyed several million books, and arrested important leaders. Li Hongzhi now (2001) lives in exile in New York.

Falun Gong supporters protest at the movement's suppression by the Chinese state authorities.

Cultural Revolution by allowing some religious activity, repairing a few monasteries, and indirectly negotiating with the Dalai Lama. However, riots led by monks in the late 1980s led to the reimposition of martial law in 1989. In the handful of Buddhist monasteries that survive, internal management by monks was replaced in 1996 with committees that include government officials, who live alongside the monks.

Even in Thailand, where Buddhism is the state religion, there are controls. Instead of allowing decentralization, as existed in early Buddhism, the government imposes a monastic hierarchy that mirrors the state structure: the Thai king appoints a monk to be "King of the Sangha" (Sangharaj), who in turn has the authority to appoint the members of a Supreme Buddhist Council (Mahatherasamakom), which administers Buddhist matters. The council is supported by the Religious Affairs Department which also regulates non-Buddhist religious groups in Thailand. The Sangha Act of 1962 sought to enforce common views among Buddhists and to enlist monks to support rural development programs. Leaders of various Buddhist reform movements who act independently of the council run the risk of being disrobed or even imprisoned. New Buddhist movements, such as Santi Asok and Dhammakaya (see pp.214–7), have faced legal proceedings.

Sri Lanka became independent from Britain in 1948 and adopted Buddhism as the state religion in 1956. The Sri Lankan government increasingly identified Buddhism with the Sinhalese people and the Sinhala language, to the detriment of the island's Tamil-speaking Hindu minority. In 1983 this divisive ideology finally resulted in a civil war costing many tens of thousands of lives.

In India, Dr B.R. Ambedkar (1891–1956), who chaired the committee that drafted the Indian constitution (1947–48), publicly converted to Buddhism in 1956, proclaiming it the best religious hope for removing the caste barriers (see pp.214–17). Himself an Untouchable by birth (see p.14), Ambedkar publicly burned those parts of the Laws of Manu, the ancient Hindu text that mandated the caste system, and worked for legal safeguards. As a cabinet member under India's first prime minister, Jawarhalal Nehru, Ambedkar proposed that the Buddhist *dharmachakra* ("wheel of law") appear on the Indian flag and was the chief proponent of India's enduring official policy of non-discrimination on grounds of caste.

Buddhism was the dominant religion in Japan under the Tokugawa shogunate (1603–1868), in particular its Pure Land forms. In the years following the restoration of imperial power in 1868, Shinto became the country's official religion ("State Shinto") and the Buddhist priesthood was deprived of its influence. The state also allowed monks to marry and as a result, Japanese Buddhism is noted as a religion of married priests, not monastics, and temples became the hereditary property of priestly families, passed down from father to eldest son. State Shinto was abolished 1945, and now all religions enjoy equal legal status. Today, most Japanese turn to Buddhism for ritual services, especially funerals and memorials for family ancestors, and these are the chief source of income for Japanese Buddhist groups.

Recent religious freedom in Japan, as well as in South Korea and Taiwan, has also fostered the growth of numerous new Buddhist movements, some of which have had a worldwide impact (see pp.214–17).

MEDITATION CENTERS

Meditation is at the heart of Buddhist life, in particular *vipashyana*, which was developed by the Buddha himself as a means to develop mental discipline and clarity (see pp.74–5). Throughout the Buddhist world today, and especially in the West, many centers have been established with the primary function of teaching Buddhist meditation. These include not only more traditional monastic institutions but also "meditation centers," many of them run by Western lay meditation movements. The most popular forms of meditation in the West today are based on Zen, but meditation centers often integrate a number of forms drawn from across the spectrum of Buddhist traditions.

A leading role in the promotion of Buddhist meditation practice in Britain was played by the Buddhist Society of Great Britain. This was established in 1907 primarily to promote the intellectual study of Buddhism, but it shifted to a more experiential basis in the 1920s under the leadership of Christmas Humphreys (1901–83), who combined Zen meditational practice with influences from Theravada and Tibet. Alan Watts (1915–73) did further work to promote Zen-based practice both in his native Britain and especially in his adopted homeland of the United States.

Today, there are more than 350 Buddhist practice centers in Britain ranging from Theravada forest retreat monasteries such as Chithurst in Hampshire, England, to Zen and Tibetan meditation groups. In 1998 one guide listed more than a thousand meditation centers in North America (over five hundred of them Zen-based), but excluded the two largest Buddhist organizations in the West, Jodo Shinshu and Soka Gakkai International, which have distinctive forms of meditation. Followers of Jodo Shinshu, a Japanese Pure Land sect, practice the *nembutsu* as a central part of their meditation practice (see p.202). Similarly, adherents of the Nichiren-inspired Soka Gakkai practice the daily chanting of homage to the Lotus Sutra (*namu myoho renge kyo*; see p201). Another popular meditation practice in the United States is a simplified Burmese style of Theravada *vipashyana* meditation promoted by the Insight Meditation Society, which was founded in 1975 by two of North America's leading meditation teachers, Joseph Goldstein and Jack Kornfield.

Buddhist meditation forms, especially Zen and *vipashyana*, are also moving into secular arenas. A Yale Law School Retreat in 1998 led to the establishment of a Contemplative Law Program as part of a new Center for Contemplative Mind in Society. In New Jersey, the Engaged Zen Foundation promotes *zazen* (seated meditation) in prisons. Other *vipashyana* movements and centers include those in India led by S. N. Goenka (1924–), who studied under the Burmese master Sayagyi U Ba Khin (1899–1971).

In the traditional Buddhist world, many lay people are increasingly adopting private, isolated meditation practice. A leading Thai meditation teacher, Upasika Kee Nanayon (1901–79), advocated simplicity and solitude, and she is still cherished through her poetry, published under the name K. Khao-suan-luang. Today, group meditation is also proving immensely popular. At Wat Dhammakaya outside Bangkok, for example, upward of one hundred thousand practitioners sometimes gather to meditate amid its splendid buildings and grounds (see p.216).

From 1981 to 1985, summer meditation retreats were held at the Tibetan Buddhist Naropa Institute in Boulder, Colorado, as the basis for a joint Buddhist-Christian dialogue that aimed not to analyze theological and ideological differences but to explore a common approach to the religious life. At the center of this approach was the practice of meditation. Today teachers of Christian contemplation practices are playing an important role in spreading Buddhist meditation. In Europe and the USA, Buddhist meditation retreats are regularly offered by Catholic and Protestant clergy and religious. For example, in Zug, Switzerland, the LaSalle Jesuit retreat house has a room designed for Zen-style meditation adjoining its chapel. In the 1990s, the head of LaSalle Haus was Father Niklaus Branschen, a Jesuit priest who is also a Zen master of the Japanese Sanbokyodan school.

Two Buddhist monks in Kandencholing temple read prayers during the birthday celebration for the 14th Dalai Lama. Dharamsala, Himachal Pradesh, India.

BUDDHISM, SCIENCE, AND TECHNOLOGY

BUDDHIST "CYBER-SANGHA"
Today the closer integration of Buddhists by electronic means offers a new illustration of Buddhist ideas of interdependence. New Buddhist communities are now forming via the internet in what is called a "cyber-sangha." Online Buddhist discussion groups began in the mid-1980s with IndraNet, which was superseded in the 1990s by other groups, including Buddha-L. In 1994 the Journal of Buddhist Ethics (JBE) was created online by Damien Keown in London and Charles Prebish in Pennsylvania—in its first year of operation it had more than 1,500 subscribers in fifty countries. In addition to articles and reviews, JBE organizes online conferences, such as one on human rights held in 2000.

Countless websites on individual Buddhist groups are now available. For example, the Falun Gong movement (see p.228) is banned in China, but its website in Hong Kong is accessible worldwide.

The relationship between Buddhism and modern Western science is relatively harmonious. The Buddhist teaching that ideas are never absolute and are subject to constant change is close to the scientific attitude that, as it has been put, truth is a set of working hypotheses. In addition, the Buddhist view of all reality as an integrated matrix in which objects and our perceptions of them are co-dependent also sits comfortably with modern physics.

Buddhist thought arises out of meditation and is more psychological than philosophical or ideological. In Buddhism, ideas of creation are not concerned with metaphysical or cosmological accounts of the origins of the heavens and earth, but rather with how we each perceive and create our own psychic world. The goal of Buddhism—the relief of suffering (*duhkha*)—is achieved through mental process, wherein the individual frees him- or herself of delusion and compulsions. For this reason, the Buddhism has attracted the interest of Western psychologists since Swiss psychiatrist Carl

A modern Buddhist monk, at ease with both a laptop computer and an ancient manuscript. Modern transport and technologies have enabled many Buddhist communities, previously separated both culturally and geographically, to exchange information and opinions. The internet and CD-ROMs mean that Buddhist scriptures in their original languages are more widely available than ever before.

BUDDHISM AND MEDICINE

Alongside the growing Western interest in ancient Buddhist healing traditions, such as those of Tibet, in recent years Western medical practitioners have also studied the therapeutic effects of Buddhist practice in general. Meditation in particular has proved to be beneficial for some patients, for example in relieving pain. In the United States, the work of the Stress Reduction Clinic at the University of Massachusetts Medical Center is noted among doctors who have encountered problems that have proved difficult to treat through surgery and drugs. For many patients, acknowledging basic bodily functions, rather than ignoring or fighting against blockages and pain, is a liberating experience. The clinic's founder, Dr Jon Kabat-Zinn, has enabled patients to find ways to acknowledge and handle their pain by directing their attention to their breathing and to each part of their anatomy. This mindfulness practice has helped many such patients to cease being victims of their pain and to recover a fuller life.

Jung (1875–1961); indeed, the Buddha has even been called the world's first psychotherapist. In 1927 two books appeared that continue to influence Western psychology today, the translation of the Tibetan Book of the Dead (see p.211) by W. Y. Evans-Wentz and Kazi Sawa Samdup, and Essays in Zen Buddhism by Daisetz Teitaro Suzuki (1870–1966). In the 1930s, Carl Jung wrote that he owed to the Tibetan Book of the Dead "not only many stimulating ideas and discoveries, but also many fundamental insights." Suzuki's work stimulated the growing interest in Zen among psychologists in the United States, where he moved in the 1950s. He collaborated with Erich Fromm, Richard DeMartino, and other leading psychologists and psychiatrists on the influential Zen Buddhism and Psychoanalysis (1960).

Suzuki attracted a Western audience by emphasizing the iconoclastic behavior of the earlier Chinese Zen masters. Reflecting the emphasis placed by American psychologist Abraham Maslow (1908–70) on "peak experience," Western Zen students in the 1960s sought *satori*, the experience of sudden enlightenment. It helped to create a popular image in Western culturer: to "be Zen" was to act with intuitive "oneness" expressed as spontaneous creativity and playful iconoclasm.

The Buddhist process of letting go of self-delusion and being mindful of the present moment has become a useful adjunct to Western psychology. The Buddhist transpersonal psychologist Ken Wilber (born 1949) concluded that the path to Buddhist liberation, in which ego is transcended, should be undertaken only if the ego is "more or less intact" in the first place, and that psychotherapy is a key tool for acquiring this healthy ego.

Developing mindfulness often requires discipline and a stable outer life, so tends to be equally suited to help a discouraged psychotherapist as well as the patient. As a result, Buddhism has been used by psychologists as "therapy for the therapist" (see also box, above).

ENGAGED BUDDHISM

On June 11, 1963, the world was shocked by the self-immolation of the South Vietnamese Buddhist monk Thich Quang Duc in protest at government restrictions limiting the public celebration of Vesak, Vietnamese Buddhism's most important annual festival. Although such self-sacrifice is an extreme example, the principle of non-violence toward others that guided Quang Duc's dramatic act characterizes most Buddhist social protest today.

Although Buddhist social practices had been restricted by state and monastic élites for two millennia, modern Buddhists are now enjoying more social freedom than ever before as a result of constitutional protections, modern media, education, increased social mobility, and international networking. This new context has prompted many Buddhists to experiment with ways to express their ideals of social equality and compassion, as well as to find international support for institutional reforms within Buddhism. While socially active Buddhism is similar to many liberal agendas, it has a distinctive flavor based on emphasizing calm mindfulness, mutual interdependency, and linking outer reform with inner transformation.

The new label for this social activism is "engaged Buddhism," a term coined during the war in Vietnam by Thich Nhat Hanh (1926–). The School of Youth for Social Service (SYSS), which he organized in 1964 to help those suffering as a result of the war, became a model for engaged Buddhists. As explained by his colleague Chan Kong, this vision was different from the usual idea of social welfare: "He wanted to teach social work and rural development as the work of personal and social transformation. Workers would not consider themselves 'helpers' nor peasants as 'people being helped.' They would cultivate the understanding that they and the poor peasants were partners in a common task."

The idea that the sick and poor could help the rich and healthy to grow beyond their ego attachments and to undergo personal growth is a recurring theme in socially engaged Buddhism. Similar teachings are found in Taiwan's Buddhist Compassion Relief Tzu-chi Association (see sidebar, p.217) and Sri Lanka's Sarvodaya movement (see pp.214–17).

Political activism is the most controversial form of engaged Buddhism. In Vietnam, Thich Nhat Hanh insisted that the SYSS should not be aligned with any political group since it cared for all people. However, in South Vietnam both government officials and the communists saw the refusal of the SYSS to join either side as disloyalty to their respective causes, and killed several SYSS volunteers. After a four-month period in 1967 in which six SYSS members had been killed and others wounded, the following public pledge was made by SYSS members: "Now, once again, we solemnly promise never to hate those who kill us, above all never to use violence to answer violence, even if the antagonists see us as enemies and kill until they annihilate us."

Thich Nhat Hanh left Vietnam in 1966 because of his opposition to the Vietnam War. In addition to his many poetic writings, he has attracted many Westerners to Buddhist meditative practices. He is seen here about to address an audience in San Francisco, United States.

One of the most memorable and shocking images from the early period of the Vietnam War is that of the monk Thich Quang Duc's public act of self-immolation in 1963 in protest at South Vietnamese government policies toward Buddhists. A picture of the event is shown here in the window of the monk's own sedan, on permanent display at his monastery of Linh Mu in Hue, Vietnam. The monk drove into the center of Saigon, drenched himself with gasoline from the car, assumed the classic Buddhist meditation posture, then to the horror of onlookers, struck a match.

Nhat Hanh emphasizes that the enemies of Buddhists are not other people, but greed, anger, ignorance, and patterns of denial and structures of privilege. Violence, he teaches, will not remove these enemies. The Fourteenth Dalai Lama (1935–) (see pp.226–9), who refuses to initiate terrorist reprisals against the Chinese occupation of Tibet, and Aung San Suu Kyi (1945–) (see pp.226–9), the leader of democratic resistance to the military junta in Burma (Myanmar), are also Buddhist role-models for non-violent political involvement.

Although the avoidance of violence has been a foundational Buddhist aims, the record shows that some Buddhists have broken this vow in the name of nationalism. In the 1590s, Korean Buddhist monks supported armies to defend Korea against Japanese invasion. During the Second World War, Japanese Buddhist leaders supported their government's military invasions of other nations. And in present-day Sri Lanka, Buddhist leaders have supported the war against the Tamil separatists. But the new international coalition of engaged Buddhists—who identify with Thich Nhat Hanh,

Robert Aitken, Sulak Sivaraksa of Thailand, and the Dalai Lama, and who are represented in the International Network of Engaged Buddhists (INEB) and the Buddhist Peace Fellowship (BPF)—reject the use of violence.

International networking is important for engaged Buddhism. As a carryover from the anti-Vietnam War protests in the 1970s, BPF was formed in 1978 in Hawaii by Robert Aitken and others to resist the proliferation of nuclear arms. Attracting the allegiance of other grassroots movements founded by Euro-American Buddhists from various Buddhist traditions, BPF has branches in America and Europe, and its work is reported in its quarterly journal "Turning Wheel."

Sulak Sivaraksa (1933–) of Thailand also works to involve an international coalition of engaged Buddhists. To be inclusive of all Buddhist traditions, in 1989 he organized the International Network of Engaged Buddhists (INEB) and edits its journal, "Seeds of Peace." More recently, Naropa Institute in Boulder, Colorado, has formed a graduate degree program on socially engaged Buddhism organized around the examples of Sulak and A.T. Ariyaratne, leader of the Sarvodaya movement (see pp.214–15).

Whereas traditional Buddhist morality emphasized ethics for individual behavior, engaged Buddhism also examines the possibility that individuals whose personal moral behavior is exemplary may still act destructively if they are part of a system or institution that is unjust. As a result, engaged Buddhists work to strengthen the position and participation in society of those whom they view as the weak and powerless, on the basis that all beings possess inherent value and need to be actively included if social structures or institutions are to be fair. In this regard, the most successful movements working today are Sarvodaya in Sri Lanka and the TBM in India (see pp.214–17).

An increased examination of social and institutional inequities has made Buddhists more self-critical of their own institutions. One result has been the push toward gender inclusiveness in the Sangha by ordaining nuns in those traditions without female monastic lineages (see pp.222–3), sharing decision-making, and financial accountability. Some Buddhists are even trying to reform the division between monastics and laity, through organizations such as the Friends of the Western Buddhist Order (FWBO). The FWBO has joined with the TBM in India to work against caste discrimination against the former Untouchables (Harijans), and also to support the empowerment of women and social development in rural areas. For an increasing number of Buddhists, social mindfulness and social change are a necessary part of Buddhist practice to achieve peace both for oneself and, as the Buddha taught, "for the good of the many, for the happiness of the many, out of compassion for the world, for the benefit, for the good, for the happiness of gods and humans" (Mahavagga Vinaya).

In a sense, Buddhism has always been "environmentalist" in outlook owing to its respect for all forms of life. From the earliest times, Buddhist monastics in India were forbidden even to plow the earth or to drink water without straining it to prevent the accidental harming of insects. This concern was applied in a new way in Thailand in March 1991, when fifty monks and lay people wrapped monastic robes around large trees in an old-growth rainforest national park, and performed a ceremony to "ordain" the

trees. By doing so, they prevented loggers from cutting down the trees for fear of injuring a "tree-monk" and thereby acquiring karmic demerit. In June that year a similar ceremony took place in Nan province with the involvement not only of local clergy and government officials, but also the Wildlife Fund Thailand, an affiliate of the international WWF (WorldWide Fund for Nature).

Environmental activism is an important emphasis of the major new Buddhist movements of recent decades, such as the Tzu-chi, Fo Kuang Shan, and Chunghwa of Taiwan, the Won and Chontae orders in Korea, and the Rissho Koseikai and Soka Gakkai of Japan. In 1989, the Fourteenth Dalai Lama proposed in his Nobel Peace Prize acceptance speech that Tibet should become an "international ecological reserve," while Thich Nhat Hanh made the environment an inherent part of his work by naming his movement the Order of Interbeing.

In the West, reinforced by the Mahayana *bodhisattva* vow to save all beings, the poet Gary Snyder began making connections between Buddhist training and ecological activism in the 1950s. Buddhist teachers such as John Seed now travel the world organizing groups—referred to collectively as the Council of All Beings—to help people work more closely to protect the environment by using various visualization, breathing, ritual, and movement techniques.

Buddhists are active in seeking to end violence and warfare worldwide. Here, monks of Nipponzan Myohoji, a Japanese-based Buddhist movement, protest during a march outside the Russian state duma (parliament) in Moscow in January 2000, calling for an end to the war in Chechnya.

GLOSSARY

NOTE: The terminology used is Sanskrit, with Pali (P) forms added where appropriate. Other languages are indicated as follows: Chinese (C), Japanese (J), and Tibetan (T).

anatman (P, *anatta*) "non-self," a Buddhist teaching that rejects the notion of an intrinsic, unchanging entity at the core of a person. With *anitya* and *duhkha* it forms one of the "three marks of existence."

anitya "impermanence," a Buddhist teaching that all phenomena are transient. With *anatman* and *duhkha* it forms one of the "three marks of existence."

avidya "ignorance" of the true nature or reality which can be dispelled by realizing the truth of "non-self" (*anatman*).

arhat (P, *arahat*) "worthy one" who has realized *nirvana* by following the teaching (Dharma) of a *buddha*. The *arhat* is enlightened but not omniscient (see also *bodhisattva, buddha*).

ashura demonic supernatural being characterized by hostility; often depicted as being in deadly combat with the *deva*s.

bardö (T) an intermediate state between death and rebirth.

bhikshu (P, *bhikkhu*) Buddhist monk who has received higher ordination and is subject to the full discipline defined in the text, the Vinaya Pitaka.

bhikshuni (P, *bhikkhuni*) Buddhist nun, see *bhikshu*.

bhumi one of the ten stages of spiritual attainment on the *bodhisattva* path: joy, purity, brightness, radiance, difficult to conquer, facing *nirvana*, far-going, immovable, spiritual intelligence, and Dharma cloud.

bodhichitta "awakening mind," which marks a shift in focus from self-concern to concern for the suffering of others, manifesting itself as compassion (*karuna*) and a commitment to pursue the *bodhisattva* path.

bodhisattva (P, *bodhisatta*) "enlightenment being," in the Theravada, this refers to the single being striving to realize *nirvana* and become the next buddha; in the Mahayana, this defines the central ideal for all which is characterized by boundless compassion and a commitment to help all other beings realize *buddha*hood (see also *arhat, buddha*).

buddha an "awakened one" who is fully enlightened and who has realized *nirvana* without the benefit of a *buddha*'s teaching in the lifetime in which he attains it. A *buddha* is generally regarded as omniscient (see also *arhat, bodhisattva*).

Buddha, the Siddhartha Gautama (ca. fifth century BCE), the historical founder of Buddhism whose teachings, the Dharma, form its core.

chakravartin "wheel turner," a righteous universal king.

dana "self-less giving" or "donation," commonly directed toward the Sangha, which brings merit—a central ideal of lay Buddhists.

deva a deity who inhabits one of the many celestial realms but who is still subject to rebirth.

dharani a spell chanted to evoke supernatural power used both for meditational and protective purposes.

dharma (P, *dhamma*) Brahmanic/Hindu "duty," eternal moral order defining one's religious obligations in accordance with one's hereditary social status; Buddhist "teaching," "truth," or "phenomenon;" central Buddhist concept (the Dharma; P, Dhamma) that includes the eternal truth that the Buddha realized, his verbal expression of that truth, and the phenomena or elements that comprise reality (see Tipitaka).

dharmaraja "just king," a righteous Buddhist ruler who governs in accordance with the Buddha's Dharma.

dhyana (P, *jhana*) "meditative trance," a set of ascending levels of meditative absorption, numbering four or eight; also used to refer to meditation more generally.

duhkha (P, *dukkha*) "suffering," "unsatisfactoriness;" the First Noble Truth states that all conditioned existence is characterized by suffering or unsatisfactoriness. With *anatman* and *anitya* it forms one of the "three marks of existence."

gandhakuti term used to refer to the Buddha's residence during his lifetime (literally "perfumed chamber") and later applied to the room in a monastery housing the central Buddha image.

guru a "spiritual teacher" who monitors a disciple's development and leads him or her toward final release from *samsara*. Translated as *lama* in Tibetan Buddhism.

icchantika category of people who have committed crimes so heinous as to be presumed incapable of attaining enlightenment.

*jakata*s accounts of the Buddha's previous lives. These texts, from the Khuddaka Nikaya, are often quoted when monks instruct the laity.

karma (P, *kamma*) "deed," an intentional action that has future consequences, including future rebirths; the consequences of past deeds largely determine one's general life situation.

karuna "compassion," an ideal particularly associated with *buddha*s, and central to the Mahayana *bodhisattva* path.

kasina ten meditation aids listed in Buddhaghosa's Visuddhimagga: earth, air, water, fire, blue, yellow, red, white, space, and light.

*klesha*s hindrances or poisons that cause beings to perform intentional deeds (*karma*) and suffer rebirth.

koan (J) accounts of deeds or utterances of Zen masters used to further a student's enlightenment; central to Rinzai Zen practice.

lama (T) translation of *guru*, someone who has mastered tantric *sadhana* meditation and ritual practice.

mahasiddha "great adept," a spiritually advanced figure associated with religious innovation in tantric Buddhism.

mandala   cosmic diagram used in meditation to visualize spiritual realms and their inhabitants.

mantra   powerful words or sounds used in meditation, particularly in tantric Buddhism.

nianfo   (C) meditational and devotional practice of reciting the name of the *buddha* Amitabha, which is central to Pure Land Buddhism; known in Japan as *nembutsu*.

nirvana   (P, *nibbana*) the state of perfect enlightenment realized by *buddha*s and *arhat*s; those who have gained this realization no longer accumulate karmic consequences and will no longer be reborn into *samsara* when they die.

papa   "bad (deed)" which brings demerit or negative karmic consequences, sometimes familiarly called "bad *karma*."

*paramita*s   "perfections," *Bodhisattvas* are directed to cultivate a list of six virtues or perfections, later expanded to ten: generosity, morality, patience, vigor, meditation, wisdom, skill in means, conviction, strength, and knowledge.

parinirvana   see *nirvana*, a term sometimes used to refer to a *buddha* or *arhat* after their final passing away from *samsara*, though also used interchangeably with *nirvana* in some Buddhist texts.

prajna   (P, *panna*) "wisdom" or "insight," the active capacity for spiritual discernment, "seeing into" the true nature of reality. This faculty is necessary for enlightenment and is central to all Buddhist schools.

preta   a restless spirit or ghost who suffers extreme hunger and thirst because of attachments in past lives.

punya   (P, *punna*) "merit"or what is familiarly called "good *karma*."

rita   the moral order of the Vedic universe, thought to be enforced by the sky god Varuna, who dealt out punishments and rewards.

sadhana   Vajrayana meditational practices commonly involving the visualization of deities

samadhi   meditative practice leading to "one-pointed concentration."

samsara   the cycle of constant rebirth in which all beings are trapped as a result of their intentional deeds (*karma*); the cycle ranges from hell states to sublime, formless realms.

samyaksambodhi   the "utterly complete" or "perfect" enlightenment realized by *buddha*s.

sangha   the Buddhist monastic community.

satori   (J) the experience of sudden awakening or enlightenment in Zen Buddhism.

sila   moral practice (right speech, right action, right livelihood) which is the starting point of the Buddhist path.

sunyata   "emptiness," Buddhist doctrine, found in nascent form in early Buddhism but central to Mahayana Buddhism, that asserts that even the *dharma*s, the conditioned elements of reality defined in the

Abhidharma ("Higher Doctrine"), are devoid or empty of their own independent nature; thus, seen from the perspective of absolute truth, the conventional distinction between *nirvana* and *samsara* is likewise void or empty.

siddha   accomplished spiritual adept with magical powers in tantric Buddhism, often translated as saint.

*skandha*s   the five components or aggregates that comprise a human being acccording to Buddhist analysis, including: physical body (*rupa*), feelings (*vendana*), perceptions (*samjna*), habitual mental dispositions (*samskaras*), and consciousness (*vijnana*).

smrti   (P, *sati*) "mindfulness," a form of meditational practice that leads to a concentrated direct awareness of transient phenomena as they arise in the present moment.

stupa   a relic monument and a focus for devotion and merit-making.

sutra   (P, *sutta*) discourse attributed to the Buddha and his early followers.

svarga   "heaven," goal of a celestial rebirth, a common lay Buddhist goal associated with the accumulation of merit (*punya*).

trikaya   Mahayana doctrine of the three bodies of the Buddha: *dharmakaya* ("truth body"), *sambhogakaya* ("enjoyment body"), and *nirmanakaya* ("emanation body").

Tripitaka   (P, **Tipitaka**) "three baskets" of the Buddha's authoritative teaching, including the monastic discipline (Vinaya), discourses (*sutra*s), and higher doctrine (Abhidharma/Abhidamma).

trishna   (P, *tanha*) "thirst" or "craving," the Second Noble Truth states that suffering (*duhkha*) arises because of craving for and attachment to sense pleasures, to continued birth, and to non-existence.

tulku   (T) enlightened *bodhisattva*s that take repeated birth in a human body in order to help humankind by teaching, healing, and by their example (Tibetan Buddhism).

upasaka   male lay follower of Buddhism.

upasika   female lay follower of Buddhism.

upaya kaushalya   "skill in means," the ability of *buddha*s and advanced *bodhisattva*s to teach beings in ways appropriate to their level of understanding.

vajracharya   advanced teacher or "*vajra* master" in the Vajrayana tradition.

vihara   monastic residence.

vipashyana   (P, *vipassana*) "insight meditation," aims to discipline the mind while fostering a profound clarity about the nature of reality.

yoga   Brahmanic/Hindu religious discipline. One form of this aims at realizing the unity of the individual's soul (*atman*) and cosmic reality (*brahman*).

zazen   (J) seated Zen meditation.

BCE | CE

IMPORTANT EVENTS

	6th Century	5th Century	4th Century	3rd Century	2nd Century	1st Century	1st Century	2nd Century	3rd Century	4th Century	5th Century	6th Century	7th Century
						BCE	CE						

Important events by period:

- **6th Century BCE:** Conjectured dates for life of Gautama Buddha in India
- **5th Century BCE:** Men's and women's monastic lineages (Sangha) established in India
- **4th Century BCE:** 1st Council at Rajagriha, 2nd Council at Vaishali; Buddhist movement fragments into Sthavira and Mahasanghika communities; these later subdivide
- **3rd Century BCE:** Ashokan empire; 3rd Council at Pataliputra; Buddhism established in Sri Lanka; Missions sent by Ashoka to the northwest, Sri Lanka, and possibly Burma
- **2nd Century BCE:** Sanchi established under Shunga patronage in India
- **1st Century BCE:** Pali Tipitaka first written down in Sri Lanka; 1st Mahayana texts composed (Perfection of Wisdom and Lotus *sutras*)
- **1st Century CE:** Buddhism spreads to China along silk routes
- **2nd Century CE:** Madhyamaka school originates in India (Nagarjuna)
- **4th Century CE:** Buddhism established in Korea; Yogacara Buddhism originates in India (Asanga and Vasubandhu)
- **5th Century CE:** life of Buddhaghosa and Pali commentaries codified in Sri Lanka; Faxian travels to India
- **6th Century CE:** Chan and Tiantai schools established in China; Buddhism established in Japan
- **7th Century CE:** developed Vajrayana school originates in India; Pure Land school becomes prominent in China; Xuanzang travels to India

Regions (with Buddhist tradition over time):

- India and Central Asia
- Sri Lanka
- Tibet
- Burma (Myanmar)
- Thailand
- Cambodia
- Laos
- Vietnam
- Indonesia / Malaysia
- China
- Korea
- Japan
- Europe / N.America

Legend:

- Theravada*
- Mahayana
- Vajrayana/Tantra

* including other Buddhist schools commonly termed Hinayana Buddhist.

Century	Events
th Century	• first Tibetan Buddhist monastery founded
9th Century	• repression of Buddhism in China and Tibet • Khmer kingdom established at Angkor in Cambodia • Tendai and Shingon schools established in Japan • Borobudur completed in Java
10th Century	• Pagan kingdom established in Burma • Pure Land and Chan schools flourish in China
11th Century	• Anawrahta converts to Theravada in Pagan (Burma) • second dissemination of Buddhism in Tibet • Atisha arrives in Tibet and initiates Sangha reform • Mahayana Tripitaka printed in Korea
12th Century	• Angkor Wat established in Cambodia • Turkish Muslim invasions in North India; Nalanda looted
13th Century	• Sukhothai kingdom established in Thailand • Zen (Eisei and Dogen); Pure Land (Honen and Shinran); Nichiren schools established in Japan
14th Century	• Ayutthaya kingdom established in Thailand • Tsongkhapa founds Gelugpa school in Tibet
15th Century	• Theravada becomes dominant in Cambodia with Thai defeat of Khmers
16th Century	• Mongols converted to Buddhism • Sonam Gyatso named Dalai Lama
17th Century	• Tokugawa era in Japan; Buddhism made state religion
18th Century	• Buddhist revival in Sri Lanka
19th Century	• British control established in Sri Lanka and Burma and French control in Cambodia and Vietnam • fifth Buddhist council in Burma. Mahabodhi Society founded in 1891. • Parliament of World Religions in Chicago • European study of Buddhism begins
20th Century	• Soka Gakkai established in Japan • Buddhist Churches of America established • 2500th anniversary of Gautama's *parinibbana* observed by Theravadins • B.R. Ambedkar founds Navayana Buddhist movement in India • exile of 6th Dalai Lama from Tibet (1959)

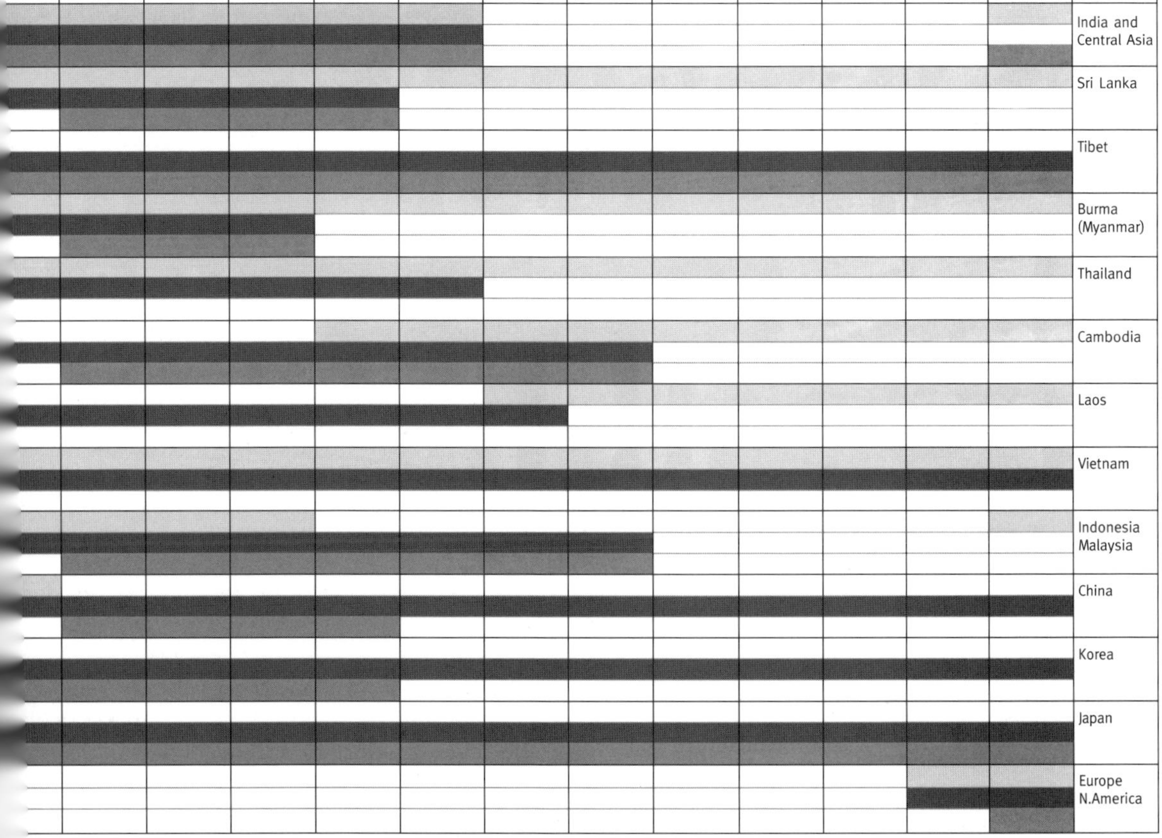
India and Central Asia
Sri Lanka
Tibet
Burma (Myanmar)
Thailand
Cambodia
Laos
Vietnam
Indonesia Malaysia
China
Korea
Japan
Europe N.America

'his timeline identifies important events in the history of Buddhism and indicates approximately when the three broad traditions of Buddhism emerged within ndaries of several modern nations and regions. The evidence for dating these movements is often fragmentary and subject to debate; the goal here is to pro-)asic temporal framework for understanding the geographical dissemination and interaction of these broad traditions, each of which was itself marked by con- e doctrinal, ritual, and cultural diversity.

BIBLIOGRAPHY

GENERAL WORKS

Bechert, Heinz and Gombrich, Richard., eds. *The World of Buddhism*. London: Thames and Hudson; New York: Facts on File, Inc., 1984.

Harris, Elizabeth J. *What Buddhists Believe*. Oxford: Oneworld Publications, 1998.

Harvey, Peter. *An Introduction to Buddhism: Teachings, History and Practices*. Cambridge and New York: Cambridge University Press, 1990.

Keown, Damien. *Buddhism: A Very Short Introduction*. Oxford and New York: Oxford University Press, 2000.

Lamotte, Étienne. *History of Indian Buddhism: From the Origins to the Saka Era*, trans. by Sara Webb-Boin. Louvain-la-Neuve: Institut Orientaliste, 1988.

Malalasekera, G.P., et al., eds. *Encyclopaedia of Buddhism*. Colombo: Government of Sri Lanka, 1961.

PART 1: ORIGINS

CHAPTER 1: ANCIENT INDIA: BELIEF AND SOCIETY
Alchin, Bridget and Alchin, Raymond. *The Rise of Civilization in India and Pakistan*. Cambridge: Cambridge University Press, 1982.

Allchin, F. R. *The Archaeology of Early Historic South Asia: The Emergence of Cities and States*. Cambridge: Cambridge University Press, 1995.

Basham, A.L. *The Origins and Development of Classical Hinduism*. New York: Oxford University Press, 1989.

Kosambi, D.D. *Ancient India*. New York: Meridian Books, 1965.

Olivelle, Patrick. *Samyasa Upanishads: Hindu Anthology*. Harmondsworth, England, and New York: Penguin Books, 1981.

Shaffer, Jim G. "The Indo-Aryan Invasions: Cultural Myth and Archaeological Reality" in *The People of South Asia: The Biological Anthropology of India, Pakistan, and Nepal*, ed. by John R. Lukacs. New York: Plenum Press, 1984, pp.77–90.

Witzel, Michael. "Rigvedic History: Poets, Cheftains and Politics" in *The Indo-Aryans of Ancient South Asia*, ed. by George Erdosy. New York: Walter de Gruyter, 1995, pp.307–352.

CHAPTER 2: THE CAREER OF SIDDHARTHA
Asvaghosa. *Buddhacarita; or, Acts of the Buddha*, ed. by E.H. Johnston. 2nd ed. New Delhi: Motilal Banarsidass, 1984.

Carrithers, Michael. *The Buddha*. Oxford: Oxford University Press, 1983.

Cummings, Mary. *The Lives of the Buddha in the Art and Literature of Asia*. Ann Arbor, Michigan: University of Michigan, Center for South and Southeast Asian Studies, 1982.

Jayawickrama, N.A., trans. *The Story of Gotama Buddha: The Nidana-katha of the Jatakatthakatha*. Oxford: Pali Text Society, 1990.

Karetzky, Patricia E. *The Life of the Buddha: Ancient Scriptural and Pictorial Traditions*. Lanham, Maryland: University Press of America, 1992.

Reynolds, Frank E. "The Many Lives of the Buddha: A Study of Sacred Biography and Theravada Tradition" in *The Biographical Process: Studies in the History and Psychology of Religion*, ed. by Frank E. Reynolds and D. Capps. The Hague: Mouton, 1976, pp.37–61.

Schober, Juliane, ed. *Sacred Biography in the Buddhist Traditions of South and Southeast Asia*. Honolulu: University of Hawaii Press, 1997.

Snellgrove, David, ed. *The Image of the Buddha*. Tokyo: Kodansha International, 1978.

CHAPTER 3: A NEW COMMUNITY
Dutt, Sukumar. *Buddhist Monks and Monasteries of India*. London: George Allen and Unwin, 1962.

Lamotte, Étienne. *History of Indian Buddhism: From the Origins to the Saka Era*, trans. by Sara Webb-Boin. Louvain-la-Neuve: Institut Orientaliste, 1988.

Nikam, N.A. and McKeon, R., eds. *The Edicts of Ashoka*. Chicago: University of Chicago Press, 1978.

Robinson, Richard and Johnson, Willard. *The Buddhist Religion: A Historical Introduction*. 4th ed. Belmost, Albany, etc.: Wadsworth, 1997.

Strong, John S. *The Legend of King Ashoka*. Princeton: Princeton University Press, 1983.

Wijayaratna, M. *Buddhist Monastic Life*. Cambridge University Press, 1987.

PART 2: PRINCIPLES AND PRACTICE

CHAPTER 1: THE HUMAN CONDITION
Collins, Steven. *Selfless Persons: Imagery and Thought in Theravada Buddhism*. Cambridge: Cambridge University Press, 1982.

Dalai Lama. *The Meaning of Life from a Buddhist Perspective*. Boston: Wisdom Publications, 1992.

Hopkins, J. *Buddhist Advice for Living and Liberation: Nagarjuna's Precious Garland*. Ithaca: Snow Lion Publications, 1998.

Kaviratna, Harischandra. *The Dhammapada*. Pasadena, California: Theosophical University Press, 1989.

Rhys-Davids, C.A.F. *Stories of the Buddha*. New York: Dover, 1988.

Rhys-Davids, T. *The Questions of King Milinda*. 2 vols. New York: Dover, 1963.

Thera, N. *The Vision of Dhamma*. Seattle: Pariyatti Publications, 2000.

Warren, Henry C. *Buddhism in Translations*, New York: Macmillan, 1966.

CHAPTER 2: THE "FOUR NOBLE TRUTHS"
Evans-Wentz, W.Y. *Tibet's Great Yogi Milarepa*. Oxford: Oxford University Press, 1974.

Mizuno, Kogen. *Basic Buddhist Concepts*. Tokyo: Kosei Publishing Company, 1988.

Rahula, Walpola. *What the Buddha Taught*. New York: Publisher Resource, 1978.

Rhys-Davids, C.A.F. *The Path of Purification by Bhadantacariya Buddhaghosa*. Seattle: Vipassana Research Publications of America reprint, 1999.

Thomas, E.J. *The History of Buddhist Thought*. London: Routledge, 1996.

Takakusu, Junjiro. *The Essentials of Buddhist Philosophy*. Westport, Connecticut: Greenwood Press, 1974.

CHAPTER 3: THE PATH OF THE BUDDHA
Bodhi, Bhikkhu. *The Noble Eightfold Path* Kandy, Sri Lanka: Buddhist Publication Society, 1994.

Bhikkhu Thanissaro. *The Wings of Awakening*. Barre, Massachusetts: Dhamma Dana Publications, 1998.

Crosby, Kate and Skilton, A., trans. *The Bodhicaryavatara*. New York: Oxford University Press, 1995.

Dalai Lama. *Stages of Meditation*. Ithaca, New York: Snow Lion Publications, 2001.

Eckel, Malcolm David. *To See the Buddha*. Princeton: Princeton University Press, 1992.

Farrer-Halls, Gill. *The Illustrated Encyclopedia of Buddhist Wisdom*. Wheaton, Illinois: Quest Books, 1999.

Harvey, Peter. *An Introduction to Buddhist Ethics*. Cambridge: Cambridge University Press, 2000.

Thera, Nyanaponika. *The Heart of Buddhist Meditation*. New York: Weiser, 1984.

Rinpoche, Patrul. *Words of My Perfect Teacher*. 2nd ed. Walnut Creek, California: Altamira Press, 1998.

CHAPTER 4: MENTAL CULTIVATION
Bhikkhu Nanamoli and Bhikkhu Bodhi, trans. *Middle Length Discourses of the Buddha* (from Bhayabherava Sutta, No. 4, in the Majjhima Nikaya, vol. 1, pp.21–22, of the Pali Text Society edition). Boston: Wisdom Pub., 1995.

Bronkhorst, Johannes. *The Two Traditions of Meditation in Ancient India*. Stuttgart: F. Steiner Verlag Wiesbaden, 1986.

Conze, Edward. *Buddhist Meditation*. London: Allen & Unwin, 1956.

Gunaratana, Henepola. *The Path of Serenity and Insight: An Explanation of the Buddhist Jhanas*. New Delhi: Motilal Banarsidass, 1985.

King, Winston. *Theravada Meditation: the Buddhist Transformation of Yoga*. University Park, Pennsylvania: Pennsylvania State University Press, 1980.

Kiyota, Minoru, and Jones, Elvin, eds. *Mahayana Buddhist Meditation*. Honolulu: University of Hawaii Press, 1978.

Nyanamoli, trans. *The Path of Purification* (translation of Buddhaghosa's Visuddhimagga). 2 vols. Sri Lanka, 1956. Reprinted, Berkeley, California and London: Shambala, 1976.

Nyanaponika, T. *The Heart of Buddhist Meditation*. London: Rider, 1962.

Ryukoku University Translation Center, trans. and ed. *The Sutra of Contemplation on the Buddha of Immeasurable Life as*

Expounded by Sakyamuni Buddha. Kyoto: Ryukoku University, 1984.

Samanaphala Sutta ("The Fruits of the Contemplative Life"), No. 2 in the Digha Nikaya.

Satipatthana Sutta ("Discourse on Mindfulness"), No. 10 in the Majjhima Nikaya, and No. 22 in the Digha Nikaya.

CHAPTER 5: THE BUDDHIST COMMUNITY
Bartholomeusz, T. *Women under the Bo Tree: Buddhist Nuns in Sri Lanka*. Cambridge: Cambridge University Press, 1994.

Buswell, Robert E. *The Zen Monastic Experience*. Princeton: Princeton University Press, 1992.

Carrithers, Michael. *The Buddha*. Oxford: Oxford University Press, 1983.

Dutt, Sukumar. *Buddhist Monks and Monasteries in India*. London, 1962.

Gombrich, Richard. *Precept and Practice: Traditional Buddhism in the Rural Highlands of Ceylon*. Oxford: Clarendon Press, 1971.

Griffiths, Paul J. *On Being Buddha: The Classical Doctrine of Buddhahood*. Albany: State University of New York Press, 1994.

Kawamura, Leslie. *The Bodhisattva Doctrine in Buddhism*. Waterloo, Ontario: Wilfred Laurier University Press, 1981.

Lopez, Donald S., ed. *Buddhism in Practice*. Princeton: Princeton University Press, 1995.

Ray, Reginald. *Buddhist Saints in India*. New York: Oxford University Press, 1994.

Spiro, Melford E. *Buddhism and Society: A Great Tradition and its Burmese Vicissitudes*. Berkeley: 1982.

Sponberg, Alan and Hardacre, Helen, eds. *Maitreya: The Future Buddha*. Cambridge: Cambridge University Press, 1988.

Tambiah, Stanley J. *The Buddhist Saints of the Forest and the Cult of Amulets*. Cambridge: 1984.

Tiyavanich, Kamala. *Forest Recollections: Wandering Monks in Twentieth Century Thailand*. Honolulu: 1997.

Williams, P. *Mahayana Buddhism*. London: Routledge and Kegan Paul, 1989.

CHAPTER 6: BUDDHISM IN PRACTICE
Carter, John R., ed. *The Threefold Refuge in the Theravada Buddhist Tradition*. Pennsylvania: Anima Books, 1982.

Coleman, Simon and Elsner, John. "Translating the Sacred: Patterns of Pilgrimage in the Buddhist World" in *Pilgrimage: Past and Present in the World Religions*. Cambridge, Massachusetts: Harvard University Press, 1995, pp.170–195.

Harvey, Peter. *An Introduction to Buddhist Ethics: Foundations, Values, and Issues*. Cambridge: Cambridge University Press, 2000.

Journal of Buddhist Ethics, internet journal: http://jbe.gold.ac.uk/ http://jbe.la.psu.edu/

Kariyawasam, A.G.S. *Buddhist Ceremonies and Rituals of Sri Lanka*. Kandy: Buddhist Publication Society, 1995.

Kinnard, Jacob. *Imaging Wisdom: Seeing and Knowing in the Art of Indian Buddhism*. Richmond, Surrey: Curzon, 1999.

Lopez, Donald S., ed. *Buddhism in Practice*. Princeton: Princeton University Press, 1995.

Schober, Juliane. "Buddhist Just Rule and Burmese National Culture: State Patronage of the Chinese Tooth Relic in Myanmar" in *History of Religions*. 1997, 36, pp.218–243.

Reynolds, Frank E. and Carbine, Jason A., eds. *The Life of Buddhism*. Berkeley, California: University of California Press, 2000.

Schopen, Gregory. *Bones, Stones, and Buddhist Monks*. Honolulu: University of Hawaii Press, 1997.

Tambiah, S.J. *World Conqueror and World Renouncer*. Cambridge: Cambridge University Press, 1976.

Trainor, Kevin. *Relics, Ritual, and Representation in Buddhism: Rematerializing the Sri Lankan Theravada Tradition*. Cambridge: Cambridge University Press, 1997.

CHAPTER 7: THERAVADA BUDDHISM
Bunnag, Jane. *Buddhist Monk, Buddhist Layman: A Study of Urban Monastic Organization in Central Thailand*. Cambridge: Cambridge University Press, 1973.

Gombrich, Richard and Obeyesekere, Gananath. *Buddhism Transformed: Religious Change in Sri Lanka*. Princeton: Princeton University Press, 1988.

Gombrich, Richard. *Precept and Practice: Traditional Buddhism in the Rural Highlands of Ceylon*. Oxford: Clarendon Press, 1971.

Gombrich, Richard. *Theravada Buddhism: A Social History from Ancient Benares to Modern Colombo*. London; New York: Routledge and Kegan Paul, 1988.

Keyes, Charles F. *The Golden Peninsula: Culture and Adaptation in Mainland Southeast Asia*. Honolulu: University of Hawaii Press, 1995.

Smith, Bardwell L., ed. *Religion and Legitimation of Power in Thailand, Laos, and Burma*. Chambersburg, Pennsylvania: Anima Books, 1978.

Strong, John S. *The Legend and Cult of Upagupta: Sanskrit Buddhism in North India and Southeast Asia*. Princeton: Princeton University Press, 1992.

Swearer, Donald K. *The Buddhist World of Southeast Asia*. Albany: State University of New York Press, 1995.

Tambiah, S.J. *Buddhism and the Spirit Cults in North-East Thailand*. Cambridge: Cambridge University Press, 1975.

Tambiah, S.J. *The Buddhist Saints of the Forest and the Cult of Amulets*. Cambridge: Cambridge University Press, 1984.

CHAPTER 8: MAHAYANA BUDDHISM

Corless, Roger. *The Vision of Buddhism*. Paragon House Publishers, 1989.

Dalai Lama. *A Flash of Lightning in the Dark of Night: A Guide to the Bodhisattva's Way of Life*. Berkeley, California, and London: Shambala, 1994.

Cowell, E.B., ed. *Buddhist Mahayana Texts*. New York: Dover, 1989.

McGovern, William. *An Introduction to Mahayana Buddhism*. AMS Press, 1971.

Williams, J. Paul. *Mahayana Buddhism: The Doctrinal Foundations*. London: Routledge, 1989.

Kalupahana, David. *Nagarjuna, The Philosophy of the Middle Way*. New York: State University of New York Press, 1986.

Kelsang Gyatso. *Ocean of Nectar: Wisdom and Compassion in Mahayana Buddhism*. Tharpa Publications, 1995.

Murti, T.R.V. *The Central Philosophy of Buddhism*. London: Allen & Unwin, 1955.

Nagao, Gadjin M. with Kawamura, Leslie S., ed. *Madhyamika and Yogacara: A Study of Mahayana Philosophies*. Albany: State University of New York Press, 1991.

Streng, Frederick. *Emptiness*. New York: Abingdon Press, 1967.

Thurman, Robert. *The Holy Teaching of Vimalakirti*. University Park, Pennsylvania: Pennsylvania State University Press, 1976.

Dutt, Nalinaksha. *Mahayana Buddhism*. Delhi: Motilal Barnasidass, 1978.

Gomez, Luis. *The Land of Bliss: The Paradise of the Buddha of Measureless Light*. Honolulu: 1996.

Inagaki, Hisao. *The Three Pure Land Sutras: A Study and Translation from Chinese*. Kyoto: Nagata Bunshodo, 1995.

CHAPTER 9: CHAN AND ZEN—THE WAY OF MEDITATION

Awakawa, Yasuichi. *Zen Painting*. Tokyo: Kodansha, date unknown.

Dumoulin, Heinrich. *Zen Buddhism: A History*. 2 vols. New York and London: Macmillan, 1988–1990.

Benoit, Hubert. *The Supreme Doctrine (Le Doctrine Suprême): Psychological Studies in Zen Thought*. New York: Pantheon Books, 1955.

Bodiford, William M. *Soto Zen in Medieval Japan*. Honolulu: University of Hawaii Press, 1993.

Faure, Bernard. *The Rhetoric of Immediacy: A Cultural Critique of Chan/Zen Buddhism*. Princeton: Princeton University Press, 1991.

Hirota, Dennis, ed. *Wind in the Pines: Classic Writings of the Way of Tea As a Buddhist Path*. Berkeley: Asian Humanities Press, 1995.

Kasulis, T.P. *Zen Action, Zen Person*. Honolulu: University of Hawaii Press, 1981.

Sasaki, Ruth. *The Record of Lin-chi*. Kyoto: The Institute for Zen Studies, 1975.

Sekida Katsuki. *Two Zen Classics: Mumonkan and Hekiganroku*. Tokyo: Weatherhill, 1977.

Shibayama Zenkei. *Zen Comments on the Mumonkan*. New York: New American Library, 1974.

Suzuki, D.T. *Essays in Zen Buddhism*. 3 vols. London: Rider and Company, 1949.

Waddell, Norman, trans. *The Essential Teachings of Zen Master Hakuin*. Boston and London: Shambhala, 1994.

CHAPTER 10: TANTRA

Beyer, Stephan. *The Cult of Tara*. Berkeley: University of California Press, 1973.

Evans-Wentz, W.Y. *Tibet's Great Yogi Milarepa*. London: Oxford University Press, 1974.

Klein, Anne. *Meeting the Great Bliss Queen*. Boston: Beacon, 1996.

Lewis, Todd T. *Popular Buddhist Texts from Nepal: Narratives and Rituals of Newar Buddhism*. Albany, New York: State University of New York Press, 2000.

Robinson, James B. *Buddha's Lions: The Lives of the Eighty-Four Siddhas*. Berkeley, California: Dharma Publishing, 1979.

Shaw, Miranda. *Passionate Enlightenment*. Princeton: Princeton University Press, 1994.

Snellgrove, David. *Indo-Tibetan Buddhism: Indian Buddhists and Their Tibetan Successors*. 2 vols. Boston: Shambhala, 1987.

White, David Gordon. *Tantra in Practice*. Princeton: Princeton University Press, 2000.

PART 3: HOLY WRITINGS

CHAPTER 1: ASSEMBLING THE DHARMA

The Asian Classics Input Project, ed. *A Thousand Books of Wisdom*, release IV. CD-ROM containing 8,000 pages of the Tibetan Kangyur texts and 29,200 pages of Tibetan Tengyur texts. New York: Asian Classics Input Project, 1999. See www.asianclassics.org/

Bhiksu Thich Minh Chau. *The Chinese Madhyama Agama and the Pali Majjhima. Nikaya*, Delhi: Motilal Barnarsidass Publishers, 1991.

Buddhist Studies Virtual Library. See www.ciolek.com/WWWVL-Buddhism.html

Ch'en, Kenneth. "The Chinese Tripitaka" in *Buddhism in China*. Princeton: Princeton University Press, 1964, pp.365–386.

Kogen, Mizuno. *Buddhist Sutras: Origin, Development, Transmission*. Tokyo: Kosei Publishing Co., 1982.

Robinson, Richard and Johnson, Willard. Appendix entitled "An Overview of the Buddhist Scriptures" in *The Buddhist Religion*. 4th ed. Belmost, Albany, etc.: Wadsworth, 1997, pp.311–314.

Vipassana Research Institute, Chattha Sangayana CD ROM Version 3. Dhamagiri, India: Vipassana Research Institute. See www.tipitaka.org/

CHAPTER 2: THE THREE BASKETS

Access to Insight, internet site: www.accesstoinsight.org/ (includes an extensive collection of Pali canonical texts in English translation).

Bond, George D. *The Word of the Buddha: The Tipitaka and Its Interpretation in*

Theravada Buddhism. Colombo: 1982.

Collins, Steven. "On the Very Idea of the Pali Canon" in *Journal of the Pali Text Society*. 1990, 15, pp.89–126.

Hinüber, Oskar von. *Handbook of Pali Literature*. Berlin and New York: Walter de Gruyter, 1996.

Kemper, Steven. *The Presence of the Past: Chronicles, Politics, and Culture in Sinhala Life*. Ithaca, New York: Cornell University Press, 1991.

Norman, K.R. *Pali-Literature*. Wiesbaden: Otto Harrassowitz, 1983.

Wijayawardhana, G.D. "Literature in Buddhist Religious Life" in *Religiousness in Sri Lanka*, ed. by John R. Carter. Colombo: Marga Institute, 1979, pp.67–77.

CHAPTER 3: MAHAYANA SCRIPTURES
Cleary, Thomas, trans. *Entry into the Realm of Reality* [*Gandavyuha Sutra*]. Boston and Shaftesbury: 1989.

Conze, Edward. *The Perfection of Wisdom in Eight Thousand Lines and Its Verse Summary* [*Ashtasahasrika Prajnaparamita Sutra*]. Bolinas, California: Four Seasons Foundation, 1973.

Conze, Edward. *Buddhist Wisdom: The Diamond Sutra and the Heart Sutra* [*Vajracchedika and Hrdaya Prajnaparamita Sutras*]. New York: Vintage Books, 2001.

Garfield, Jay. *The Fundamental Wisdom of the Middle Way: Nagarjuna's Mulamadhyamakakarika*. New York and London: Oxford Univesity Press, 1995.

Hakeda, Yoshito, trans. *The Awakening of Faith* [*Qixin Lun*]. New York: Columbia Paperback, 1967.

Lamotte, Etienne, trans. *La Concentration de la Marche Heroique* [*Surangamasamadhi Sutra*]. Bruxelles: Institut Belge des Hautes Etudes Chinoises, 1975.

Powers, John. *An Introduction to Tibetan Buddhism*. Ithaca, New York: 1995.

Samuel, Geoffrey. *Civilized Shamans: Buddhism in Tibetan Societies*. Washington, D.C., 1993.

Stcherbatsky, F.Th., trans. *Buddhist Logic* [*Nyayabindu, Nyayabindu-tika*]. vol. 2. London and New York: Dover Publications, 1962.

Suzuki, Daitetsu Teitaru, trans. *The Lankavatara Sutra*. London: Routledge & Kegan Paul, 1932.

Thurman, Robert A.F. *The Holy Teaching*

of Vimalakirti: A Mahayana Scripture [*Vimalakirtinirdesa Sutra*]. Pennsylvania: Pennsylvania University Press, 1987.

Tucci, Guiseppe. *The Religions of Tibet*. London, 1980.

Watson, Burton, trans. *The Lotus Sutra*. New York: Columbia University Press, 1993.

Wayman, Alex and Hideko, trans. *The Lion's Roar of Queen Srimala* [*Srimala Sutra*]. New York: Columbia University Press, 1974.

PART 4: BUDDHISM TODAY

CHAPTER 1: THE EXPANDING COMMUNITY
Baumann, Martin. *Deutsche Buddhisten. Geschichte und Gemeinschaften*. 2nd ed. Marburg: Diagonal, 1995.

Boucher, Sandy, *Turning the Wheel: American Women Creating the New Buddhism*. 2nd ed. Boston: Beacon, 1993.

The Buddhist Society, ed. *The Buddhist Directory*. 8th ed. London: 2000.

DeJong, J.W. *A Brief History of Buddhist Studies in Europe and America*. Delhi, India: Sri Satguru, 1987.

Fields, Rick. *How the Swans Came to the Lake*. 3rd ed. London & Boston: Shambhala, 1992.

Hubbard, Jamie, and Swanson, Paul L., eds. *Pruning the Bodhi Tree: The Storm Over Critical Buddhism*. Honolulu: University of Hawaii Press, 1997.

Jones, Charles Brewer. *Buddhism in Taiwan: Religion and the State 1660–1990*. Honolulu: University of Hawaii Press, 1999.

Obadia, Lionel. *Bouddhisme et Occident: La diffusion du bouddhisme tibetain en France*. Paris: Editions L'Hartmattan, 1999.

Prebish, Charles S. and Tanaka, Kenneth K., eds. *The Faces of American Buddhism*. London and Berkeley: University of California Press, 1998.

Tsomo, Karma Lekshe, ed. *Buddhist Women Across Cultures*. Albany, New York: State University of New York Press, 1999.

Williams, Duncan R. and Queen, Christopher S., eds. *American Buddhist: Methods and Findings in Recent Scholarship*. Surrey, England: Curzon, 1999.

CHAPTER 2: SOCIETY AND THE SANGHA
Ariyanatne, A.T. *Buddhism and Sarvodaya:*

Sri Lankan Experience. Delhi: Sri Satguru, Indian Books Centre, 1996.

Chan Khong (Cao Ngoc Phuong). *Learning True Love: How I Learned and Practiced Social Change in Vietnam*. Berkeley: Parallax Press, 1993.

Chappell, David, ed. *Buddhist Peacework*. London and Boston: Wisdom, 1999.

Dumoulin, Heinrich, and Maraldo, John C., eds. *Buddhism in the Modern World*. London and New York: Collier Macmillan, 1976.

Goldstein, Melvyn and Kapstein, Matthew, eds. *Buddhism in Contemporary Tibet: Religious Revival and Cultural Identity*. London and Berkeley: University of California Press, 1998.

Kabat-Zinn, Jon. *Full Catastrophe Living: Using the Wisdom of Your Body and Mind to Face Stress, Pain, and Illness*. New York: Delta, 1990.

Kaza, Stephanie, and Kraft, Kenneth. *Dharma Rain: Sources of Buddhist Environmentalism*. Boston and London: Shambhala, 2000.

Morreale, Don, ed. *The Complete Guide to Buddhist America*. London and Boston: Shambhala, 1998.

Queen, Christopher S. and King, Sallie, eds. *Engaged Buddhism: Buddhist Liberation Movements in Asia*. Albany, New York: State University of New York Press, 1996.

Queen, Christopher S., ed. *Engaged Buddhism in the West*. London and Boston: Wisdom, 2000.

Sivaraksa, Sulak. *Seeds of Peace: A Buddhist Vision for Renewing Society*. Berkeley: Parallax Press, 1992.

Tambiah, Stanley J. *Buddhism Betrayed? Religion, Politics, and Violence in Sri Lanka*. Chicago: University of Chicago Press, 1992.

Wilber, Ken, Engler, Jack, and Brown, Daniel. *Transformations of Consciousness: Conventional and Contemplative Perspectives on Development*. London and Boston: Shambhala, 1986.

INDEX

PICTURE CREDITS

PICTURE CREDITS
The publisher would like to thank the following people, museums and photographic libraries for permission to reproduce their material. Every care has been taken to trace copyright holders. However, if we have omitted anyone we apologize and will, if informed, make corrections in any future edition.

Abbreviations:

BM   British Museum
BPK   Bildarchiv Preussischer Kulturbesitz
RHPL   Robert Harding Picture Library
Stone   gettyone Stone

Page 1 Tony Stone Images, London/Masaharu Uemura; **2** Tony Stone Images, London /Kevin R. Morris ; **7** AKG, London/Gilles Mermet; **8** Tibet Images/Ian Cumming; **10** BM (OA 1880–11); **15** Axiom/Paul Quayle; **16** Panos Pictures/Daniel O'Leary; **17** BM (BMC59); **18** RHPL; **19** Michael Willis; **20** Todd Lewis; **21** AKG/British Library; **23** BM (OA1919.1–1.088); **24** AKG/Jean Louis Nou; **25** BPK/Museum für Indische Kunst, Berlin; **26** BM (BM 49, Barratt 70); **27** Corbis/Owen Franken; **29** British Library (Or 14297 f.10–11); **30** Corbis/Nevada Wier; **32/33** BPK/Museum für Indische Kunst, Berlin; **34** Kevin Trainor; **35** British Library (Or 14297 f.19–20); **37** Corbis/Wolfgang Kaehler; **38** Christie's Images; **39** Stone/David Hanson; **40** AKG/Jean–Louis Nou; **42** BM (1948.7–10.0–12); **43** BM (OA 1907.12–28.1); **44** Corbis/Kevin R. Morris; **47** Stone/Paul Chesley; **48** BM (Sanchi 30); **49** BM (OA 1880.257); **51** BM (BM 70, Barrett 100); **52** Graham Harrison; **53** Graham Harrison; **54** AKG/Erich Lessing; **55** AKG/Jean-Louis Nou; **56** Stone/James Strachan; **59** Corbis/Leonard da Selva; **60** BM (OMPB Or. 13538); **63** DBP Archives; **65** Todd Lewis; **66** AKG/Gilles Mermet; **68** Stone/Hilarie Kavanagh; **71** Christie's Images; **73** Corbis/Peter Turnley; **74** Stone/James Strachan; **75** Tibet Images/Greta Jensen; **76** BM (OA 1973, S–14.2); **78–79** Spinks, London; **79** BM (OA 1887.7–17–81); **81** Stone/Hugh Sitton; **82** Stone/Nicholas Devore; **84** British Library (Or. 13813); **85** Graham Harrison; **86** Graham Harrison; **87** AKG/Erich Lessing; **88** BM (OA 1991.3–28.1); **89** BM (OA 1944.4–1.05); **90** AKG/Erich Lessing; **91** BM (1992,12–14.36); **93** Stone/Keren Su; **94–95** Stone/James Strachan; **96** BM (OA 1942,4–16.1); **97** Stone/Glen Allison; **98** Corbis/Chris Lisle; **100** Corbis/Carmen Redondo; **101** Tibet Images/Ian Cumming; **102** Tibet Images/Ian Cumming; **105** Corbis/Nevada Wier; **107** Corbis/Kevin R. Morris; **109** Kevin Trainor; **110** Tibet Images/Ian Cumming; **111** Kevin Trainor; **113** Graham Harrison; **114** Michael Willis; **115** Graham Harrison; **116** Stone/Rex A. Butcher; **117** British Library (Or 14297 f.4–5); **118** Graham Harrison; **119** BM (1922–4–24–127); **122** British Library (Or 14297 f.43–44); **125** Panos Pictures/D. Sansoni; **126** Corbis/Luca Tettoni; **127** Stone/Mervyn Rees; **128** Stone/Hugh Sitton; **131** Stone/Glen

Allison; **134** Stone/Jerry Alexander; **135** Graham Harrison; **137** BM (OA 1898.4–8,0.33); **138** Stone/Dave Jacobs; **139** BM (OA 1973.05–14.1); **140–141** Shokuku-ji Temple, Kyoto, Japan/ Photo courtesy of Kyoto National Museum; **142** Corbis/Chris Lisle; **145** Christie's Images; **146** Corbis/Nik Wheeler; **147** Christie's Images; **148** DBP Archives; **149** BM (OA 1919.1–1.047); **150** Christie's Images; **151** Corbis/Kevin R. Morris; **152** Graham Harrison; **155** Eisei Bunko; **156** Graham Harrison; **157** Graham Harrison; **158** BM (OA 1983.11–11.04); **160** Werner Forman Archive; **161** Art Archive; **163** Todd Lewis; **164–165** Tibet Images/Ian Cumming; **167** BM (OA 1908,5–15.10); **168–169** Tibet Images/Ian Cumming; **171** Tibet Images/Christopher Langridge; **172** Panos Pictures; **174** BM (OA 1919.1–1–0279); **177** Corbis/Christine Kolisch; **178** Corbis/Wolfgang Kaehler; **181** Corbis/Galen Rowell; **182** BM (Or 12010/J); **183** British Library (Or 74.D.5); **184–185** BM (OA 1983,5–26.1); **187** Graham Harrison; **188** Sam Fogg Rare Books, London; **189** Bridgeman Art Library/Private Collection; **190** Corbis/Howard Davies; **192** Kevin Trainor; **193** Corbis/Luca Tettoni; **194** Corbis/Tim Page; **195** Kevin Trainor; **196** CWB; **197** Sam Fogg Rare Books; **199** Christie's Images; **200** Christie's Images; **201** Bridgeman Art Library/ Victoria and Albert Museum; **202** Sam Fogg Rare Books; **204** Sam Fogg Rare Books; **205** Graham Harrison; **206** Stone/Paul Chesley; **207** Sam Fogg Rare Books; **209** Corbis/Lindsey Hebberd; **210** British Library (Or 15190.3); **212** Corbis/Stephanie Maze; **215** BLIA, South Africa; **216** Soka Gakkai, Taiwan; **219** Corbis/Kevin R. Morris; **220** Graham Harrison; **221** Corbis/David Muench; **222** Corbis/Michael Freeman; **223** Corbis/Ted Streshinsky; **224** Corbis/Alison Wright; **226** Frank Spooner Agency; **227** Frank Spooner Agency; **228** Associated Press; **231** Corbis/David Samuel Robbins; **232** Stone/ Glen Allison; **234** *San Francisco Chronicle*/Eric Luse; **235** Corbis/Nik Wheeler; **237** Corbis/Reuters Newmedia

ACKNOWLEDGMENTS
Most of the quoted material reproduced in the book has been supplied by the authors, who have translated from the original texts. Every effort has been made to establish the identity of the copyright holders of any other quoted extracts and to contact them. However, if there are omissions we apologize and will, if informed, make corrections in any future edition. The publisher would like to thank the following sources for permission to reproduce extracts:

Page 68 W.Y. Evans-Wentz *Tibet's Great Yogi Milarepa*, London: OUP, 1974, p.246; **87** *Buddhist Texts Through the Ages*, Harper Torchbooks, 1953, pp.252–53.